WELCOME TO THE MACHINE

The Systemic Failures of Digital Transformation

ERIC KIMBERLING

Welcome to the Machine
The Systemic Failures of Digital Transformation

Published by Third Stage Consulting
www.thirdstage-consulting.com

Table of Contents

Acknowledgements

Thank you to my wife Kelly, Cooper, and Colton – along with my extended family – for making this book possible.

Thank you to the many clients, teams, and colleagues that I have worked with over the last 30 years. All of your knowledge has inspired and informed this book.

~Eric

INTRODUCTION

THE MACHINE

Chapter 1

Welcome to the Machine

Here is a number that should stop you cold: between 55 and 75 percent of all enterprise software implementations fail outright or significantly underperform expectations.

Let that sink in. Not 10 percent. Not 20. The majority.

Here is another number: 189 percent. That is the average cost overrun for ERP implementations, the backbone technology projects that companies undertake to run their core operations. If you budgeted $10 million, plan on spending nearly $29 million. If you budgeted $50 million, you might be looking at $145 million before anyone admits there is a problem.

And one more: only 23 percent of all ERP implementations are considered successful by the companies that paid for them. Fewer than one in four.

I have spent the better part of twenty-five years inside these numbers. Over the course of my career, I have helped more than 1,000 organizations through their digital transformations. At Third Stage Consulting alone, we have worked with nearly 500 paying client organizations. Before that, there were years of advising steering committees, hundreds of conversations with executives and project team members, and a long trail of client engagements stretching back to the late 1990s when I began my career at PricewaterhouseCoopers. I worked my way through the large consulting firms, and eventually founded my own advisory practice. First Panorama Consulting Group in 2005, then Third Stage Consulting Group in 2018. I made those moves because I could no longer reconcile what the industry was selling with what the industry was delivering.

My team and I have also analyzed over 50 implementations embroiled in litigation, including Waste Management v. SAP and California v. SAP. In each case, we dug into how decisions were made, how projects were managed, how failures originated. We reviewed internal documents, emails between executives, sales presentations that promised the moon, and post-mortem reports that catalogued the wreckage. Over time, very common patterns emerged. The same mistakes, the same misaligned incentives, the same breakdowns in governance and accountability, showing up again and again across different industries, different vendors, and different consulting firms. I have sat across the table from CEOs who spent $100 million and had nothing to show for it but a lawsuit and a board that wanted their head.

And after all of that, after the thousands of hours in conference rooms and courtrooms, after the hundreds of readiness assessments and risk reviews, after two decades of watching the same patterns repeat themselves with eerie precision, I can tell you this with absolute certainty:

Digital transformation failure is not a bug. It is a feature.

It is a feature of a system so thoroughly designed around the economic interests of technology vendors, consulting firms, and system integrators that the client, the organization actually paying for and undergoing the transformation, is often the least important participant in the process. The system does not fail despite its design. It fails *because* of it.

I call this system the machine.

The Machine

Picture the Pink Floyd album cover. Not the prism and the rainbow, but the other one. *Wish You Were Here*. The man in the suit, shaking hands, on fire. Or better yet, picture the lyrics from "Welcome to the

Machine" itself: *"What did you dream? It's alright, we told you what to dream."*

That is what happens to organizations that enter the world of digital transformation unprepared. They are told what to dream. They are told what the technology can do, what the consultants will deliver, what the timeline will look like, what the return on investment will be. They are told these things by people who have a profound financial interest in the telling. And by the time the organization realizes that the dream was someone else's, crafted not for their benefit but for the benefit of the machine, it is almost always too late to turn back.

The machine has three interlocking gears.

The first gear is the client, the organization undergoing the transformation. Clients enter the machine with some combination of genuine need and manufactured urgency. They are told their legacy systems are dying, that their competitors are pulling ahead, that the cloud is the future and the future is now. Some of this is true. Much of it is exaggerated. Almost none of it comes with an honest assessment of what the transformation will actually require. Not just in dollars, but in organizational pain, cultural upheaval, and executive courage. The client is the fuel. The machine cannot run without organizations willing to feed themselves into it.

The second gear is the technology, the enterprise software platforms and the vendors that sell them. SAP, Oracle, Microsoft, and their competitors have built extraordinarily sophisticated products. I am not here to tell you the technology does not work. By and large, it does. What I am here to tell you is that the business model surrounding the technology, the subscription revenue, the forced migrations, the platform lock-in, the ecosystem of analyst firms and industry events that exist primarily to validate vendor marketing, has created a set of incentives that have almost nothing to do with whether your specific implementation succeeds or fails.

The technology is the engine. It runs whether you are ready for it or not.

The third gear is the consultant, the system integrators, value-added resellers, and advisory firms that are hired to guide the transformation. This is where the machine gets truly insidious, because the consultant is supposed to be on the client's side. They are supposed to be the expert, the sherpa, the trusted advisor. Instead, the largest consulting firms in the world, Deloitte, Accenture, Capgemini, and others, operate with a business model that is fundamentally misaligned with client success. They are paid by the hour. They need to staff hundreds of thousands of consultants on projects to justify their economic model. Their vendor partnerships mean they walk into your organization with a pre-determined answer. And the longer your project runs, even if it is failing, the more money they make. The consultant is the operator. They run the machine.

These three gears mesh together with a terrible precision. The vendor creates artificial urgency. The consultant validates it. The client believes it. The vendor sells the software. The consultant sells the implementation. The client funds it all. When it goes sideways, and the statistics tell you it goes sideways far more often than not, the vendor blames the implementation, the consultant blames the client's "readiness," and the client is left holding the bag.

Not much has really changed in the industry within the last twenty years. In the early 2000s, you had well-publicized failures at Hershey's, Nike, and FoxMeyer Drug. In recent years, we have seen ERP failures at Lidl, Revlon, SPAR Group, and others. Technology has seen quantum improvements. The end results are largely the same.

This is not a coincidence. This is the machine working exactly as designed.

A Brief History of Wreckage

If these failure rates applied to any other industry, we would call it a crisis. If 55 to 75 percent of commercial aircraft crashed or underperformed, no one would fly. If 189 percent cost overruns were standard in homebuilding, no one would buy a house. But in digital transformation, these numbers have been stable for decades, and somehow the industry keeps growing.

Let me make the numbers real.

In 1999, Hershey, one of the most iconic brands in American consumer goods, attempted to simultaneously implement SAP, Siebel CRM, and Manugistics supply chain software. It was an ambitious program with an ambitious timeline, and it went live just before the Halloween candy season, the single most important revenue period for a candy company. The result was catastrophic. The systems could not process orders. Hershey was incapable of fulfilling roughly $100 million worth of orders for Hershey's Kisses and Jolly Ranchers. Distributors could not get product. Shelves sat empty. The company's stock price plummeted. They had tried to implement SAP in an unreasonably short period of time during an unreasonably busy season.

In 2005, Waste Management, the largest waste disposal company in North America, initiated an enterprise-wide ERP project with SAP. The contract was awarded based on SAP's claims that the solution was out-of-the-box, adapted to U.S. standards, and could fulfill the company's goals with minimal customization. SAP promised that Waste Management would realize annual benefits somewhere in the neighborhood of $100 to $200 million per year, and that the system would go live by 2007. None of this turned out to be true. Waste Management found SAP's claims to be false, was unable to glean any benefit from the software, and filed a $100 million lawsuit that was later raised to $500 million before settling out of court in 2010. The company spent far more money than it was ever able to recover.

In 2011, the United Kingdom's National Health Service abandoned its National Programme for IT, an initiative intended to create a unified electronic health record system across the entire NHS. The program consumed £12 billion. Twelve billion pounds. It was the largest civilian IT failure in history, and it delivered virtually none of its intended benefits.

In 2018, Lidl, one of the largest discount grocery chains in the world, walked away from seven years and approximately €500 million worth of investment in an SAP implementation. Seven years. Half a billion euros. And in the end, the German retailer simply reverted to their legacy systems and started over. They had insisted on replicating their existing pricing and inventory processes within SAP rather than adapting to the software's standard capabilities, and the gap proved unbridgeable.

Also in 2018, Revlon's SAP S/4HANA cloud implementation disrupted the cosmetics company's ability to fulfill orders and manage inventory so severely that it contributed to a $64 million inventory write-down and, according to many analysts, played a role in the company's eventual bankruptcy in 2022.

I could go on. Nike lost over $100 million and $200 million in sales from a botched demand-planning system. Target Canada's data migration failures contributed to a $7 billion market exit. Ford spent over $400 million on a global ERP initiative before abandoning it. FoxMeyer Drug, once one of the largest pharmaceutical distributors in the United States, went bankrupt after a failed SAP implementation combined with warehouse automation problems. Hewlett-Packard spent $160 million on an ERP project where, as their CIO said at the time, "We had a series of small problems, none of which individually would have been too much to handle." Together, they created the perfect storm.

These are not obscure companies. These are global enterprises with deep pockets, sophisticated leadership teams, and access to the best technology and consultants money can buy. They still failed. And for every headline-making disaster, there are thousands of smaller failures that never make the news. The mid-market manufacturer that spent $15 million and got a system nobody uses. The distributor that went live and immediately started losing orders. The services company that is three years and two system integrators into a project with no end in sight.

Fifty-four percent of companies experience a material operational disruption at the time of go-live. The duration of these disruptions varies from a few weeks to several months. The costs of these disruptions increase the initial cost of the implementation by anywhere from 50 to 300 percent. And yet somehow, when the next organization steps up to the plate, they believe it will be different for them.

The machine counts on that belief.

The Formula

It took years of watching the same patterns repeat across hundreds of engagements before my team at Third Stage Consulting was able to articulate a simple equation that captures the essence of most digital transformation failures:

NS + OP = EOP

New Software + Old Processes = Expensive Old Processes

This is what happens when organizations spend tens or hundreds of millions of dollars on new enterprise technology but refuse to change the way they actually work. They automate their dysfunction. They pave the cow paths, taking the winding, inefficient trails that their business has followed for decades and putting a fresh layer of asphalt on top. The cows still walk the same route. But now it costs a fortune to maintain.

I have seen this pattern so many times that I can usually spot it within the first few hours of an engagement. A company with 1,800 "requirements" that should be 400, because most of what they are asking for is not a legitimate business need but a refusal to change. Sixty percent of the so-called requirements I see in discovery workshops are not requirements at all. They are change resistance wearing a business analyst's hat.

The inverse of the formula is equally simple:

NP + NT + CM = DEO

New Processes + New Technology + Change Management = Digital Enterprise Operations

This is what success looks like. New processes, designed deliberately around the business outcomes the organization is trying to achieve. New technology, selected to enable those processes rather than dictate them. And change management, the sustained effort to prepare the people, the culture, and the organization to absorb the disruption and adopt the new way of working. All three are required. Remove any one of them and the formula collapses back to EOP.

It requires an organization to fundamentally rethink how it operates *before* it selects technology, not after. It requires the courage to tell a warehouse manager who has been running things his way for twenty years that his way is about to change. It requires executive leadership that does not just sponsor the transformation in name but champions it with authority, resources, and the willingness to make unpopular decisions. And it requires a deliberate, funded, sustained investment in helping people navigate the change -- not a two-week training program bolted onto the end of the implementation, but a comprehensive change management effort that begins before the project starts and continues long after go-live.

In my experience, this kind of courage is rare. The machine does not reward it. The machine rewards compliance. Buy the software, hire the consultants, stay on the timeline, go live on the date, and hope for the best. Organizations that push back, that slow down, that ask hard questions, are told they are being difficult. They are told they are behind their peers. They are told the technology is proven and the risk is manageable. They are told these things by the people who profit from the telling.

How I Became a Heretic

I did not set out to write a book about the failures of my own industry. I set out to be a consultant. I started my career at PricewaterhouseCoopers in 1998, and for the first several years I was a true believer. I believed the technology was transformative. I believed the consulting firms were acting in their clients' best interests. I believed the failures I saw were exceptions, the result of bad luck or bad planning, not bad incentives.

What I did not set out to be was a technologist. In graduate school, I studied business. I imagined myself as a business consultant, someone who helped organizations think strategically about their operations. When PricewaterhouseCoopers told me I was going to get SAP certified and work on SAP implementations, I kicked and screamed. I did not want to be a technologist. I wanted to be a business advisor. I lost that argument, of course. I was a junior, entry-level consultant and had about as much influence over my career path as a leaf has over the direction of the wind. But in hindsight, the forced combination of business training and technical immersion gave me something that most people in this industry never develop: the ability to see that technology alone never solves business problems. It is always about the people and the operations first. That understanding became the foundation of everything I have done since.

The disillusionment started earlier than I expected. One of the first projects I was assigned to was an ERP evaluation. A large client had paid our firm close to a million and a half dollars in consulting fees to assess their operations and determine which technology would be the best fit. It was supposed to be an objective, rigorous analysis. When I got into the project, I quickly realized the answer had been decided before we ever walked in the door. We were going to recommend SAP. That was the predetermined outcome from day one. Our Denver office had a large SAP practice, and our job, whether anyone said it out loud or not, was to feed that practice as much business as possible. Every software selection I participated in at that firm ended with the same recommendation.

I still remember the moment it clicked. I was sitting in a team meeting, the new guy, twenty-four years old, on my very first consulting engagement. There were twenty or thirty of us on the project, and the partner had just laid out the scope. I raised my hand and asked what I thought was a reasonable question: at what point do we start evaluating different technology options? I was excited to learn about the alternatives -- Baan, Microsoft, whatever else was out there. The room went quiet. The senior consultants exchanged a look that I did not understand at the time but have never forgotten. It was the look of people who could not believe someone had said the quiet part out loud. There was no evaluation. There was no decision to be made. Our job was to work backwards from a conclusion that had already been reached and build a justification around it.

The client was paying us handsomely for what they believed was independent advice. What they were actually getting was a sales channel for our own consulting services. Being a new consultant, I thought it seemed odd. It seemed unethical. But it turned out this was not a quirk of one project. It was how the entire model worked.

The disillusionment did not come in a single moment. It accumulated.

I remember being on projects as a newbie when I had absolutely nothing to do but yet I was billing full-time on the project because I was expected to. Nobody questioned it. Nobody thought it was unusual. The firm needed bodies on the project, and I was a body. The client was paying my fully loaded rate, which at the time seemed like an absurd amount of money for someone who did not yet know what he was doing, and I was learning on their dime. I remember looking around the room at a dozen other consultants doing the same thing, all of us collecting hours against a client's budget while we figured out what our jobs were supposed to be.

By the time the implementation started, the team had scaled to forty or fifty consultants. I was adding maybe five to ten hours of real value per week, yet I was expected to bill fifty to sixty. I remember the creeping dread of impostor syndrome, the feeling that at some point the client was going to find me out, that someone was going to look at my timesheets and ask what exactly I had been doing for the other forty-five hours. They never did. The client had no idea what each of us was doing. The team had grown like an amoeba, absorbing more bodies at every opportunity, and the client simply did not have the visibility or the expertise to question it. The big system integrators are notorious for this: employing people right out of school and charging their clients to train them. They are also notorious for outsourcing a majority of work to people with limited skillsets.

But the staffing was only the beginning. What really got to me was watching how the entire engagement was structured around the consulting firm's interests, not the client's. The vendor had already been selected before we arrived, often based on a relationship between the vendor's sales team and the SI's partner group. The scope had been defined to maximize billable hours, not to address the client's actual business problems. The timeline was whatever the sales team had promised to win the deal, regardless of whether it was realistic. And when things started to go wrong, as they almost always did, the response was never to stop and reassess. It was to add more consultants.

I moved from PwC to the Convergent Group and then to Schlumberger, and at each stop the pattern was the same. The consulting firms existed to staff consultants. The clients existed to pay for them. The technology existed to justify the engagement. The measure of success was not whether the client's transformation delivered value. It was whether the consulting firm hit its revenue targets and the vendor closed the deal.

I became jaded. There is no other word for it. I watched clients get steamrolled by the very firms they had hired to help them. I watched vendors make promises in sales presentations that their own implementation teams knew were impossible. I watched projects go off the rails in slow motion while the system integrator quietly submitted change orders and extended timelines, because every additional month was another month of revenue. And I watched clients accept all of it, because they did not know any better. They did not have anyone in the room who was truly on their side.

That realization is what changed the trajectory of my career. Most ERP consultants, system integrators, and value-added resellers represent the software vendors rather than clients' best interests. Someone needed to sit on the other side of the table. Someone needed to be in the room whose only job was to protect the client, to call out the conflicts of interest, to challenge the unrealistic timelines, and to hold the vendors and the system integrators accountable for what they had promised.

I left Schlumberger in 2003 and started my own practice. In 2005, I founded Panorama Consulting Group with a simple premise: be the independent voice in a room full of conflicted parties. For over a decade, that firm grew into one of the most recognized names in independent ERP consulting.

But over time, I came to believe that independence alone was not enough. The machine was too powerful, too deeply embedded, too skilled at co-opting even well-intentioned advisors. What clients needed was not just an independent consultant. They needed a client-side advocate. Someone whose entire purpose was to help them navigate the machine, protect their own best interests, and completely dismantle the machine's negative impact on their organization.

That is why I started Third Stage Consulting Group in 2018. Not as a career move. As a mission. Every engagement we take on starts from the same place: we work for the client, full stop. We do not represent vendors. We do not partner with system integrators. We do not earn referral fees or commissions. When we walk into a room, there is exactly one set of interests we are there to serve, and it is the interests of the organization that is about to put itself through one of the most difficult and expensive undertakings it will ever face. We exist to fight the machine on their behalf.

Two decades into this work, the machine has only grown stronger. The firms are bigger. The technology is more sophisticated. The sales pitches are slicker. But the underlying dynamics, the misaligned incentives, the information asymmetry, the structural conflicts of interest, are identical to what I saw in 1998. The machine has simply grown more efficient at processing its fuel.

What This Book Is, and What It Isn't

This is not an anti-technology book. Technology, when implemented well, can be genuinely transformative. I have seen organizations completely reinvent themselves through digital transformation. I have seen supply chains become faster, finance functions become more transparent, customer experiences become seamless. When it works, it works beautifully.

This is a book about why it usually does not work, and whose fault that is.

This is the third book in what has become an unplanned trilogy. My first book, *The Final Countdown*, was about defining a comprehensive digital strategy and roadmap, the work that should happen before an organization commits to any specific technology or partner. My second book, *Welcome to the Jungle*, was about how to navigate the pitfalls and failures that so many organizations face once a transformation is underway. This book is different. This book is about understanding how the technology industry machine itself works, so that your team can dismantle its negative effects and create a foundation for success. The first two books assumed the machine existed and tried to help you survive it. This one pulls it apart and shows you every gear, every lever, every incentive that makes it run.

The conventional wisdom in the industry is that digital transformation failures are primarily the client's fault. Poor readiness, weak executive sponsorship, resistance to change, unrealistic expectations. There is truth in this. Clients bear real responsibility, and Part I of this book will examine that responsibility in unflinching detail.

But the conventional wisdom conveniently ignores the two other parties in the room. It ignores the technology vendors that make promises they cannot keep, force migrations on timelines that serve their investors rather than their customers, and build products with deliberate lock-in. And it ignores the consulting firms that profit from failure, overstaff projects to maximize revenue, and systematically eliminate independent oversight.

When I have sat across from the three parties, the finger-pointing always follows the same pattern. The vendor blames the implementation. The consultant blames the client. The client does not know whom to blame because no one ever told them how the machine actually works.

This book tells them.

There is an analogy I will return to at several points in this book, because it captures something about the machine's structure that no amount of neutral business language quite conveys. The enterprise technology industry operates on the same organizing principles as organized crime. Not in the legal sense -- the machine is largely lawful, which is one of the more disturbing things about it. But in the structural sense. The vendor is the Don, collecting tribute and setting the terms. The system integrators are the capos -- mid-level operators who keep clients in line, take their cut of every engagement, and protect their territory from outside interference. The analyst firms are the consigliere -- advisors with divided loyalties whose counsel is shaped by who is paying for their access. And the client is the mark who believes they are entering a legitimate business relationship. I will return to this analogy in the chapters that follow. By the time we reach the end of this book, I suspect it will not feel like an exaggeration.

I should note that writing this book, like running an independent consulting firm, is not without personal cost. Being tech-agnostic, being a trusted client advisor rather than a vendor ally, being someone who refuses to drink the Kool-Aid -- these positions make powerful people uncomfortable. Over the years, I have received anonymous threatening phone calls from people who did not appreciate what I had to say. One voicemail, left by someone who did not identify themselves, said simply: "Eric, I saw your article and I would be careful if I were you." It sounds like a scene from a fictional movie about the mafia, but this has happened to me on multiple occasions. The technology industry is a trillion-dollar ecosystem, and there are people within it who do not welcome scrutiny. I mention this not to dramatize my own experience but to illustrate the depth of the machine's self-protective instincts. When the incentives are this large, the resistance to transparency is fierce.

Part I examines the transformation from the *client's perspective*. Why organizations start transformations for the wrong reasons, how leadership failures create vacuums that consultants fill with billable hours, why culture and change resistance sabotage even the best-funded programs, and what happens when testing is sacrificed and go-live becomes a catastrophe. Real case studies, real organizations, real consequences. Client names have been anonymized where confidentiality requires it, but every story in this book is true.

Part II examines the transformation from the *technology perspective*. How the cloud business model reshaped the entire ecosystem for investors rather than customers, the specific tactics vendors use to win deals, why integration and data migration are perpetually underestimated, the customization paradox that traps organizations between rigid standardization and runaway complexity, and why AI is poised to repeat every mistake of the previous technology waves.

Part III examines the transformation from the *consultant's perspective*. The fundamental conflict of interest at the heart of the system integrator model, the bait-and-switch between sales teams and delivery teams, why every SI proposes an eighteen-month timeline regardless of complexity, how consultant dependency becomes permanent, and how the selection process itself is rigged.

There is a paradox at the center of all of this that has baffled me for twenty-five years. The executives who lead digital transformations are, in most cases, smart, capable, and experienced business leaders. They would never approve a $100 million factory build without a detailed architectural blueprint, a qualified general contractor, rigorous safety inspections, and a clear understanding of what the finished building should look like. They would never approve a major acquisition without months of due diligence, independent financial analysis, and legal review. They would never open a new regional office without a site plan, a budget, and a project manager who reports to them. These are not reckless people. They are disciplined operators who manage large capital investments with appropriate rigor.

And yet these same executives routinely approve digital transformations -- often the largest capital investment and the highest-risk initiative their organization has ever undertaken -- with a fraction of the diligence they would apply to any other investment of comparable size. They accept an eighteen-month timeline from a system integrator without independent validation. They let the SI run the program without client-owned governance. They skip the organizational readiness assessment because the vendor says they are running out of time. They fund change management at 3 percent of the program budget. They approve go-live dates that their own project teams know are unrealistic. When is the last time you heard of a leadership team completely botching a new factory build? It happens, but it is rare, because the discipline around physical construction is embedded in how organizations operate. Digital transformation has no equivalent discipline, no building codes, no inspections, no general contractor who answers to the owner rather than to the subcontractors. And the failure rate reflects it.

Part IV offers a way out. Not a silver bullet, because there are none, but a set of principles grounded in twenty-five years of evidence about what separates the rare successes from the common failures.

Why This Book, Why Now

Every major enterprise software vendor in the world is simultaneously forcing its customers to migrate from on-premise systems to the cloud. SAP has set a deadline of 2027, recently extended to 2030 under pressure, for customers to move to S/4HANA. Oracle and Microsoft are on parallel tracks.

If this playbook sounds familiar, it should. We saw a version of it twenty-five years ago with Y2K. The technology industry convinced the world that every computer system on the planet was going to collapse at midnight on January 1, 2000, and the only solution was to buy new software. Some of the risk was real. A lot of it was manufactured. But it did not matter, because the fear was enough. Companies spent billions replacing systems that would have run just fine, and the vendors and consultants who stoked the panic were the ones who profited most. Today's forced cloud migration is built on the same logic. After all, what better way to sell something than convincing someone that they have no choice but to buy your product?

This is not happening because cloud systems are somehow superior. In many cases, they are not. It is not happening because it saves companies money. It usually does not. It is happening because investors simply love the cloud business model too much. The recurring revenue, higher profit margins, and high customer switching costs make cloud ERP vendors an investor's dream. The economic incentives cascade through every level of the industry. Investors drive stock prices up for vendors that convert more customers to the cloud, rewarding cloud adoption with market capitalization gains that dwarf the actual value delivered to customers. Executives at these vendors are compensated handsomely -- through bonuses, stock options, and promotions -- for accelerating cloud migration. Sales representatives earn higher commissions on cloud subscriptions than they ever did on on-premise deals. The entire industry, from Wall Street to the individual account executive sitting across from your CIO, has enormous financial incentive behind the cloud push. And that incentive often conflicts directly with the needs and wants of the businesses being pushed.

With investors and vendors both investing heavily in cloud, the rest of the ERP ecosystem falls into line. Consultants and system integrators, paid by the vendors, reinforce the vendors' pro-cloud philosophy. Industry analysts, who are also paid by the vendors, have been touting the death of on-premise for years. The industry has built a fully integrated ecosystem that is crushing on-premise into oblivion.

The result is the largest wave of forced digital transformations in history. Tens of thousands of organizations, whether ready or not, are being thrust into the process of transformation. Many of them have never done this before. Most of them do not understand how the machine works.

This book is for them.

It is for the CEO who has been told by her board that the company needs to "go digital" but is not sure what that means or what it will cost. It is for the CIO who suspects the system integrator is not telling the whole truth but cannot prove it. It is for the CFO who approved a $20 million budget and is about to learn it will be $60 million. It is for the project manager who is drowning in change orders and does not understand why the timeline keeps slipping. It is for the mid-level employee who has been told the new system will make their job easier and suspects, correctly, that nobody actually designed the system with their job in mind.

It is for anyone who has been told what to dream and is beginning to suspect the dream is not their own.

Welcome to the machine. Let me show you how it works.

Part I: THE CLIENT

Fuel for the Machine

"Why do organizations keep feeding themselves into a system designed to consume them?"

Chapter 2

The Burning Platform That Isn't Burning

There is a concept in change management called the "burning platform." The idea is simple: people will not change unless they have to. Unless the platform they are standing on is literally on fire, they will stay put. So if you want to drive transformation, you need a crisis. You need urgency. You need a reason compelling enough that staying the same becomes more frightening than the pain of change.

It is a useful concept. It is also one of the most abused ideas in the technology industry.

Because here is what happens in practice: when a real burning platform does not exist, the machine creates one. Vendors manufacture urgency through end-of-life announcements and sunset deadlines. System integrators amplify the fear by warning clients that they are "falling behind." Analyst firms publish reports declaring that companies that do not transform will be irrelevant within five years. And boards of directors, reading those same reports, hand down mandates to their executive teams without understanding what they are actually asking for.

The result is that a staggering number of organizations begin their digital transformations not because they have a clear strategic rationale, not because they have defined measurable business outcomes, not because they have honestly assessed whether they are ready for the upheaval, but because someone told them they had no choice.

This is how the machine gets fed.

The Manufactured Crisis

In my career, I have seen many legitimate reasons to transform. An organization running a system so old that the original vendor no longer exists. A company that has grown through acquisitions and is running fifteen different platforms that cannot talk to each other. A manufacturer whose supply chain processes are so manual and fragmented that they are losing millions in inefficiency every year. These are real burning platforms. The fire is genuine, the heat is measurable, and the case for change can be built on facts rather than fear.

But increasingly, the organizations I work with are not starting from that place. They are starting because their software vendor told them their current system is going away.

SAP is forcing its customers to migrate to S/4HANA whether they want to or are ready to or not. The company announced that it would end normal support for its legacy ECC platform by December 31, 2027, with extended support available through 2030. For the roughly 30,000 organizations worldwide running SAP ECC, the message was unmistakable: move to our new product, or you are on your own.

On the surface, this sounds like a reasonable business decision by a technology company. Products have lifecycles. Support cannot last forever. Companies need to modernize.

But look closer, and the picture gets more complicated.

A lot of these organizations that they are forcing to upgrade just implemented ECC five, ten, fifteen years ago, so they have not been using that software long enough to get a full ROI on the systems, and they are still paying maintenance on the system, yet SAP is still telling them it does not matter. Think about that for a moment. A company spends $50 million implementing an ERP system. They are still paying annual maintenance fees to the vendor. They have not yet realized the full return on that investment. And now the vendor is telling them they need to spend another $50 million, or more, to move to a new platform. Not because the old one is broken. Not because the business needs have fundamentally changed. Because the vendor has decided it is time.

As of the fourth quarter of 2024, 61 percent of SAP ECC customers had not yet licensed S/4HANA. Nearly two thirds of SAP's installed base, with the original deadline less than three years away, had not even begun the process. That is not a statistic that suggests eager adoption. That is a statistic that suggests an industry being dragged somewhere it does not want to go.

I work with these organizations every day. I hear the same conversation over and over. The CIO or the VP of IT sits across from me and says some version of the same thing: our current system works fine. It is stable. It serves the business well. We do not see the business case for this disruption. But SAP says we have to, so here we are.

One client, a $7 billion global manufacturer running 17 SAP instances, told us plainly that they would not upgrade to S/4HANA if they did not have a deadline. They did not see the value. Their current system ran well. It felt, in their words, like an asymmetrical fight. Nothing was broken. They could not see a business case for the disruption. Their estimated total cost of ownership for the migration was between $50 million and $100 million. For a system they did not need and did not want.

Another client, a major apparel manufacturer, had their CDO pause the S/4HANA upgrade entirely. They did not like how aggressive SAP had been with time-based discounts and pricing pressure. They met with Accenture and Infosys to discuss implementation options and came away underwhelmed. There were not a lot of good examples of people moving from ECC to S/4HANA. Not a lot of "that's amazing, I want to sign a contract" moments.

This whole forced migration is causing SAP to lose a lot of goodwill in the industry. So much so that a lot of legacy customers are actually questioning their decision to be on SAP and are secondguessing that decision and evaluating other options. When your best customers are considering leaving you, that should tell you something about the nature of the "urgency" you have created.

And SAP is not alone. Oracle and Microsoft are on parallel tracks, pushing their customer bases toward cloud versions of their flagship products. This is the first time in my career where all the leading ERP vendors have replaced their flagship products at essentially the same time. SAP S/4HANA, Oracle Cloud ERP, Microsoft Dynamics 365, and Infor CloudSuite are all relatively new and unproven systems. That is an enormous amount of risk being pushed onto the market simultaneously, and most of it is being pushed not by customer demand but by vendor strategy.

We Have Seen This Before

The current spike in ERP deployments reminds me of when I started my career in the late 1990s amid the frenzy of organizations replacing their pre-Y2K systems. Back then, companies had no choice but to replace their systems to avoid the sky from falling when their legacy systems switched over to the year 2000.

The Y2K scare was, in many ways, the original manufactured burning platform. The technology industry convinced the world that every computer system on the planet was going to collapse at midnight on January 1, 2000. The only solution, we were told, was to rip out the old systems and buy new ones. Billions of dollars were spent. Entire IT departments were consumed by the effort. Consulting firms posted record revenues.

Some of the risk was real. Legacy systems that stored dates as two-digit years could indeed have produced errors. But the scale of the response was wildly disproportionate to the actual threat. Many of the systems that were replaced would have required nothing more than a patch. Many would have continued to function without any intervention at all. The fear, not the technical reality, drove the spending.

That wave of replacements produced a corresponding wave of failures that led to some of my first expert witness engagements in the early 2000s. Companies that rushed to implement new systems under artificial deadlines made predictable mistakes. They compressed timelines. They skipped testing. They failed to prepare their organizations for the change. The urgency was manufactured, but the consequences were real.

Like then, companies are now largely replacing systems because of the migration to cloud systems. Also like the Y2K situation, companies are myopically focusing on quick-hit deployments rather than doing it right. The playbook has not changed. The technology industry has simply found a new way to convince organizations that they have no choice. And once again, the vendors and consultants who stoke the urgency are the ones who profit most.

The Business Case That Does Not Exist

One of the most troubling trends I have observed in recent years is the declining rigor around business cases for digital transformation. More client executives that I speak with are becoming less inclined to develop a business case for their digital transformation initiatives. They are skipping the most fundamental step in any major investment: defining why they are doing it and what success looks like.

Part of this is fatigue. When the vendor tells you that you have to migrate, developing a business case can feel like an academic exercise. You are not choosing to transform. You are being forced to. So why bother building a case for something you cannot say no to?

The answer is that the business case is not just about justifying the investment. It is about defining the scope, setting priorities, and establishing the measurable outcomes against which the entire program will be judged. Without it, you are writing a blank check. You are telling the vendor and the system integrator that you will spend whatever it takes to get to the finish line, without ever defining where the finish line is or what it looks like when you get there.

"Why are we changing?" is a fundamental question that needs a more comprehensive answer than just upgrading technology or being forced to move to a new system. Organizations need to have a clear and comprehensive reason for going through a digital transformation. One of the best ways to unpack the "why" of doing this project is to define the business value that is expected from the transformation. These should be measurable metrics that affect the performance, metrics, and results of the organization.

When I conduct organizational readiness assessments, I always ask executives and project team members to articulate the strategy behind their transformation. What are you trying to achieve? What business outcomes will define success? How will you know, two years from now, whether this was worth it?

In a disturbing number of cases, most interviewed individuals are not able to articulate the organization's strategy. They know they are implementing SAP, or Oracle, or D365. They know the go-live date. They know the budget, or at least the original budget. But they cannot tell you why. Not in any way that connects to measurable business value.

One of the top causes of failure is a disconnect between what the C-suite expects and what the program delivers. And in my experience, this disconnect almost always traces back to the beginning, to a transformation that was launched without a clear definition of what it was supposed to accomplish. A weak business case focuses only on system cost and headcount reduction. A strong one connects the technology investment to operational improvements, customer experience, competitive positioning, and long-term strategic goals. The weak version is far more common.

The Vendor's Business Case

When clients do not build their own business case, the vendor is more than happy to provide one. This is where things get dangerous.

The Waste Management case is the most instructive example I know. In 2008, Waste Management, North America's largest waste services company, partnered with SAP to implement a comprehensive ERP system. The project was supposed to deliver $100 million in benefits within 18 months while streamlining operations across the company's complex network of facilities and services.

Read that again. One hundred million dollars in benefits. Eighteen months. For the largest waste services company in North America, with thousands of facilities, tens of thousands of employees, and a web of operational complexity that would make most technology implementations look simple by comparison.

SAP had promised that the company could achieve $106 million to $220 million in annual benefits from a consolidated ERP system that could be implemented in 18 months. These were not Waste Management's numbers. These were SAP's numbers, presented during the sales cycle to justify the investment and win the deal.

The contract was awarded to SAP based on claims that the solution was out-of-the-box, adapted to U.S. standards, and could fulfill the company's goals with minimal customization. However, Waste Management found these claims to be false. The system did not work as promised. The benefits did not materialize. The 18-month timeline was a fantasy.

The company was unable to glean any benefit from the software and filed a $100 million lawsuit against SAP in 2008, later raising that amount to $500 million before settling out of court in 2010. Waste Management said they were part of a fraudulent sales scheme on the part of SAP, whereas SAP turned the tables and pointed the finger at Waste Management, saying that they did not make key business decisions and define requirements in a timely manner.

That finger-pointing is the machine in miniature. The vendor blames the client. The client blames the vendor. And the truth, as is usually the case, involves failures on both sides. Waste Management failed to verify SAP's claims adequately before making executive decisions. They accepted the vendor's business case as their own. They let SAP define the "why" of their transformation.

Waste Management sued SAP for over $1 billion in damages and from their financial records showed that they had realized gains of $77 million as a result of their settlement with SAP. They recovered some money. They spent far more than they recovered. And the years of litigation, disruption, and organizational damage cannot be measured in dollars alone.

The Waste Management case is public, well-documented, and extreme. But the dynamic it illustrates is not extreme at all. It is ordinary. In my work analyzing over 50 implementations embroiled in litigation, my team and I have seen this pattern again and again. The vendor makes promises during the sales cycle that the implementation team cannot deliver. The business case is built on the vendor's projections, not the client's analysis. And when reality diverges from the sales pitch, which it almost always does, the client discovers that the business case they relied on was never really theirs.

In one case, the vendor's sales team over-promised and exaggerated solution benefits that their own solution team could not back up with results. A configurator they claimed was 80 percent built did not work and was slower than the legacy system. They promised 25 to 50 percent efficiency gains. Not only did those gains fail to materialize, but there is a good argument that there would have been problems even with ideal execution.

This is what happens when you let someone else define your burning platform.

The Board Deck That Launched a Thousand Disasters

There is another flavor of manufactured urgency that comes not from the vendor but from the boardroom. I see this most often with private equity-backed companies, though it is by no means limited to them.

The scenario goes like this. A PE firm acquires a company. The company is running older systems, maybe a legacy ERP, maybe QuickBooks, maybe a patchwork of spreadsheets and standalone applications. The PE firm, looking to increase the value of its portfolio company before an eventual exit, decides that a digital transformation is needed. A board mandate is issued. A budget is allocated. A timeline is set. And the organization, which may or may not be ready for any of this, is told to make it happen.

In one case, a PE firm acquired a company and immediately identified the legacy ERP system as a risk. The PE firm had a bias toward Tier I products like SAP and Oracle, and they were looking for their next deal at some point, which was part of what drove the urgency. The transformation was not being pursued because the business needed it. It was being pursued because the PE firm's investment thesis required it.

In another case, a PE-backed apparel company found itself in a similar position. The private equity firm had very little understanding of retail and production. The board did not know or understand the complexities of ERP. They did not even like the term "ERP" because it sounded too technical and too expensive. So they referred to it as an "IT initiative" instead, as if changing the label would change the complexity.

These board-driven mandates share a common feature: the people making the decision to transform are not the people who will live with the consequences. The PE partner or the board member who approves the budget will not be the one sitting in the conference room at 10 PM trying to reconcile inventory discrepancies two days before go-live. They will not be the warehouse worker who has to learn an entirely new system while still shipping orders.

They will not be the project manager who has to explain, six months in, why the timeline has doubled and the budget is gone.

The distance between the decision and the impact is where a lot of damage gets done. When the people who authorize a transformation do not understand what they are authorizing, the organization enters the machine without a compass. The vendor and the system integrator are happy to provide direction. But their direction, as we have discussed, tends to serve their interests more than the client's.

There is a specific PE dynamic that makes the timeline pressure even more dangerous: the hold period. Private equity firms typically plan to hold a portfolio company for three to seven years before exiting. That hold period drives every strategic decision, including technology. A PE firm with a two-to-three-year hold horizon will push for a light, low-cost technology investment -- enough to clean up the books for a resale, not enough to genuinely transform the business. A PE firm with a five-to-seven-year hold will push for a comprehensive ERP implementation -- but they want it done fast, because every month of implementation is a month without the operational improvements that justify the investment thesis.

In both cases, the PE firm's financial timeline, not the organization's operational readiness, dictates the pace. The result is that PE-backed transformations carry a built-in accelerant: board-level pressure for speed that compounds the SI's already-compressed timeline and the vendor's already-aggressive migration deadline. The eighteen-month lie, which I will discuss in Chapter 19, becomes even harder to challenge when the PE partner sitting on the board has modeled the returns based on a go-live date that was set before anyone assessed whether the organization could meet it.

A Technology Project Is Not a Transformation

Beneath all of these manufactured burning platforms lies a fundamental confusion that is worth addressing directly, because it is the root cause of so much of the dysfunction described in this book.

The difference between an ERP implementation and digital transformation is the holistic, full-scope essence that comes with evolving as an organization. Everything from effective organizational change management plans, business process management, and other people and process aspects of a project are much more important than the technology. Your project can succeed with subpar technology, but it cannot succeed without strong business processes and people enablement.

Read that last sentence again. Your project can succeed with subpar technology. It cannot succeed without strong business processes and people enablement. That is not a philosophical abstraction. That is a finding from the data we have collected across more than a thousand implementations.

Yet the way most transformations begin, you would think the technology is the only thing that matters. The first major decision is which software to buy. The second major decision is which system integrator to hire. The people, the processes, the organizational readiness, the change management, the business case, the strategic alignment: all of these get addressed later, if they get addressed at all. The sequence is backwards, and it is backwards because the machine is designed to sell technology first.

There is another dimension to this problem that has become more acute in recent years: technology is changing exponentially faster than any single organization can absorb. The gap between what technology can potentially do and what a business is actually ready to implement is widening, not narrowing. Every year, the vendors release new capabilities, new modules, new AI-powered features, new cloud services. And every year, the organizations that are supposed to adopt these capabilities fall further behind, because human beings and organizational cultures do not change at the speed of software releases. This widening chasm makes transformations more risky, more complicated, and more costly than they were even five years ago. Yet the industry continues to sell speed and innovation as though the constraint is the technology, when in reality the constraint is, and has always been, the organization's capacity to change.

A vendor is not going to tell you to slow down and get your organization ready before you buy their software. That is not how they get paid. A system integrator is not going to tell you to spend six months on business process redesign before you start configuring the system. That is not how they get paid either. The machine is designed to move fast, close deals, start billing hours, and get to go-live as quickly as possible. Organizational readiness is an inconvenience. Strategic clarity is a delay. And the business case, if it exists at all, is something that was written to justify a decision that has already been made.

The organizations that succeed are the ones that resist this pressure. They define their strategy first. They assess their readiness honestly. They build a business case grounded in measurable outcomes. They make the technology serve the business, not the other way around.

But resisting the pressure requires knowing that the pressure exists. And most organizations, when they step onto what they believe is a burning platform, do not realize that the fire was lit by someone who profits from the heat.

The Questions Nobody Asks

Before any organization commits to a digital transformation, there are questions that should be answered honestly. Not by the vendor. Not by the system integrator. Not by the analyst firm. By the organization itself.

Why are we doing this? Not "because SAP told us to" or "because the board said so" or "because our competitors are." Why, in terms of specific, measurable business outcomes, is this investment worth the disruption it will cause?

What will be different when we are done? Not in terms of technology, but in terms of how the business operates. What processes will change? What capabilities will we have that we do not have today? How will our customers, our employees, and our bottom line be affected?

Are we ready? Not "do we have the budget" but are our people ready for this level of change? Does our leadership team agree on the objectives? Do we have the governance structure to make difficult decisions quickly? Is our organizational culture capable of absorbing this kind of disruption?

What happens if we do nothing? This is perhaps the most important question, and the one that is asked least often. In some cases, the answer is genuinely alarming: the system is failing, the vendor has no support path, the business is at risk. In those cases, the burning platform is real. But in many cases, the honest answer is that the current system works fine, that extended support is available, that the risks of doing nothing are manageable and the risks of doing something are substantial. The machine does not want you to reach that conclusion. The machine wants you on the platform, burning or not.

Only about 10 percent of the transformation projects I have seen achieve what I would consider genuine success: completed as expected, on time and on budget, with the intended ROI realized. Roughly 80 percent get stuck somewhere in the middle, delivered partially, over budget, over timeline, with limited return and significant operational disruption. And about 10 percent never complete at all. Those are sobering numbers for any organization, but they are especially sobering for an organization that did not need to be on the platform in the first place.

The burning platform is a powerful concept. But its power depends on whether the fire is real. Too many organizations are standing on a platform that is perfectly solid, being told by people with matches and gasoline that they had better jump.

The first step in dismantling the machine is learning to tell the difference.

Chapter 3

The Leadership Vacuum

Every digital transformation has an executive sponsor. It says so right there on the project charter, usually on the first page, in a box near the top. The name of a senior executive, often the CIO, sometimes the CFO, occasionally the CEO. Their title is listed. Their role is defined. On paper, they are the person accountable for the success of a program that will cost tens of millions of dollars and consume the organization for years.

On paper.

In practice, executive sponsorship is one of the most consistently misunderstood and underperformed roles in digital transformation. I have conducted hundreds of organizational readiness assessments over the course of my career, and in a disturbing number of them, the executive sponsor is a figurehead. They attend the steering committee meetings, or some of them. They sign off on the budget, or the original version of it. They make an appearance at the project kickoff, say a few words about how important this initiative is, and then disappear into the demands of their day job. The project team does not hear from them again until something goes badly wrong.

By then, it is usually too late.

The absence of genuine executive leadership is not just one more risk factor on a long list of things that can go wrong with a transformation. It is the risk factor that enables all the others. When leadership is absent, governance becomes theater. When governance becomes theater, the system integrator fills the vacuum. When the system integrator fills the vacuum, the project starts serving the consultant's interests instead of the client's. And when the project serves the consultant's interests, the machine is in full control.

The Title Without the Authority

There is a meaningful difference between sponsoring a transformation and championing one. A sponsor approves the budget. A champion fights for the program when it gets hard. A sponsor delegates decisions to the project team. A champion makes the difficult calls that only a senior executive can make: reallocating resources from other priorities, resolving political conflicts between business units, telling a department head that their processes are going to change whether they like it or not.

Executive sponsors must understand that digital transformation is not just a technology project. It is a business transformation that affects every aspect of the organization. They must be prepared to make difficult decisions about resource allocation, process changes, and organizational restructuring.

Most are not prepared. Most do not even understand what they are being asked to do.

Forty percent of organizations report a lack of executive buy-in as a significant factor in digital transformation failures. That number alone should be staggering. Four out of ten organizations cannot get their own leadership genuinely behind the most expensive initiative the company will undertake. But the number undersells the problem, because it only captures the organizations that recognize the gap. In my experience, many more organizations believe they have strong executive support when what they actually have is a name on a charter and a standing calendar invitation that gets declined more often than accepted.

I see this pattern in nearly every readiness assessment we conduct. We interview executives, project team members, and end users.

We ask them to describe the level of executive engagement they are seeing. And what comes back is a consistent story of absence.

In one assessment at a mid-market industrial company, the pattern was textbook. The executive team had kicked off the transformation with the usual fanfare, town halls, internal announcements, reassurances that this was a priority. But within a few months, the executives had retreated to their day jobs. Project team members told us that leadership was no longer visible. They were not walking the floor, not showing up to project meetings, not checking in with the people doing the work. Employees told us they appreciated management visibility, that it mattered to them to see executives in the room, being on the floor to reassure and provide encouragement. But that visibility had faded. The finding was clear: if employees do not sense executive support, buy-in will not be easily achieved.

When we scored that organization on executive support in our readiness framework, they came in at a 3 out of 10. Strategic clarity scored a 3 as well. Internal communications, also a 3. And accountability, the dimension that measures whether people believe commitments are honored and follow-through is real, scored a 1 out of 10.

Those numbers paint a picture of an organization where the people at the top have checked out, the people in the middle do not know where the program is headed, and the people at the bottom do not believe anyone will be held to their word. That is not an edge case. It is closer to the norm than most executives would like to believe.

When the C-Suite Cannot Agree

Executives and stakeholders need to be aligned on how and why an organization needs to go through a change or transformation. The larger your organization, the higher the probability that your team will be misaligned.

This sounds obvious. Of course the leadership team should agree on what they are trying to accomplish. But in practice, executive misalignment is one of the most common and most destructive dynamics I encounter.

The CEO sees the transformation as a growth enabler, a way to scale operations and enter new markets. The CFO sees it as a cost-reduction play, a way to automate manual processes and reduce headcount. The CIO sees it as a technical modernization, a necessary upgrade to aging infrastructure. The COO sees it as a disruption to operations that need to keep running while the technology is being swapped out underneath them. Each of these perspectives contains a piece of the truth. None of them, on its own, constitutes a strategy.

Executives must be aligned on the scope of transformation, whether it is a technology-only effort or a full process redesign. They must agree on the timeline, whether they are pursuing quick wins or a multi-year roadmap. And they must understand the effort required, the investment in change management and data that will be necessary to succeed. When they are not aligned on these fundamentals, every decision downstream becomes a negotiation, a compromise, or a conflict.

I worked with one large manufacturing company where the rupture between the executive team became visible only weeks before go-live. The CTO and CIO were on one track, focused on the technical deployment. The COO was on another, concerned about operational readiness and the impact on production. For months, these two camps had been moving in parallel without truly collaborating. It was only in the final weeks, when the consequences of misalignment became impossible to ignore, that they started working together as a team. By then, decisions that should have been made months earlier were being made under pressure, with incomplete information and no time to get them right.

At another organization, a global industrial company, the dynamics were even more corrosive. The key supply chain executive, the person with the most business benefits at stake, had no voice in the program. He had advocated for a specialized supply chain planning tool, but the system integrator, in this case Deloitte, pushed the organization toward the ERP vendor's own planning module instead. The executive was overruled. The supply chain workstream went into red status. A large part of the leadership team was new and did not have ERP experience, which meant they lacked the context to challenge the SI's recommendation. The system integrator filled the decision-making gap with its own preferences, which happened to align with its own revenue model.

This is what happens when executives are not aligned. Somebody fills the vacuum. And that somebody is almost never acting in the client's best interest.

Governance Theater

Most transformation programs have a governance structure. There is a steering committee. There is a project management office. There are status reports and dashboards and escalation protocols. On a slide deck, it all looks very organized.

The question is whether any of it actually works.

In one implementation readiness review, we did not find evidence that the steering committee was being used to full effect. Presentations to the steering committee lacked specific requests or information that would allow executive decisions to be made. The committee was meeting. People were showing up. PowerPoints were being presented. But the meetings were informational, not decisional. The steering committee was being briefed on the status of the project without being asked to actually steer anything.

At another organization, we found that data migration, the single most exposed workstream in the program, had recorded only one tracked decision against 209 action items, 368 requirements, and 144 open items. One decision. For a workstream that was drowning in complexity and risk. That is not governance. That is the absence of governance disguised as process.

Every transformation program maintains what the industry calls a RAID log, a running register of Risks, Action Items, Issues, and Decisions. It is supposed to be the program's early warning system, the place where problems are documented, tracked, and escalated to leadership for resolution. In a well-governed program, the RAID log is a living document that forces uncomfortable truths to the surface before they become crises.

The volume and age distribution of overdue items in that program suggested that either the RAID status was not being reported to the steering committee with sufficient granularity, or that escalations were not resulting in timely resolution. In other words, either the problems were not reaching the people with the authority to solve them, or they were reaching them and nothing was being done. Neither scenario is acceptable. Both are common.

I have come to think of governance in digital transformation as serving three essential functions. The first is information: consolidating key data from all program areas so that leadership has a clear picture of reality, not the sanitized version that project teams are incentivized to present. The second is alignment: ensuring that all parts of the program are heading in the same direction. The third is control: the ability to intervene when something is going wrong, in the same way that the purpose of a chief engineer on a ship is to ensure the engines do not blow up.

When governance fails at any of these three functions, the program drifts. And when it drifts, the system integrator steps in to provide the direction that leadership should be providing. That direction will be informed by the SI's own interests, which are not the same as yours.

There is an additional danger worth noting: governance can sometimes overtake the purpose of the program and become an industry unto itself. I have seen transformation programs where the governance process consumed so much time and produced so many reports that the people who were supposed to be building and configuring the system were spending half their days in meetings about the meetings. The more layers and complexity a program adds to a governance model, the more likely it is to lose value. The goal is not to have the most elaborate governance framework. The goal is to make decisions quickly, escalate risks effectively, and hold people accountable for their commitments.

The Leadership Revolving Door

There is another dimension to the leadership vacuum that deserves its own discussion, because it is remarkably common and remarkably destructive: executive turnover during a transformation.

Digital transformations take time. Even well-run programs typically span two to three years. Complex, multi-phase programs can run five years or more. Over that kind of timeline, leadership changes are almost inevitable. CEOs retire. CIOs take new jobs. Executive sponsors get promoted, or pushed out, or simply burn out.

The half-life of a CIO is 2.8 years at a company, usually because the board gets frustrated with an IT project gone wrong. Think about what that means for a three-year transformation program. There is a meaningful probability that the executive who started the initiative will not be the one who finishes it. And when the executive sponsor changes, everything changes with them. The new person has different priorities, different relationships, different opinions about what the program should accomplish. They may not even believe the program should continue.

The Lidl case illustrates this dynamic at its most damaging. Throughout the seven-year implementation, Lidl experienced significant executive turnover. The company appointed a new CEO in 2014 who subsequently stepped down in 2017, during the most critical phases of the project. The Head of IT also departed during this period, creating a leadership vacuum at precisely when strong, consistent direction was most needed.

This executive instability meant that key strategic decisions, such as whether all stores should operate under the same process model or whether certain geographies should maintain autonomous operations, were left unresolved. Without consistent leadership championing the transformation and making difficult decisions about process changes, the project lost momentum and coherence. The result, as we know, was €500 million spent over seven years with nothing to show for it.

The US Air Force's ECSS program suffered from the same disease. The Air Force's lack of leadership, especially at the executive level, was perhaps the biggest problem. There was no clear executive sponsor, and the organization's leaders delegated most major project decisions to the project team without providing adequate strategic direction. The result was over $1 billion spent on a system that was never deployed.

At a municipal government we worked with, the leadership picture was fragmented in a different way. The city had experienced turnover in its city manager position. The CIO was not included in the management leadership team. The result was unclear executive sponsorship, trust issues across the organization, and a transformation that lacked a visible champion at the top.

Each of these situations is different in its specifics. But the pattern is the same. When the person at the top changes, the center of gravity shifts. Decisions that were settled become unsettled. Priorities that were clear become contested. And the project team, caught in the middle, tries to keep building a house while the architects keep changing the blueprints.

The Vacuum Gets Filled

Nature abhors a vacuum, and so does a system integrator's revenue model.

When executive leadership is absent, disengaged, or constantly turning over, someone has to make decisions. The project cannot stand still. Configuration choices need to be made. Scope questions need to be resolved. Timelines need to be set. And if the client's leadership is not in the room to make those calls, the system integrator will make them instead.

This is not always malicious. In many cases, the SI consultants on the ground are genuinely trying to keep the project moving. They see that decisions are not being made, that risks are not being escalated, that the steering committee is a rubber stamp, and they step in because someone has to.

The problem is that their frame of reference is different from yours. They are optimizing for what they know: the technology, the methodology, the timeline they committed to in the statement of work. They are not optimizing for your business strategy, your organizational culture, or your long-term operating model, because those things are not their responsibility. They were supposed to be yours.

It is often easier and more straightforward to just let some big-name integrator handle it. But your SI is most likely not a stakeholder in your business outcomes, and therefore should not be making the staffing and organizational decisions or managing all activities of the implementation.

One industry peer put it well: "I think when we read about large-scale IT failures, we are often seeing organizations make large IT investment decisions when they were not fit to understand those dependencies. Therefore, they are left with the very large risk of failure because they outsource the decision-making to a party who may be taking a fairly narrow view that ignores many of those dependencies."

That narrow view is the crux of the issue. A system integrator knows how to configure SAP or Oracle or D365. They may know it very well. But they do not know your business the way your own people do. They do not understand the informal power structures, the unwritten rules, the relationships between departments that make the organization actually function.

When they fill the leadership vacuum, they bring technical competence but organizational blindness. And the decisions they make in that vacuum, about scope, about process design, about what to customize and what to leave standard, will shape the organization for years after the consultants are gone.

This is why we tell every client the same thing: do not turn over all of the project budget responsibility to your SI. You should own this. The client needs to own the project management and lead through partnership. Do not rely on the SI alone.

But owning the project requires leaders who are present, engaged, and willing to make hard decisions. When they are not, the client loses control of its own transformation. And once control is lost, getting it back is extraordinarily difficult.

The Accountability Crisis

Leadership is not just about making decisions at the top. It is about creating an environment where decisions are made and honored at every level of the organization. This is where accountability enters the picture, and it is where many organizations fall apart.

At one large food and agriculture conglomerate we assessed, accountability was perhaps the most widely cited risk for successful change. As an organizational culture that grants a large amount of autonomy to individual business units, central leadership does not favor dictating practices. This has caused managers and other employees historically to feel enabled to opt out of change initiatives, practices, processes, and tools.

Let that register. This was an organization about to undertake an enterprise-wide digital transformation, and its own culture permitted people to opt out of enterprise-wide initiatives. The organization bought tools and then gave people the option of not using them. It launched programs and then allowed business units to decide for themselves whether to participate.

The interviews we conducted painted a vivid picture. "Up until recently, leaders would still be able to choose if they were in or out. Because everyone operates their own business, they had the freedom to pick and choose what they wanted to participate in on a global business scale."

"People pay lip-service to stuff. They think it will go away. There is no accountability, and it will not be followed up on."

"People not wanting to change and are being allowed to not change. Small pockets of people still going back to the way they were doing things before, and the managers on the site are allowing them to do that."

This organization scored accountability at 37 percent favorable in their employee engagement survey. The culture survey came in at 43 percent. These are not ambiguous numbers. They describe an organization where nearly two thirds of the workforce does not believe that commitments are honored or that there are consequences for inaction.

Now imagine deploying a new ERP system into that environment. Imagine asking thousands of employees to abandon the processes they have used for years and adopt entirely new ways of working, in an organization where the prevailing belief is that if you wait long enough, the new initiative will go away and things will go back to normal.

This is not an isolated case. In another readiness assessment, accountability scored a 1 out of 10. One out of ten. The perception was that there was no accountability. The messaging employees received was "you are input only, let someone else solve on the back end." When individuals feel there are no consequences for their actions, user adoption becomes very challenging.

I have now seen accountability scores of 1 out of 10 at multiple client organizations. It is more common than anyone in the industry wants to admit. And it is not something that can be fixed by a better project plan or a more capable system integrator. It is a leadership problem. It is a culture problem. And if it is not addressed before the transformation begins, it will quietly destroy everything the program is trying to build.

Change Fatigue and the Organization That Has Had Enough

There is a related condition that I encounter with increasing frequency, and it compounds every leadership challenge described in this chapter. It is the organization that has been through so much change that it simply does not have the capacity to absorb any more.

One client had gone through eight ownership changes in recent years. The employees had coined a term for their experience: ASC. "Always Something Changing." There was a lot of change fatigue in this part of the business and an inconsistent way of managing change.

Eight ownership changes. Each one bringing new leadership, new priorities, new systems, new processes, new uncertainty about who would still have a job in six months. And now someone was asking these same people to embrace yet another major change, this time a full ERP implementation, and to do it with enthusiasm and commitment.

Change fatigue is not laziness. It is not resistance. It is a rational response to an environment where change has consistently been imposed without clear purpose, without adequate support, and without follow-through. When employees have seen three "transformative" initiatives come and go in five years, each one announced with great fanfare and then quietly abandoned or half-implemented, they learn to keep their heads down and wait it out. The current initiative, no matter how well-intentioned, gets treated as just another wave that will pass.

This is a leadership failure, not an employee failure. Every abandoned initiative, every half-finished program, every change that was launched without the resources or commitment to see it through, has deposited a layer of cynicism in the organization. That cynicism does not disappear when a new project charter is signed. It has to be acknowledged, addressed, and overcome through consistent, visible, sustained leadership behavior. And that takes time and energy that most transformation programs do not budget for.

What Real Leadership Looks Like

I do not want to leave this chapter entirely in the dark. I have seen organizations get this right. They are the minority, but they exist, and they share common characteristics worth naming.

In organizations that succeed, the executive sponsor is not a name on a charter. They are a visible, active presence in the program. They attend steering committee meetings and use them to make real decisions, not to receive status updates. They walk the floor. They talk to end users. They understand, at a detailed level, what the transformation requires and what it will disrupt. They do not delegate the hard conversations to consultants. They have them personally.

The leadership team is aligned. Not perfectly, because perfect alignment is an illusion, but sufficiently. They have debated the scope, the priorities, the trade-offs. They have agreed on what success looks like. And when disagreements surface during the program, as they inevitably do, they have a mechanism for resolving them that does not involve months of political maneuvering or punting the decision to the system integrator.

Governance is real. The steering committee has decision-making authority and uses it. Risks are escalated and resolved, not logged and forgotten. Status reports reflect reality, including the uncomfortable parts. And when something is going wrong, the response is to address the root cause, not to reclassify the risk as medium and hope it resolves itself.

Accountability is built into the culture, or at least into the program's operating model. Commitments are tracked. Deadlines are honored. When someone does not deliver, there are consequences. Not punitive consequences, necessarily, but real follow-through that makes it clear this program is not optional and this timeline is not aspirational.

And perhaps most importantly, the organization owns its own transformation. The system integrator is a partner, not a surrogate. The client's project management team leads the program. The client's business leaders make the business decisions. The client's change management team prepares the organization. The SI provides technical expertise and implementation capacity, which is what they are good at. But the strategy, the governance, the accountability, and the leadership belong to the organization. They cannot be outsourced. When they are, the machine takes over.

Governance must be business-led, independent, and enforceable. That is a simple sentence. It is one of the hardest things in this book to actually do. But every successful transformation I have been part of has had it, and every catastrophic failure I have investigated has lacked it.

The leadership vacuum is not inevitable. It is a choice. It is the choice to treat executive sponsorship as a ceremonial role instead of the most important job on the program. It is the choice to let the steering committee become a status meeting instead of a decision-making body.

It is the choice to tolerate misalignment at the top because the conversations required to resolve it are uncomfortable. It is the choice to let the SI fill the gaps that only internal leadership can fill.

These choices are made quietly, incrementally, often without anyone recognizing what is happening until the consequences are undeniable. The machine counts on this. The machine thrives in the space that leadership leaves empty. It is designed to fill vacuums, and to fill them in ways that serve its own interests.

The organizations that break free are the ones whose leaders refuse to leave that space empty in the first place.

Chapter 4

The Accountability Gap

In the previous chapter, I described the leadership vacuum: the absence of genuine executive sponsorship, the misalignment at the top, the governance theater that passes for oversight. Those are failures of the people in charge. This chapter is about something deeper and harder to fix. It is about the organizational culture that exists beneath the leadership layer, the invisible operating system that determines whether any initiative, no matter how well-led, will actually take hold.

Culture is not on the project plan. It does not appear as a line item in the budget. It is not a deliverable in the statement of work. No system integrator will tell you that your culture is the reason their project is going to fail, because they do not get paid to diagnose culture. They get paid to configure software. And so culture operates in the background, shaping everything, accountable to no one, and acknowledged by almost nobody until the damage is done.

Peter Drucker is credited with the observation that culture eats strategy for breakfast. In my experience, culture eats strategy, technology, project plans, change management programs, and billion-dollar ERP investments for breakfast, lunch, and dinner. I have watched technically flawless implementations fail because the culture rejected them like an immune system attacking a transplant. I have watched modest, imperfect implementations succeed because the culture was healthy enough to absorb the disruption and adapt. The technology is the organ being transplanted. The culture is the body that decides whether to accept it or destroy it.

And the machine does not care about culture. The machine sells software and bills hours. Culture is someone else's problem. Which is precisely why it becomes everyone's problem the moment the system goes live.

The Accountability Paradox

There is a paradox at the heart of enterprise transformation that I have never seen adequately addressed in any methodology, any vendor presentation, or any SI proposal. It is this: the organizations that most need enterprise-wide transformation are often the ones whose cultures are least capable of executing it.

Enterprise transformation, by definition, requires the entire enterprise to move in the same direction at the same time. It requires standardization. It requires common processes, common data definitions, common ways of working. It requires departments that have operated independently for decades to suddenly adopt shared workflows, shared systems, and shared accountability for outcomes that cross organizational boundaries.

But the organizations that most need this standardization are typically the ones that have spent years, sometimes decades, cultivating the opposite. They have grown through acquisition, inheriting different systems and processes with each deal. They have empowered regional or divisional leaders to run their operations as they see fit. They have built cultures that prize autonomy, entrepreneurship, and local decision-making. These are not bad values. In many cases, they are the values that made the company successful in the first place.

The problem is that these values are fundamentally incompatible with enterprise-wide systems implementation. You cannot give every business unit the freedom to define its own processes and simultaneously deploy a single ERP system that requires everyone to follow the same process. You cannot celebrate autonomous decision-making and simultaneously demand compliance with a centralized data model. The transformation asks the organization to become something it has never been, and the culture, which is the accumulated expression of everything the organization has rewarded and tolerated for years, pushes back.

This is not resistance in the way we discussed in the chapter on the human firewall. Individuals are not consciously opposing the change. The culture itself is opposing it. The antibodies are organizational, not personal. And they are far harder to see and far harder to address.

I have conducted readiness assessments at organizations where every individual I interviewed said they supported the transformation. Every one of them. And yet the organization, collectively, was incapable of executing it. The individuals were willing. The culture was not. The gap between individual intent and organizational behavior is the accountability gap, and it is where more transformations die than anyone in the industry wants to admit.

One of the most counterintuitive manifestations of the accountability gap I have encountered was at a large food and agriculture conglomerate where the culture was, by every measure, genuinely kind. People cared about each other. Relationships were deep and long-tenured. The organization had built its identity around being a good place to work, and it was. But that kindness had a shadow. The organization had developed an internal shorthand for the dynamic, a phrase that everyone recognized: the culture was too nice. Managers did not feel comfortable having tough conversations with direct reports or peers. Hard things were not discussed. People did not debate. They did not disagree. They did not engage in effective conflict. The result was that poor performance was tolerated, passive resistance went unaddressed, and a heavier focus on relationships came at the detriment of accountability. There is a direct line between a culture that cannot have difficult conversations and a culture that cannot execute enterprise transformation, because transformation is one long series of difficult conversations: about which processes will change, about which roles will be redefined, about which business units will lose autonomy, and about what happens when someone does not comply. When the culture's immune response to discomfort is avoidance, those conversations never happen, and the transformation stalls in a swamp of politeness.

The Opt-Out Culture

In the previous chapter, I briefly described a large food and agriculture conglomerate where the culture of autonomy had created an environment in which managers could simply opt out of enterprise initiatives. I want to return to that organization now, because what we found there illustrates the accountability gap at a depth that the previous chapter could only introduce.

This was not a small company. It was a multi-billion-dollar global enterprise with operations spanning continents. It had grown through acquisitions, absorbing companies with their own systems, their own processes, their own ways of doing things. Central leadership had historically taken a light touch, allowing business units to operate with a high degree of independence. This approach had served the company well during its growth phase. Regional leaders knew their markets. Local operations were responsive and agile. The autonomy was a competitive advantage.

Until it was not.

When the organization decided to pursue an enterprise-wide digital transformation, it ran headlong into the culture it had built. The autonomy that had been a strength in a decentralized operating model became a fatal weakness in an initiative that required centralized coordination, standardized processes, and universal adoption.

We found that the organization had tried to implement enterprise tools before, and the results were telling. Tools had been purchased and deployed, and then adoption was made optional. Business units that did not see the value simply did not use them. "Every group believes that the way they do business is fine. They've already done things necessary to be as efficient as possible." That belief, held simultaneously by dozens of business units, each with their own processes and their own definition of "efficient," made enterprise standardization nearly impossible.

The organization had a cultural mantra that had served it well during its growth years: "run your own rig." It was an expression of the entrepreneurial spirit that had built the company from a regional operation into a global enterprise. Local leaders were trusted to make decisions, solve problems, and operate with minimal interference from the center. But what had once been a competitive advantage had become an organizational liability. When the enterprise attempted to make decisions around common tools or processes, the independent streak reasserted itself. People took off and did their own thing. Decisions were customized based on the business group and what they thought would work for them, leading to a patchwork of workarounds. The culture had also produced what I came to think of as a "heroes and spreadsheets" operating model. There was tons of tribal knowledge and nothing was documented. Individual expertise had become a form of job security -- the person who knew how the pricing logic worked or how the intercompany transfers were handled held power precisely because that knowledge lived nowhere but in their head. Tribal knowledge had become certain employees' competitive edge. It gave them security, and it was a risk for the organization.

An enterprise ERP system, by design, eliminates this kind of individual dependency. It codifies processes, standardizes workflows, and makes institutional knowledge accessible to everyone. For people whose value was tied to being the only one who knew how something worked, the new system was not a tool. It was a threat.

The pattern went deeper than tool adoption. It extended to how the organization made and enforced decisions. When we surveyed the organization, accountability scored 37 percent favorable. The culture dimension scored 43 percent. These were not scores that reflected isolated pockets of dysfunction. They reflected an organizational norm. Nearly two-thirds of the workforce did not believe that commitments were followed through on or that there were meaningful consequences for non-compliance.

What made this finding so dangerous was not just the score itself. It was what the score predicted about the transformation's chances. An ERP implementation requires thousands of decisions to be made and honored. Business process owners must define future-state workflows and commit to them. Department heads must release their best people to the project team and keep them released for the duration. Testing cycles must be completed on schedule. Training must be attended and absorbed. Data must be cleaned and validated by the business, not by the SI.

Every one of those activities depends on accountability. Every one of them requires someone to make a commitment and someone else to hold them to it. In an organization where accountability scores 37 percent favorable, where the prevailing expectation is that commitments are aspirational rather than binding, each of those activities becomes unreliable. Not because the individuals are incompetent or unwilling, but because the organizational culture has taught them, through years of reinforcement, that commitments are negotiable and follow-through is optional.

The Hub-and-Spoke Problem

Many of the organizations I work with operate on what I think of as a hub-and-spoke model. There is a corporate center, the hub, which sets strategy, manages finances, and provides shared services. And there are the business units, the spokes, which operate with varying degrees of autonomy depending on the company's history and management philosophy.

In a healthy hub-and-spoke model, the hub sets the standards and the spokes adapt them to local needs within defined boundaries.

There is a balance between central coordination and local flexibility. The hub provides the framework. The spokes provide the execution. Decisions flow in both directions, and there is a shared understanding of which decisions belong to the center and which belong to the business unit.

In the organizations that struggle most with transformation, this balance has broken down. The spokes have become so autonomous that they no longer recognize the hub's authority. Or the hub has become so passive that it no longer exercises it. The result is an organization that looks unified on the org chart but operates as a loose confederation of independent fiefdoms, each with its own processes, its own systems, its own data definitions, and its own ideas about how things should work.

When you deploy an enterprise ERP system into this environment, you are not just implementing technology. You are attempting to rebuild the relationship between the hub and the spokes. You are asking business units that have operated independently for years to surrender process autonomy to a centralized system. You are asking the hub to assert authority it may never have exercised.

You are, in effect, restructuring the organization's power dynamics through a technology project, without ever calling it that.

This is why so many ERP implementations devolve into political warfare. The technology is the visible battlefield, but the real fight is about power. Who gets to define the process? Who decides which exceptions are permitted? Who determines the data standards? In a well-governed transformation, these questions are resolved through a structured decision-making process with clear escalation paths. In an organization with a broken hub-and-spoke model, these questions become proxy wars for deeper disagreements about organizational identity and control.

I have seen implementations where individual plant managers refused to adopt the standard process because it did not accommodate their specific workflow. I have seen division presidents overrule enterprise-wide decisions because they believed their business was "different." I have seen regional IT teams quietly maintain shadow systems alongside the new ERP because they did not trust the centralized solution to meet their needs. In each case, the technology implementation was technically sound. The cultural infrastructure required to support it simply did not exist.

At the food and agriculture conglomerate, the incentive structures reinforced the dysfunction. People were rewarded within their group. The metric was group profitability, not enterprise performance. The prevailing thought was: how do I make my group successful? When one location's profitability came at the expense of another location's, the system rewarded the behavior anyway. Some individuals had been there for so long that they controlled knowledge and power. They were rewarded for being the one expert in something. The incentive structure was not broken by accident. It was the logical expression of a decentralized culture that had never needed to operate as a single enterprise. But an ERP implementation demands exactly that: a single enterprise, with common processes, common data, and common measures of success. When the incentives point in the opposite direction, the technology cannot override the economics. People follow the money, and the money was telling them to stay in their silos.

The Inheritance Problem

There is a particular version of the accountability gap that has become more common in recent years, and it deserves specific attention because of how effectively it undermines transformation from the inside.

It is the problem of inherited initiatives. A transformation is approved by one leadership team and then executed by another. The executive who championed the business case retires, or gets promoted, or moves to a different company. The new executive inherits a program that is already in flight, already funded, already committed, but that they did not choose and may not believe in.

At one organization, the employees had gone through eight ownership changes in recent years. Eight. Each change brought new leadership, new priorities, new strategic direction. Each change required the organization to recalibrate, to figure out what the new owners valued, what they would fund, what they would cut. And each change deposited another layer of scar tissue, another reason to believe that whatever was happening now would not last.

The employees had coined a term for their experience: ASC. "Always Something Changing." It was said with the weary resignation of people who had learned that the only constant in their organization was instability. They had stopped investing emotionally in new initiatives because experience had taught them that the initiative would change, the leaders would change, and the only people who would still be there in three years were the ones on the shop floor.

This is not cynicism. This is pattern recognition. When employees have watched five strategic initiatives launch and three of them get abandoned, they are not being negative when they assume the sixth one will meet the same fate. They are being rational. And their rationality creates an enormous problem for the transformation program that is trying to earn their commitment.

The inheritance problem is compounded when the new leadership team is not just indifferent to the inherited program but actively skeptical. I have worked with organizations where a new CEO arrived with a mandate from the board to "clean house" and immediately began questioning every initiative the previous leadership had approved. The ERP implementation, which was already twelve months into execution and had consumed $15 million, was suddenly on the chopping block. Not because it was failing, but because it belonged to the old regime.

The uncertainty that follows is devastating. The project team does not know if the program will continue. The system integrator does not know if the contract will be honored. Business users who were starting to engage with the new processes pull back, waiting to see which way the wind blows. The transformation enters a limbo that can last weeks or months, during which momentum is lost, talent leaves the project, and the window of organizational energy that existed when the program launched closes permanently.

Even when the new leadership decides to continue the program, the commitment is different. They did not build the business case. They did not select the vendor. They did not design the governance model. They are running someone else's program, and their ownership of it is, at best, intellectual rather than emotional.

The depth of commitment that comes from having fought for a program, having staked your reputation on it, having personally made the case to the board, that commitment cannot be transferred from one executive to another. It has to be rebuilt from scratch. And in most cases, it is not.

The Layers of Cynicism

Every organization carries a history of change, and that history shapes how the next change is received. In organizations with a track record of successful transformation, the history is an asset. People have seen change work before. They trust the process. They believe that if leadership says this is important, it probably is.

In organizations with a track record of failed or abandoned initiatives, the history is a liability. Each failure leaves behind a residue of cynicism that accumulates over time, like sediment at the bottom of a river. The river keeps flowing. New initiatives keep launching. But the sediment is always there, silently shaping the current.

At the food and agriculture conglomerate, we found that a previous ERP implementation had been "patchy" due primarily to a lack of consensus and buy-in. The result was partial adoption of solutions, further resistance, burnout, unresolved emotions, and in some cases a return to previous business practices. The organization was carrying that history into its next transformation. Every employee who had lived through the previous attempt brought their memories of what happened, and those memories were not encouraging.

The cynicism is not uniform. It is layered. At the executive level, there may be genuine enthusiasm for the new initiative. The executives are new, or they were not involved in the previous failure, or they genuinely believe this time will be different. At the director level, there is cautious optimism mixed with fatigue. They remember the last time and they have concerns, but they are willing to try again if the conditions are right. At the manager level, there is skepticism. They were the ones who had to explain to their teams why the last initiative did not deliver what was promised, and they do not want to make promises they cannot keep again. At the frontline, there is indifference bordering on resignation. They have stopped listening to the announcements. They will believe it when they see it.

This layered cynicism creates a communication challenge that most transformation programs are not equipped to handle. The standard change management playbook calls for cascading communication: the message starts at the top and flows downward through the organization. But when each layer of the organization has a different level of trust and a different relationship with change, the message gets filtered, diluted, and distorted as it moves down. By the time it reaches the frontline, the inspiring vision that the CEO articulated in the town hall has been reduced to an eye roll and a whispered prediction: "Give it six months."

Breaking through this cynicism requires something that the machine is structurally incapable of providing: honesty about the past. Before you can earn credibility for the current initiative, you have to acknowledge what happened with the previous ones. You have to name the failures. You have to explain what went wrong and what is different this time. You have to demonstrate, through actions rather than words, that this initiative has the leadership commitment, the resources, and the accountability mechanisms that the previous ones lacked.

Most organizations do not do this. They launch the new initiative as if the previous failures never happened. They use the same language, the same slides, the same promises. And the organization, which has an institutional memory far longer than any executive's tenure, recognizes the pattern and responds accordingly.

At the same food and agriculture conglomerate, this dynamic had a name that employees used among themselves. The prevailing sentiment was simple: "Things are just fine. We're making money." If the current state was profitable, the case for disruption was abstract at best. The organization was, in their own description, change-averse. Comfortable in the way things were. The attitude was: change is okay as long as it doesn't happen to me. People paid lip service to initiatives. They assumed it would go away, that there would be no accountability and no follow-up. Our assessment found that this was not mere cynicism. It was a phenomenon recognized in social psychology as loss aversion: the tendency to prefer avoiding losses over acquiring equivalent gains. The business units, departments, and individuals were not feeling the pain of not changing. Their current state was tolerable, even comfortable. The future state promised improvement but guaranteed disruption. In the absence of a burning platform -- and as we discussed in Chapter 2, the burning platform was often manufactured rather than real -- the rational response was to wait it out. The result was predictable: people not wanting to change and being allowed not to change. Small pockets of people going back to the way they were doing things before, with managers on the site allowing them to do it. The cynicism was not a character flaw. It was an adaptive response to an environment that had never enforced the consequences of not changing.

Everyone Is Responsible, No One Is Accountable

There is a phrase I hear in nearly every readiness assessment, in one form or another. It goes something like this: "Everyone is responsible for this, but no one is accountable."

The distinction between responsibility and accountability is not academic. It is the difference between a transformation that sticks and one that dissolves the moment the consultants leave. Responsibility means you have a role to play. Accountability means there are consequences if you do not play it.

In many organizations, the transformation is positioned as a shared responsibility. Everyone is expected to contribute. Everyone is encouraged to embrace the change. Posters go up in the break room. The CEO sends an email. The intranet features a countdown to go-live. But beneath the shared messaging, there is a void where accountability should be. Nobody's performance review includes a line item for transformation readiness. Nobody's bonus is tied to adoption metrics. Nobody's career consequences are linked to whether the new processes are followed or the old ones persist.

When there are no consequences for non-compliance, compliance becomes optional. And when compliance is optional in an enterprise transformation, the enterprise does not transform. Individual pockets of the organization adopt the new system because the local leader happens to be supportive or because the old system was painful enough that the new one is a genuine improvement. Other pockets resist, revert, or simply ignore the mandate. The result is a partially adopted system running in parallel with legacy processes, shadow spreadsheets, and manual workarounds that negate most of the benefits the transformation was supposed to deliver.

At one organization where accountability scored a 1 out of 10, the perception was that employees were told "you are input only, let someone else solve on the back end." When individuals feel there are no consequences for their actions, user adoption becomes very challenging. The message that employees received, whether intentionally or not, was that their role in the transformation was passive. They were to provide information when asked and then wait for someone else to do the hard work. They were not expected to change. They were not held to account for changing. And predictably, they did not change.

The accountability void is especially damaging in the months following go-live, when the initial energy of the launch has faded and the daily grind of using the new system has set in. This is the period when adoption either solidifies or erodes, and it is the period when leadership attention typically shifts to the next priority. If there is no mechanism for tracking adoption, no process for identifying and addressing non-compliance, no visible consequence for reverting to old practices, the erosion is silent and steady. Six months after go-live, the organization has technically implemented the new system. Functionally, it is running the old one with a new interface.

This is one of the most common and least discussed outcomes in the industry. It does not show up as a failed go-live. It does not trigger a lawsuit. It does not make headlines. It is a quiet, slow failure that manifests as unrealized benefits, persistent workarounds, and an organization that spent tens of millions of dollars to arrive at a destination that looks remarkably similar to where it started. It is, in its own way, the purest expression of the formula: new software plus old processes equals expensive old processes. But in this case, it is not the processes that remained old. It is the culture.

Diagnosing the Gap Before It Destroys the Program

The accountability gap cannot be closed by a system integrator. It cannot be configured into the software. It cannot be addressed by a change management consultant who arrives six months into the program and is given a budget that represents 3 percent of the total investment. It can only be addressed by the organization itself, and only if the organization is willing to look at itself honestly before the transformation begins.

This is why we start every engagement with an organizational readiness assessment. Not a technology readiness assessment. Not a "are your servers ready for cloud migration" assessment. An organizational readiness assessment that examines the culture, the leadership, the governance, the accountability structures, and the history of change in the organization. We interview executives, middle managers, and frontline employees. We ask them what they think about the upcoming initiative, how they experienced previous changes, whether they trust leadership to follow through, whether they believe commitments are honored, whether they have the capacity to absorb another major disruption.

The findings are often uncomfortable. Executives who believe their organization is ready discover that the people three levels below them do not share that confidence. Leaders who believe accountability is strong discover that their employees view it as nonexistent. Organizations that believe they have a culture of innovation discover that their frontline workers describe a culture of survival.

But uncomfortable findings are useful findings. They tell you where the gap is before the gap swallows the program. They give you a chance to address the cultural deficiencies before you layer a multi-million-dollar technology implementation on top of them. They allow you to design a change management approach that is calibrated to the actual culture of the organization, not the culture that leadership wishes it had.

At the food and agriculture conglomerate, this diagnostic work revealed the depth of the challenge in quantitative terms that could not be argued away. Transformation management scored a 2 out of 10. Business process alignment scored a 3 out of 10. The assessment concluded that the organization's strong culture could also be a liability, and that the validity of the entire implementation plan was highly dependent on its level of alignment with the reality of who this organization actually was. The change infrastructure dimension scored 1.75 out of 5. Implementation readiness scored 2.10 out of 5. Communications scored 2.25 out of 5. The highest-scoring dimension was trust, at 3.50 out of 5. That last number was the most telling. The people in this organization trusted each other. They trusted their colleagues, their managers, their leadership. What they lacked was not trust but machinery: the organizational infrastructure, the governance mechanisms, the decision-making frameworks, and the accountability systems required to translate trust into coordinated action at enterprise scale. Trust without infrastructure is goodwill without execution. And goodwill alone has never delivered an ERP implementation.

The organizations that skip this step, and most do, are building on a foundation they have never tested. They are assuming that the culture will support the transformation because the leadership has said it will. They are treating organizational readiness as a checkbox rather than a diagnostic. And they are feeding themselves into the machine without understanding the single most important variable in whether they will come out the other side intact.

Culture is not a soft topic. It is not a nice-to-have. It is the operating system of the organization, and if it is not compatible with the transformation you are attempting, no amount of hardware, no amount of software, and no amount of consulting hours will make the installation succeed. The machine does not test for cultural compatibility. The machine does not care whether the organization can absorb what is being imposed on it. That test is your responsibility. And if you do not conduct it, you will discover the results on the morning after go-live, when it is too late to do anything about them.

The accountability gap is the space between what the organization says it will do and what it actually does. Every transformation lives or dies in that space. And the only way to close it is to see it clearly, name it honestly, and address it before the first line of code is written.

Chapter 5

Paving the Cow Paths

There is an old story, possibly apocryphal, about the streets of Boston. The city's road layout is famously irregular, a tangle of curves and dead ends and streets that seem to follow no logic at all. The explanation, according to legend, is that the original roads were built on top of the paths that cows had worn into the landscape as they wandered between pastures, water sources, and barns. The cows walked where it was easy. The colonists paved over the cow paths. And three hundred years later, the city is still navigating a road system designed by livestock.

This is exactly what most organizations do when they implement new enterprise technology.

They take the winding, inefficient, often irrational processes that their business has followed for decades, and they pave over them with a multi-million dollar ERP system. The processes do not change. The workflows do not improve. The inefficiencies are not addressed. They are simply automated. What the organization had before was a slow, manual, paper-based version of dysfunction. What they have afterward is a fast, digital, extremely expensive version of the same dysfunction.

It took years of watching this pattern repeat itself before my team at Third Stage Consulting could articulate it as a formula. But once we saw it, we could not unsee it:

NS + OP = EOP

New Software + Old Processes = Expensive Old Processes

This is, in my experience, the single most common way that organizations waste their transformation investment. Not through a catastrophic go-live failure. Not through a lawsuit with the vendor. Not through a project that gets canceled outright. But through the slow, quiet, entirely preventable outcome of spending a fortune to stay exactly the same.

The Most Neglected Workstream

Despite big investments in new enterprise technologies, companies leave far too much money on the table because of inefficient post-go-live business processes. Too many organizations simply automate their subpar processes. I have been saying this for years, and every year the evidence grows stronger. The technology is not the problem. The processes are the problem. And the processes are the problem because nobody wants to do the hard work of changing them.

The most successful implementations invest the time and money defining current-state and future-state business processes, with an emphasis on the latter. They understand their strong areas, their areas of competitive advantage, and areas that need improvement. They also understand that technology is simply an enabler of change, not the end all be all.

But here is the reality of how most transformation programs are structured. The first major milestone is software selection. The second is hiring the system integrator. The third is kicking off the implementation. Somewhere in the project plan, usually buried between configuration and testing, there is a line item for business process design. It is allocated a few weeks. It is staffed with whoever is available. And it is the first thing that gets compressed when the timeline starts slipping, which it almost always does.

A deliberate business process management workstream also helps clearly define a more appropriate system design, a more effective organizational change strategy, and clear opportunities to reengineer business processes. In other words, the process work is not just about processes. It shapes the system design, the change management approach, and the scope of the transformation itself. Skip it, and you are building on a foundation of sand.

Most organizations skip it. Not deliberately, and not completely. But they treat business process redesign as something that happens alongside the implementation rather than something that drives it. The system integrator shows up with a methodology, a timeline, and a set of workshops. The workshops are focused on configuring the software, not on questioning whether the underlying business processes make sense. And the organization, which has never done this before, follows the SI's lead.

This is how you end up paving the cow paths. Not because anyone decided to. Because nobody decided not to.

The Requirements Factory

The mechanism through which cow paths get paved is the requirements-gathering process. In every ERP implementation, there is a phase, usually early in the project, where the organization defines what it needs the system to do. Business users are brought into workshops. They describe their current processes. They explain what they need. They document their requirements.

This sounds reasonable. The problem is what actually happens in those rooms.

What happens is that people describe how they work today, and those descriptions get written down as requirements for the future system. The warehouse manager explains his picking process. The accounts payable clerk explains her three-way match. The procurement director explains the approval workflow he built fifteen years ago. Each of these descriptions becomes a requirement. Each requirement becomes a line item in a spreadsheet. And by the end of the discovery phase, the organization has produced a document with hundreds or thousands of "requirements" that are, in large part, a detailed description of the status quo.

I have seen organizations come out of discovery with 1,800 requirements when 400 would have been more than sufficient. The excess is not because the business is exceptionally complex. It is because nobody in the room had the authority or the inclination to push back and ask whether a stated requirement was truly a business need or simply a description of how things happen to be done today.

In my experience, roughly 60 percent of the requirements I see in discovery workshops are not legitimate business requirements at all. They are change resistance wearing a business analyst's hat. They are people saying, in the language of requirements documentation, "I want the new system to work exactly like the old one." And when those requirements are accepted at face value, the new system is designed to replicate the old one. The cow paths get paved.

At one client, I learned that none of the nearly 1,900 requirements that had been generated during discovery were turned down. Not one. The system integrator and the vendor had said yes to everything. Every wish list item, every "nice to have," every legacy process that someone wanted preserved, had been accepted as a valid requirement and added to the scope. The result was a project that was wildly over-scoped, over-budget, and on a trajectory toward failure before the first line of configuration had been written.

Why does this happen? Because saying no to a requirement takes courage. It means telling a department head that their process is going to change. It means having a difficult conversation about why the way things have been done for twenty years is not the way they should be done going forward. It means risking political conflict within the organization. And neither the system integrator nor the vendor has any incentive to have that conversation. The SI gets paid to build what the client asks for. The vendor gets paid when the software is licensed. More requirements mean more scope. More scope means more hours. More hours mean more revenue. The machine does not reward efficiency. It rewards volume.

Fit-to-Standard and Its Discontents

There is a concept in the ERP world called "fit-to-standard." The idea is that instead of customizing the software to match your current processes, you adapt your processes to match the software's standard capabilities. The software, after all, was designed around industry best practices. Thousands of companies have implemented it before you. The standard processes represent accumulated wisdom about how things should be done. Why not take advantage of that?

The philosophy is sound. The execution is brutal.

"Fit-to-standard" is not about recreating today's processes step by step in the software. It is about stepping back and asking what outcomes you are actually trying to achieve. If you focus too much on how you do things now, you risk carrying forward inefficiencies just because they are familiar.

That sounds elegant in a conference room. It sounds very different when you are the warehouse manager who has been running the same picking process for fifteen years and someone is telling you that the software does it differently and you need to change. Or when you are the controller who has built an entire reporting structure around a specific chart of accounts and the new system uses a different one. Or when you are the plant manager who has developed a scheduling method that works perfectly well for your operation and some consultant is explaining that the "standard" approach requires you to do it another way.

The interviews I conduct at client organizations tell a consistent story. "Things are just fine, we're making money." "Every group believes that the way they do business is fine. They've already done things necessary to be as efficient as possible." "There is a little bit of defensiveness. People are easily threatened by change, their decision rights and authority."

And my personal favorite, a quote from an employee at a large food and agriculture conglomerate that captures the sentiment perfectly: "Change is okay as long as it doesn't happen to me."

This is the reality that fit-to-standard runs into. It is philosophically right and practically brutal. The people on the receiving end of the change are not abstract stakeholders on a change management slide. They are real people with real expertise, real pride in how they do their work, and real fear about what happens when the rules change. Dismissing their concerns as "resistance" does not make the resistance go away. It drives it underground, where it becomes far more dangerous.

The challenge, then, is not whether to adopt standard processes. It is how to do it in a way that respects the organization's knowledge while still achieving genuine transformation. And this is where most programs fail, because they lack the frameworks, the leadership, and frankly the patience to get it right.

The 80/20 Illusion

About 80 percent of ERP business processes do not differentiate a company in the market. So why deviate from the standard process if it does not provide a competitive advantage?

This is the argument that vendors and system integrators make, and in principle it is correct. Most of what happens inside an ERP system is not what makes your company special. Accounts payable is accounts payable. General ledger is general ledger. Procurement, inventory management, order processing: these are commodity processes that every company in your industry performs in roughly the same way. For these processes, adopting the software's standard approach makes sense. It is cheaper to implement, easier to maintain, and simpler to upgrade.

The problem is in the other 20 percent. Or more precisely, the problem is in figuring out which 20 percent actually matters.

Every department believes that its processes are in the 20 percent. Every business unit is convinced that its way of doing things is unique, that it provides a competitive advantage, that standardizing it would destroy value. Some of these claims are legitimate. A manufacturer's proprietary scheduling algorithm. A distributor's unique pricing model. A retailer's inventory valuation method. These may genuinely differentiate the business and may genuinely warrant customization.

But most of the claims are not legitimate. Most of them are simply the natural human tendency to believe that the way you do things is the right way, combined with the organizational tendency to confuse "how we have always done it" with "how it should be done." Sorting the legitimate from the illegitimate requires deep knowledge of the business, deep knowledge of the technology, and the willingness to have uncomfortable conversations with powerful people. Most implementation teams lack at least one of those three things, and many lack all three.

At one chemical company we worked with, the culture of customization was deeply ingrained. People were used to getting what they wanted in the system. If something did not work the way they liked, they would go to IT and have enhancements made. Twenty years of squeaky wheels had created a culture where everyone knew that if they screamed loud enough, they could get the system changed to suit them. The organization had put a hold on new customization requests because of the impending transformation, but the underlying culture had not changed. The expectation was still that the new system would be bent to fit individual preferences.

This is the opposite of fit-to-standard. This is fit-to-me. And when it prevails, the new system inherits all the idiosyncrasies, workarounds, and accumulated compromises of the old one, plus the cost of building them into a platform that was never designed to accommodate them.

But I want to be careful not to leave the wrong impression. This book argues against mindless customization, not against all customization. There are cases where the standard software genuinely does not do what the business needs it to do, and in those cases, the organization has a right and an obligation to solve the problem rather than accept a degraded process in the name of staying standard.

The key is knowing what your options are, because "customize the ERP" is not the only answer and is often not the best one.

The first option is genuine customization of the core system. This is appropriate when the requirement is deeply embedded in the ERP's transactional flow, when it touches core data structures like inventory, financials, or order management, and when no external tool could reasonably handle it without creating integration complexity that exceeds the complexity of the customization itself.

A manufacturer with a truly proprietary scheduling algorithm that needs to interact in real time with shop floor data, material availability, and capacity planning may have a legitimate case for building that logic into the ERP. But this should be the option of last resort, not the default, because every customization to the core system carries the technical debt burden described later in this chapter.

The second option is a custom application built outside the ERP. Modern development platforms and low-code tools have made it far more practical to build standalone applications that handle specialized business logic without touching the core system. The application communicates with the ERP through APIs, pulling and pushing data as needed, but it lives outside the upgrade path and can be maintained independently.

This is often a better answer for processes that are unique to the business but do not need to be embedded in the transactional backbone. A distributor with a proprietary pricing engine, for example, might be better served by a custom pricing application that feeds results into the ERP's order management module rather than trying to build that pricing logic into the ERP itself.

The third option is a third-party bolt-on or best-of-breed solution. The ERP market is surrounded by an ecosystem of specialized software vendors that do specific things very well. Warehouse management, transportation management, advanced planning and scheduling, configure-price-quote, field service management: for each of these domains, there are products that are purpose-built and often superior to what the ERP vendor offers natively. When a business requirement falls into the legitimate 20 percent, one of these specialized tools may be the right answer. It avoids customizing the core ERP, it provides functionality that was designed for exactly this kind of problem, and it can often be implemented faster and more reliably than a custom build.

The decision among these three options should be made deliberately, with clear criteria. How central is this process to the ERP's transactional flow? How often will it change? How critical is real-time integration with core data? What is the long-term maintenance burden? What happens when the ERP vendor releases an upgrade? Organizations that think through these questions for each legitimate gap end up with a technology architecture that is sustainable. Organizations that default to "just customize the ERP" end up back where they started, trapped on a system they cannot upgrade.

The point is not that every process should be forced into the standard. The point is that the standard should be the starting assumption, and departures from it should be justified, deliberate, and implemented through the approach that creates the least long-term risk. Too many organizations never get to this level of rigor because they never distinguish the legitimate 20 percent from the illegitimate 60 percent. Everything gets treated the same, and everything gets built into the core, and the technical debt piles up until the system becomes unmaintainable.

Configuration Versus Customization

Before going further, it is worth clarifying a distinction that is often misunderstood, because it has enormous implications for the cost, timeline, and long-term sustainability of any implementation.

Configuration means the software already knows how to do something. You are just choosing which option you want. For example, choosing between net-30 and net-60 payment terms. Those are standard options. Customization, on the other hand, is when you ask the system to do something it was not designed to do.

Configuration is expected. Every implementation involves configuration, because every organization has unique data, unique structures, and unique preferences within the range of options the software provides. Configuration is built into the product. It does not create technical debt. It does not interfere with upgrades. It is how the system is meant to be adapted.

Customization is a different animal entirely. When you customize an ERP system, you are writing code that changes the software's fundamental behavior. You are asking it to do something that the vendor did not anticipate or did not intend. This code sits outside the standard product. It has to be maintained separately. It has to be tested against every upgrade, every patch, every security update. And over time, as the customizations accumulate, they create a version of the software that is increasingly different from the version the vendor supports.

This is technical debt, and it compounds like interest on a credit card. A few customizations in year one become a dozen in year three become fifty in year five. Each one makes the system a little harder to upgrade, a little more expensive to maintain, a little more fragile. Eventually, the organization finds itself in the same position it was in before the transformation: trapped on an aging, heavily modified system that it cannot easily replace. The cycle begins again.

The dynamics play out differently depending on the vendor. SAP's rigidity creates culture shock and forced adaptation. Organizations either accept the standard or face painful, expensive customization. Microsoft D365's flexibility enables over-customization and avoidance of change, because the system is so accommodating that it lets organizations replicate virtually anything, which means they often do. Oracle's complexity absorbs so much bandwidth just getting the baseline configured that there is little energy left for the process redesign work that should accompany it. Each vendor presents its own version of the trap, but the trap is the same: the organization uses the implementation to preserve the status quo rather than to change it.

The Half-Billion Dollar Cow Path

No case study illustrates the cost of paving the cow paths more vividly than Lidl.

With close to €100 billion in annual revenue and operations spanning thousands of stores across multiple countries, Lidl needed a modern, scalable system to support its rapid growth. The project assembled approximately 1,000 internal staff members and hundreds of external consultants, making it one of the largest retail system implementations ever attempted.

The scale was enormous, and so was the ambition. But the ambition was pointed in the wrong direction.

Lidl had built its business model around purchase-price-based inventory valuation, which allowed them to maintain their low-cost structure and rapid decision-making processes. However, SAP for Retail used a retail-price-based valuation model as its standard approach. This seemingly technical difference represented a fundamental clash between Lidl's core business operations and the software's built-in assumptions.

Now, there is a legitimate argument that inventory valuation methodology is part of the 20 percent. It touches pricing, margin calculation, reporting, and strategic decision-making. A discount retailer's approach to valuation may genuinely be a source of competitive advantage. I am not here to say that Lidl was wrong to value the way it valued.

But I am here to say that if your core business process is fundamentally incompatible with the software's standard approach, that incompatibility needs to be identified, understood, and addressed before you spend seven years and half a billion euros trying to force the software to comply.

Rather than adapting their business processes to align with SAP's proven methodology, used successfully by numerous other retailers worldwide, Lidl insisted on customizing the system to mirror their legacy approach. This decision revealed a critical failure in strategic thinking: the company was not willing to change their processes to leverage the benefits of a modern, standardized system. Instead, they tried to recreate their old system using expensive new technology.

NS + OP = EOP. New Software + Old Processes = Expensive Old Processes. Except in Lidl's case, it was even worse. They did not even get the expensive old processes. They got nothing. The over-customization created a cascade of problems. The heavily modified system became more complex to implement, test, and maintain. Integration with other systems became more difficult. Upgrades to newer versions of SAP became nearly impossible.

The company's decision to ultimately abandon the project and revert to developing their old system further illustrates this resistance to change. After seven years, after €500 million, after 1,000 internal staff and hundreds of consultants, Lidl went back to what it had before. The cow paths won.

The €500 million write-off represents more than just a financial loss. It reflects seven years without meaningful system modernization during a period of intense retail industry transformation. While Lidl was fighting with SAP over inventory valuation methodology, its competitors were modernizing their operations, improving their supply chains, and gaining ground. The cost of paving the cow paths is not just the money you spend. It is the opportunity you lose while you are spending it.

Woolworths Australia provides a stark illustration of what happens when future-state processes are never defined. The company spent six years on an SAP project, replacing a thirty-year-old homegrown system. Six years. And yet when the system went live, they could not produce a store-level profit and loss statement -- the most basic financial report in retail operations. The reason was simple: they had never defined what their future-state business processes should look like before they began configuring the system. They carried forward the assumptions of the legacy system without questioning whether those assumptions still applied. The technology was new. The processes were old. The result was exactly what the formula predicts.

When the Sales Force Walks Out

Lidl's failure was driven from the top, by strategic decisions about process design that were made at the executive level. But paving the cow paths can also destroy a transformation from the bottom up, when the system is so poorly aligned with how people actually work that they simply refuse to use it.

The case of Avon's SAP failure in 2013 illustrates how employee resistance can doom even well-intentioned projects. The system was so complex that sales representatives could not log into the website, and when high-level sales staff could not operate the system, other workers simply gave up on the ERP entirely. Employee frustration reached such levels that many began leaving the company rather than adapting to the new system.

Avon's direct-sales model depended on a vast network of independent sales representatives, many of whom were not particularly technical. The new system needed to work for them, intuitively and reliably, or it would not work at all. Instead, the implementation produced something so complex and so disconnected from the way these people actually sold products that they could not even get past the login screen.

Instead of making processes easier for the organization, the SAP implementation made operations too intricate for users to handle. The system's complexity had a snowball effect. When high-level sales representatives could not operate the system, other workers gave up entirely. This is what happens when the system is designed around technology requirements rather than human requirements. When the people who have to use it every day were not meaningfully considered in the design.

Avon abandoned the project. The company wrote off the investment and went back to its old processes. Another set of cow paths, paved at enormous expense, leading nowhere.

The Courage to Change

The inverse of the formula is just as simple:

NP + NT + CM = DEO

New Processes + New Technology + Change Management = Digital Enterprise Operations

This is what success looks like. The organization redesigns its processes first, or at least concurrently with the technology implementation. It selects technology to enable the new way of working rather than to preserve the old one. And it invests in change management -- the sustained, deliberate effort to prepare the people, the culture, and the organization to adopt and sustain the new way of working. All three elements are essential. New processes without new technology remain aspirational. New technology without new processes produces expensive old processes. And new processes with new technology but without change management produces a system that works on paper but that nobody uses, because the people were never brought along. The focus shifts from "what do we do today?" to "what should we be doing tomorrow, and how do we bring our people there?" The technology becomes a tool for transformation rather than a monument to the status quo.

Getting there requires three things that are in short supply in most transformation programs.

The first is knowledge. Someone in the room needs to understand both the business and the technology well enough to distinguish a legitimate requirement from a legacy habit. This is harder than it sounds. The business experts know the processes but not the software's capabilities. The technology experts know the software but not the business context. The fit-to-standard process only works when someone is carefully evaluating and vetting each requirement or gap, asking whether a request is strategically aligned, whether it might be short-sighted, and whether resistance to change might be influencing it.

There is a technology that can help organizations break this pattern, and it is one of the few emerging tools I recommend without reservation: business process mining. Tools like Celonis can quantitatively analyze how your current processes actually run -- measuring workflow steps, identifying breakdowns, and showing process variations across departments, locations, and individuals. Rather than relying on workshop participants to self-report their processes -- which invariably produces the cow paths, because people describe what they believe they do, not what they actually do -- process mining shows you the reality. It reveals the workarounds, the bottlenecks, the variations between sites that nobody knew existed. It gives you an evidence-based current-state picture that is far more accurate than any facilitated workshop, and it provides the foundation for a future-state design that is grounded in data rather than anecdote.

The second is leadership. As we discussed in the previous chapter, someone with authority needs to be willing to tell departments that their processes are going to change. This is not the system integrator's job. It is the organization's job. The SI can recommend. The SI can present options. But the decision to change a business process is a business decision, and it has to be made by business leaders who are willing to absorb the political cost.

The third is time. Process redesign cannot be compressed into a two-week workshop at the beginning of the implementation. It needs to start before the technology is selected, it needs to continue through the implementation, and it needs to be revisited after go-live as the organization learns to operate in the new environment. The focus should be on defining requirements from the perspective of what the organization expects to look like in three to five years, not on replicating the current state. That is a fundamentally different conversation than the one most organizations have during discovery.

The approach should be to bend the business to fit the system as much as possible, minimizing technical debt. During fit-to-standard workshops, the team should document requirements and determine what truly needs customization. The key phrase is "truly needs." Not "wants." Not "has always had." Not "would be nice to have." Truly needs, in the sense that the business cannot function without it or that it provides a genuine competitive advantage that justifies the cost and complexity of building and maintaining custom code.

The fewer requirements and gaps you log, the faster and more standard your system will be, making it more sustainable in the long run. That is not a popular message. It is an honest one.

The organizations I have seen succeed at this share a common trait. They treat the transformation as an opportunity to question everything about how they operate, not as an obligation to preserve everything about how they operate. They are willing to be uncomfortable. They are willing to tell the warehouse manager that his picking process is going to change. They are willing to tell the controller that the chart of accounts is being restructured. They are willing to sit with the discomfort of people being upset, because they understand that the alternative, spending $50 million to stay the same, is worse.

That takes courage. It takes leadership. And it takes a clear-eyed understanding that the machine is designed to make this as difficult as possible. The vendor wants to sell you the software. The SI wants to build whatever you ask for. Nobody in the room is incentivized to tell you that your requirements list is too long, your processes are outdated, or your organization is not ready to change. That message has to come from within. And it has to come from people with the authority to act on it.

The cow paths are comfortable. They are familiar. They are the way things have always been done. But they were designed by cows. And if you pave them with a hundred million dollars of new technology, all you will have is very expensive cow paths.

The question every organization must answer before it begins a transformation is whether it has the courage to build new roads.

Chapter 6

The Human Firewall

We were called in to help a company that was two weeks from going live with a new ERP system. The situation was already deteriorating when we arrived, but nothing prepared us for what happened next.

More than 80 percent of their most tenured employees retired or resigned in the two weeks preceding the go-live date. These employees represented more than one-third of their workforce and were a major source of tribal knowledge for the company. Their departure was directly related to the ERP initiative and how it was handled.

Eighty percent of the most experienced people in the building walked out the door rather than use the new system. They did not stage a protest. They did not write angry letters to the CEO. They simply left. Some retired early. Others resigned and found jobs elsewhere. They made a calculation, one that is made quietly in organizations all over the world during transformation programs, and they concluded that leaving was preferable to staying.

That calculation is the human firewall. It is the invisible barrier that organizations hit when they push technology changes onto people who have not been prepared, have not been consulted, have not been given a reason to believe that the change is worth the disruption it will cause. The technology may work perfectly. The configuration may be flawless. The data may be clean. But if the people who are supposed to use the system do not want to use it, or cannot use it, or are afraid of what it means for their future, the system will fail.

Seventy percent of all change initiatives fall short of their intended goals. That statistic comes from John Kotter's 1996 work Leading Change, and it has been validated repeatedly in the decades since.

McKinsey conducted a survey of 3,199 executives in 2008 and found that only one in three culture transformations succeed. Although some of these references date back over twenty years, little has changed to move the success meter.

The reason it has not changed is that the industry continues to treat the human dimension of transformation as a secondary concern. The technology comes first. The people come second. And by the time anyone realizes that the people are the ones who determine whether the technology succeeds or fails, the damage has already been done.

The Iceberg

Resistance to change does not surface right away. In fact, at the beginning of a project, most employees are excited for change. They hear about the new system. They attend the kickoff meeting. They see the demonstrations. There is energy and optimism. The old system was clunky and frustrating, and the new one looks modern and capable. People are genuinely interested in what is coming.

But lurking underneath the tip of that iceberg are dark and murky human fears and quirks. We are okay with the idea of transformation until we realize that our own interests might be thwarted by it. Some of the everyday tasks might be automated. That spreadsheet that someone spent years creating, fine-tuning, and managing is about to become useless. All the tribal knowledge that has made a team so indispensable to the company for twenty years is about to become data.

When word of the ERP initiative reaches your employees, they will begin to question their role, tasks, skills, value. Your goal may not be to eliminate jobs, but this thought, or worry, will be in many of your employees' minds. Some will also wonder if they will be able to learn the newly required routines in a drastically changing environment. They will carry this stress to their family's dinner table only to impact their personal life.

This is the part that the project plan does not capture. The Gantt chart has milestones for configuration, testing, data migration, and go-live. It does not have a milestone for the moment a fifty-year-old warehouse supervisor realizes that the job he has done for twenty-five years is about to fundamentally change, and he is not sure he can learn the new way, and he is afraid to ask for help because asking for help feels like admitting he is no longer valuable.

That fear is real. It is rational. And it is the single most powerful force working against your transformation.

The Four Faces of Resistance

Over the years, my team and I have developed a framework for understanding the different types of resistance that surface during digital transformations. There are four, and each requires a different response.

The first is intentional resistance. This is the most visible and, paradoxically, the least dangerous, because at least you can see it. Intentional resistance is when people are actively opposed to the changes. It is typically concentrated among key stakeholders and influencers. It manifests as sabotage, refusal to accept changes, and open defiance. It can spread like a cancer if not mitigated. The department head who announces in a meeting that the new system is a disaster and he will not be using it. The plant manager who instructs his team to keep using the old process and ignore the new one. These people are making a conscious choice to resist, and their resistance is contagious.

Intentional resistance is serious, but it can be addressed directly. You can have a conversation with the department head. You can escalate the plant manager's behavior to executive leadership. The resistance is on the surface, which means it can be confronted.

One of the most difficult manifestations of intentional resistance I have encountered involved a single-point-of-failure employee at a mid-sized consumer services company. This individual had been at the company for years. She had helped build the legacy systems. She knew the processes inside and out. She was the only person in the organization who understood how to do certain things with the software. Her institutional knowledge was enormous, and the organization was completely dependent on it. When the digital transformation was announced, she did not just resist -- she became actively obstructive. She withheld information. She challenged every decision. She leveraged her indispensability as a weapon, because she understood that the new system would eliminate the dependency that made her powerful. The organization was, in a real sense, held hostage by the very person whose knowledge they needed most to succeed.

She was eventually terminated. She did not survive the transformation. But the damage she inflicted along the way -- the delays, the political turmoil, the knowledge gaps she left behind -- was substantial. Her case illustrates a pattern I have seen at organizations of every size: the person who holds the most institutional knowledge about the legacy system often has the most to lose from its replacement, and that misalignment of incentives can turn your most knowledgeable employee into your most dangerous adversary. Identifying these individuals early, addressing their concerns honestly, and building redundancy around their knowledge before the transformation begins is not optional. It is a prerequisite for survival.

The second type is far more dangerous precisely because it is not on the surface.

Unintentional resistance is a more widespread and common challenge. It is harder to detect and mitigate. It stems from fear of loss, a perceived lack of personal value in the future. It comes in the form of watering down the future state vision.

Unintentional resistance is the employee who does not realize they are resisting. They are not trying to sabotage the project. They genuinely believe they are being helpful. But their fear, which they may not even be able to articulate, expresses itself through behavior that quietly undermines the transformation. They insist on customizations that preserve their current workflow. They raise objections in workshops that are framed as business requirements but are really expressions of anxiety. They agree to the changes in meetings and then continue doing things the old way at their desks. They water down the future state, one small compromise at a time, until the "transformation" is just a more expensive version of what existed before.

Stakeholders start to unintentionally work against the change initiative. Not because they want to sabotage the transformation, but because they revert to the survival layer of Maslow's hierarchy of needs. Everything will still seem okay on the surface, but the fear of change just beneath everyone's calm, even positive exteriors will lead to distrust, turn into politicking and power plays within your organization that will slow your progress or worse, destabilize it entirely.

This is the resistance that kills most transformations. Not the loud refusal. The quiet erosion.

There is a particularly sophisticated form of resistance that disguises itself as compliance: the regulatory excuse. In workshop after workshop, I have encountered team members who claim that customers or government regulations require certain existing processes to remain unchanged. Sometimes this is legitimate -- there are genuine regulatory requirements that must be preserved. But frequently, the regulatory claim is invoked as a shield against change. The team member is not citing a specific regulation. They are citing the idea of regulation, the general sense that "the regulators would not allow us to change this," without having verified whether the regulation actually says what they claim it says.

When you hear "we cannot change that because of regulations," investigate. Ask for the specific regulation. Ask for the specific clause. Ask whether the current process is the only way to satisfy the requirement, or whether a different process could achieve compliance while also improving efficiency. In many cases, the regulation is being interpreted far more broadly than its actual text requires, and the broad interpretation is the resistance -- not the regulation itself.

The third type is misunderstanding. This manifests as confusion about future-state processes, roles and responsibilities, and a lack of awareness regarding new software functionality. New roles and responsibilities are not clear. People are not resisting the change. They simply do not understand it. They do not know what the new system will require of them, how their jobs will be different, or what is expected. This type of resistance is the easiest to address, because it responds to clear communication and effective training. But it is also the most common symptom of a change management program that started too late or communicated too little.

The fourth type is misalignment. People, processes, and technology do not align. The future state does not support the bigger-picture corporate goals. This is not an individual problem. It is a structural problem. The transformation is headed in a direction that does not make sense for part of the organization, and the people in that part can feel it even if they cannot explain it. Misalignment resistance is a signal that something is wrong with the strategy, not with the people.

The symptoms of all four types overlap and can be difficult to distinguish. Refusal to accept changes. Workarounds. Too much customization. Operational disruption. Paving the cow paths. These are the outward signs. The root cause might be fear, confusion, defiance, or legitimate misalignment. Treating them all the same, which is what most programs do, guarantees that none of them will be addressed effectively.

Why People Really Resist

Beneath the framework, there is a simpler truth that I share with every client at the beginning of every engagement.

People are comfortable with what they know. Forced initiatives make them question things: their jobs, their roles and tasks, their teams, their skills.

That is the raw material of resistance. Not stubbornness. Not ignorance. Not an unwillingness to improve. Fear. Fear of losing the job they have. Fear of being unable to do the job that replaces it. Fear of losing their team, their status, their sense of competence. Fear that the thing that made them valuable yesterday will not make them valuable tomorrow.

I have sat in workshops where employees broke down describing what the transformation meant to them. Not in terms of technology or processes, but in terms of their identity. The controller who had built a reporting system from scratch over fifteen years and knew it was about to be replaced. The procurement specialist whose entire value to the organization was her knowledge of a legacy system that nobody else understood.

The operations manager who had spent a decade building workarounds that kept a flawed system running, and who knew that the new system would make all of those workarounds, and all of that expertise, obsolete.

These are not hypothetical examples. These are people I have met, in conference rooms and on factory floors, who are being asked to accept that the skills and knowledge they have accumulated over decades are about to be devalued. That is not a training problem. That is an existential problem. And treating it as anything less than that is one of the reasons 70 percent of change initiatives fail.

People change for their own personal reasons. They change because they understand and believe in the new direction. Because they follow leaders they trust. Because their peers are on board and they do not want to be left behind. Because they are excited to learn something new. Because problems they are aware of are finally being addressed. Because changing enables them to keep their jobs. Because they are rewarded for changing.

Notice what is not on that list. Nobody changes because the project plan says they should. Nobody changes because the system integrator told them to. Nobody changes because a slide deck explained the benefits of the new ERP. People change when the change is personal, when they can see themselves in the future state, when they believe that their lives will be better on the other side. Everything else is theater.

The Voices from the Floor

Some of the most illuminating moments in my career have come not from executive presentations or steering committee meetings, but from workshops and interviews with the people who actually do the work. When you ask frontline employees what they think about the transformation, they will tell you things that no project status report will ever capture.

"Things are just fine, we're making money."

"There isn't always 100 percent adoption of new practices. Sometimes folks say 'screw it' because I've been doing it okay for a long time."

"Every group believes that the way they do business is fine. They've already done things necessary to be as efficient as possible."

"Change is okay as long as it doesn't happen to me."

"Difficult to change from something that has been a successful model. There are many sacred cows with how we do things today. Control mechanisms that leaders feel they own today, they may not own that process in the future."

"People pay lip-service to stuff. They think it will go away. There is no accountability, and it will not be followed up on."

These are not complaints from disgruntled employees. These are honest assessments from people who have been through change before and have learned, through experience, that most change initiatives do not stick. They have seen the company buy tools and then make them optional. They have seen programs launch with great energy and then quietly fade. They have learned that the safest strategy is to keep your head down, agree in the meetings, and wait for the initiative to pass.

At one large food and agriculture conglomerate, we found that prior transformation attempts had left a clear residue of cynicism. A previous ERP implementation had been "patchy" due primarily to a lack of consensus and buy-in. The result was partial adoption of solutions, further resistance, burnout, unresolved emotions, and in some cases a return to previous business practices. The organization was carrying the scar tissue of past failures into its next initiative, and that scar tissue was thicker than anyone in leadership wanted to admit.

The contrast was instructive. At the same organization, an HRIS implementation had been relatively successful, and the reason was clear: leadership awareness and support, frequency of meetings with stakeholders, and overcommunication. Same company, same culture, dramatically different outcomes. The difference was not the technology. It was how the change was managed.

The Middle Management Problem

If executive leadership is the engine of transformation, middle management is the transmission. It does not matter how powerful the engine is if the transmission cannot transfer the force to the wheels.

Middle managers are the people who translate executive vision into daily reality. They are the ones who sit with their teams, answer questions, model new behaviors, and hold people accountable for adopting new processes. When middle management is engaged and supportive, change flows through the organization. When they are disengaged, skeptical, or actively resistant, change stops at their level and never reaches the people who have to use the system every day.

"People not wanting to change and are being allowed to not change. Small pockets of people still going back to the way they were doing things before, and the managers on the site are allowing them to do that."

That quote captures the middle management problem in a single sentence. The employees are reverting to old practices, and their managers are letting them. Not because the managers are sabotaging the project. Because the managers themselves have not been equipped to lead the change. They have not been told what is expected of them. They have not been given the tools or the training to coach their teams through the transition. And in many cases, they are just as uncertain and afraid as the people who report to them.

"One thing we underestimated and should learn for the future is the way the organization behaves. Getting leaders engaged and to understand what happens two, three, four levels below them."

Most transformation programs focus their change management effort on two groups: executives and end users. Executives get the strategic briefings. End users get the training. Middle managers, the people who actually determine whether the change sticks, get almost nothing. They are expected to champion a transformation they may not fully understand, to their teams who are looking to them for reassurance they may not be able to provide. It is an impossible position, and it is one of the most consistent gaps I see in every change management program.

When the Firewall Breaks: Hershey and Queensland Health

The consequences of ignoring the human dimension range from disappointing to catastrophic. Two cases illustrate the extremes.

Hershey's attempt to simultaneously implement SAP, Siebel CRM, and Manugistics supply chain software resulted in a $100 million revenue loss during the critical Halloween candy season. Orders went unfulfilled, distributors could not get products, and the company's stock price plummeted. The failure stemmed from an overly aggressive timeline, inadequate testing, insufficient user training, and a fundamental underestimation of the complexity involved in integrating multiple enterprise systems simultaneously.

Employees were not adequately trained on the new systems, backup procedures were insufficient when systems failed, and support resources were overwhelmed by the volume of user problems and questions. The technology went live. The people did not. And the gap between what the system required and what the organization could deliver produced one of the most famous ERP failures in history.

Queensland Health is the case that haunts me more than any other, because the human cost went far beyond financial losses.

What began as a $6.19 million payroll system replacement project ultimately cost taxpayers $1.25 billion and led to over 35,000 payroll errors affecting healthcare workers. The system was supposed to manage payroll for over 80,000 employees across the

Queensland Health system, dealing with more than 24,000 different combinations of wage payments.

When the system went live, over 35,000 healthcare workers experienced payroll errors that created significant personal financial stress. Many employees had to take out loans or seek financial assistance to cover basic living expenses while the system problems were resolved. Some healthcare workers left the profession entirely, contributing to staffing shortages that affected patient care quality.

Think about what that means at a human level. Nurses who could not pay their rent. Doctors who had to borrow money to cover their mortgage. Healthcare workers who had dedicated their careers to taking care of other people, and who were now unable to take care of their own families because a payroll system did not work. Some of them left the profession. Not the hospital. The profession. The system that was supposed to make payroll more efficient drove experienced healthcare workers out of healthcare entirely.

That is the human firewall at its most consequential. The technology failure was real, but the human failure was worse. The people who built the system did not adequately consider the people who depended on it. And the people who depended on it paid the price.

Training Is Not Change Management

There is a persistent myth in the industry that I have spent years trying to dismantle. It is the belief that organizational change management means training and communications. Send out some emails. Build some e-learning modules. Hold a town hall. Train the users on the new system. Check the box.

This conflation is the first myth we address with every client: OCM does not equal training plus communications. New technology does not equal transformation. And consultants do not manage the actual change.

Training is just one of several critical change management workstreams. Training should almost seem like a formality, one where employees have already worked through the "freak out" moments of understanding how their jobs will be impacted but are just learning the details of how the new world will look. If employees are hearing any of these changes for the first time in the last stages of your implementation, you are in for a rough go-live.

Read that again, because it is one of the most important concepts in this book. By the time you get to training, the hard work of change management should already be done. The employees should already know why the transformation is happening. They should already understand how their roles will change. They should already have had the opportunity to express their concerns, ask their questions, and work through their anxieties. Training is the final step, the technical instruction on how to use the new system. It is not the beginning of change management. It is the end.

When organizations treat training as the whole of change management, they compress months of psychological and organizational preparation into a few weeks of system demonstrations. Employees sit through training sessions while still processing the fundamental questions: Will I still have a job? Will I be able to do this? Why is this happening? They are not learning. They are surviving. And the organization mistakes their physical presence in the training room for genuine readiness.

Real change management starts long before the first line of code is configured. It starts with understanding the current culture. It starts with assessing who will be most affected by the change, and how. It starts with identifying the informal leaders, the people whose opinions carry weight regardless of their title, and getting them on board early. It starts with honest, consistent, relentless communication about what is changing, why it is changing, and what it means for each person in the organization.

"We need to translate the message down into individual users, teams, departments. The WIIFM has not been developed." WIIFM stands for "What's In It For Me," and it is the question every employee is asking, whether out loud or silently. If the change management program cannot answer that question for each person in the organization, in terms that are specific, personal, and credible, the human firewall will hold.

The System Integrator Cannot Do This for You

Too many companies fail to recognize that their new ERP system is not a silver bullet to address all of their needs. Systems integrators are good at configuring and building software, not at managing the change that results from the implementation process and go-live.

The problem is that many organizations get "Accentured," or Deloitted, or Capped, into thinking that the system integrator can and should handle organizational change, when they should not. The SI will offer change management services. They will have a methodology. They may even have a dedicated OCM team. But their version of change management is typically a technology-centric exercise focused on training plans, communication templates, and readiness checklists. It is not the deep, culturally sensitive, emotionally honest work that genuine organizational change requires.

ERP vendors and integrators often miss out on some of the most effective strategies like change impact assessments, benefit realization, go/no-go change readiness, communication plans, internal capability uplift, and process improvements. Organizational change strategies become a result of their myopic focus on the technology side of the process and more of an afterthought that will simply take care of itself.

This is not because the people at the SI are incompetent. It is because the SI's business model is built around technology delivery, not organizational transformation. Their consultants are trained in configuration, not psychology. Their methodologies are designed to move through phases and reach go-live, not to navigate the messy, nonlinear, deeply human process of helping thousands of people adopt a new way of working. And as we discussed in the introduction, there is a fundamental conflict of interest: the SI that is also providing change management is essentially grading its own homework. If the OCM team identifies a readiness gap that could delay go-live, they are creating a problem for the implementation team that sits down the hall and reports to the same partner.

This is why we advocate for change management that is led by the organization itself, supported by independent advisors who are accountable to the client rather than to the implementation timeline. The people who manage the change need to be free to tell the truth, even when the truth is that the organization is not ready, the timeline is too aggressive, and the go-live should be delayed.

The J-Curve

There is one more concept that every leader should understand before their organization enters a transformation, because it explains something that catches nearly every organization off guard.

When a transformation begins, most leaders expect a trajectory that goes up and to the right. You invest in the new system. You go live. Things get better. Performance improves. Value is realized.

That is not what happens. What happens is the J-curve.

Productivity dips after go-live. Sometimes it dips significantly. People are learning a new system while still trying to do their jobs. Processes that were automatic under the old system now require conscious effort. Reports that took five minutes now take thirty because nobody has built the shortcuts yet. The organization gets slower, more frustrated, and less efficient before it gets better.

With strong change management, the dip is shallow and the recovery is fast. People were prepared. They knew it was coming. They have support systems in place. They work through the discomfort and begin to see the benefits on the other side.

Without change management, the dip is deep and the recovery is slow, if it comes at all. People were not prepared. They are surprised by how hard the transition is. They blame the system, the SI, the executives who approved the project. Morale drops. Workarounds proliferate. Some people leave. The ones who stay lose confidence in the initiative and begin the quiet process of reverting to old practices wherever they can.

The difference between these two curves is not the technology. It is the investment in people. Organizations that fund change management at 15 to 20 percent of the total program budget typically experience the shallow curve. Organizations that allocate 5 percent or less, which is far more common, experience the deep one. The machine does not encourage the larger investment, because change management hours do not generate the same revenue for SIs as configuration hours, and they do not sell additional licenses for vendors. The economics of the machine are aligned against the single most important workstream in the entire program.

Making Change Personal

I want to close this chapter by returning to the fundamental truth that underlies everything we have discussed.

People change for their own personal reasons.

Not for the company's reasons. Not for the project's reasons. Not for the vendor's reasons. For their own reasons. This is not a flaw in human nature. It is human nature. And any change management approach that does not start from this reality is doomed to produce the same 70 percent failure rate that has persisted for decades.

Research by management thought leader Danah Zohar revealed that managers and employees alike were motivated by five factors: the impact on society, the impact on the customer, the impact on the company, the impact on the team, and the impact on them personally. Notice the hierarchy. The broadest impact comes first in principle, but the personal impact is what actually drives behavior. People need to see themselves in the future state. They need to understand what the change means for them, specifically, concretely, honestly.

This means that change management cannot be generic. A company-wide town hall that explains the strategic benefits of the new ERP system is necessary but not sufficient. What each employee needs to hear is: here is how your job will change. Here is what you will be doing differently. Here is what support you will have. Here is what this means for your career. Here is why this is better for you, not just for the company.

The organizations that do this well invest in what we call change impact assessments, a detailed mapping of how each role in the organization will be affected by the transformation. Not at the department level. At the role level. What does the accounts payable clerk do today, and what will she do tomorrow? What skills does she need to acquire? What tasks will be automated? What new tasks will she take on? This level of specificity is labor-intensive and unglamorous. It does not show up well on a steering committee dashboard. But it is the foundation of genuine adoption, because it answers the only question that matters to the person sitting at the desk: what does this mean for me?

The human firewall is not a problem to be solved. It is a reality to be respected. The people in your organization are not obstacles to your transformation. They are the transformation. If they do not change, nothing changes. No amount of software, no configuration, no system integrator, no vendor, no project plan can substitute for the hard, slow, deeply human work of helping people move from where they are to where the organization needs them to be.

The machine is not designed to do this work. The machine is designed to sell software, bill hours, and go live on schedule. The human dimension is inconvenient. It is messy. It does not fit neatly into a project methodology. And it is, without question, the single most important factor in whether your transformation succeeds or fails.

Seventy percent of the time, the firewall wins. The organizations in the other thirty percent are the ones that took the firewall seriously from the beginning.

Chapter 7

Testing – The Last Line of Defense That Nobody Funds

Somewhere around the midpoint of every ERP implementation, a quiet compression begins. The project is behind schedule. It is almost always behind schedule. Requirements took longer than expected. Configuration ran into complications. Key decisions were delayed because the steering committee could not align. The go-live date, which was set during the sales cycle and has been repeated in every executive presentation since, has not moved. But the work that remains has grown.

Something has to give, and what gives is testing.

Testing is the last honest conversation an organization has with itself before it goes live. It is the moment when theory meets reality, when the configured system is measured against the actual business processes it is supposed to support. It is the point at which defects are found, gaps are exposed, and the organization has to decide whether the system is ready for the people who will depend on it every day.

It is also the workstream that is most consistently underfunded, understaffed, compressed, and compromised. In more than twenty-five years of working with organizations going through digital transformations, I have never once seen a program where the testing phase received too much time or too many resources. Not once. What I have seen, over and over, is testing treated as the buffer that absorbs all the delays accumulated earlier in the project. Configuration ran long? Compress testing. Integration development was late? Compress testing. The business could not finalize its requirements? Compress testing.

The logic, if you can call it logic, is that testing is the last major phase before go-live, and the go-live date is immovable. So the testing window shrinks, the scope is reduced, the standards are lowered, and the organization proceeds to go-live with a system that has not been adequately validated. Then everyone acts surprised when things go wrong.

Of all companies in our study, 51 to 54 percent experienced a material operational disruption at the time of go-live. More than half. And the data showed a clear correlation: the more thoroughly a company tested its processes and systems, the less likely they were to experience disruption. This is not a complicated finding. Testing works. The organizations that invest in it suffer less. The organizations that cut it suffer more. And yet, project after project, testing is the line item that gets sacrificed.

What Testing Actually Means

Before I describe how testing goes wrong, it is worth explaining what it looks like when it goes right, because many of the executives and business leaders reading this book may not have a clear picture of what a proper testing program involves.

Testing in an ERP implementation is not a single activity. It is a layered process, with each layer building on the one before it.

The first layer is unit testing. This is where individual components of the system are tested in isolation. Does the purchase order workflow function correctly? Does the invoice approval route to the right person? Does the inventory transaction post to the correct accounts? Unit testing verifies that the individual building blocks work as configured.

The second layer is integration testing. This is where the building blocks are connected and tested as a system. When a sales order is created, does it trigger the correct inventory reservation, generate the correct pick list, update the correct financial accounts, and send the correct information to the warehouse management system? Integration testing is exponentially more complex than unit testing, because it tests the connections between modules, between systems, and between business processes that span multiple areas of the organization.

The third layer is user acceptance testing, or UAT. This is where business users, the people who will actually operate the system every day, walk through end-to-end business scenarios and verify that the system supports their work. UAT is not a technical test. It is a business test. It is the moment when the warehouse manager runs through his receiving process in the new system and confirms that it works, or discovers that it does not. It is the last quality gate before the organization commits to go-live.

Beyond these core layers, a thorough testing program also includes performance testing (can the system handle the expected transaction volume?), regression testing (when a defect is fixed, does the fix break something else?), data migration testing (is the data that was moved from the old system accurate and complete?), and cutover rehearsals (can the organization execute the transition from old system to new system within the planned window?).

Each of these layers takes time, expertise, and resources. Each produces findings that need to be addressed before the next layer can begin. And each is dependent on the layers before it being done properly. You cannot run meaningful integration testing if the unit testing was incomplete. You cannot run meaningful UAT if the integration testing did not catch the cross-module defects. The layers are sequential, and compressing any one of them compromises all the ones that follow.

It is also worth emphasizing that each of these layers is not a single pass. Unit testing is not one round. It is multiple cycles of test, find defects, fix, retest. Integration testing typically requires three or more complete cycles, because the first round surfaces defects that, once fixed, need to be validated again, and those fixes sometimes introduce new issues that require yet another cycle. UAT often requires at least two full rounds, sometimes three: the first to identify gaps and usability issues, the second to confirm that fixes have been applied correctly, and sometimes a third when the volume of changes between cycles warrants additional validation. When a project plan shows one line item for "integration testing" and one line item for "UAT," it is almost certainly underestimating the work. A realistic testing plan accounts for the iterative nature of each phase, builds in time for defect resolution between cycles, and assumes that each cycle will surface issues that were not visible in the previous one. This is why testing takes as long as it does when done properly, and why compressing it is so destructive. You are not just cutting one round short. You are eliminating the iterations that catch the defects the first round missed.

Testing Is Where Change Management Gets Real

There is another dimension to testing that is almost never discussed, and it connects directly to everything we covered in the previous chapter about the human firewall.

Testing is the first time most employees encounter the new system in a context that resembles their actual work. Before testing, the transformation is abstract. Employees have heard about it in town halls. They may have seen a demonstration. They may have attended a workshop where future-state processes were described on a whiteboard. But they have not sat down at a screen and tried to do their job in the new system. Testing, particularly UAT, is where abstraction becomes reality.

This is why testing is not just a quality assurance exercise. It is a change management event. It is the moment when the accounts payable clerk discovers that the three-way match process she has performed for fifteen years now works differently. It is when the warehouse supervisor learns that the picking logic has changed and his team will need to work in a different sequence. It is when the plant manager realizes that the production scheduling screen looks nothing like what he is used to and he does not know where to find the information he needs.

These are not defects. These are change impacts. And they represent one of the most important deliverables to come out of the testing process, though most organizations do not think of them that way.

Change impact assessments are the mechanism through which the change management team connects the dots between the current state and the future state for every affected employee. They document not just how the new system works differently from the old one, but how processes will change, how job roles and responsibilities will shift, how team structures and reporting relationships may be affected, and what new skills will be required. A well-executed change impact assessment tells the procurement manager that her approval workflow is moving from email to system-based routing, that she will now be responsible for supplier performance data she never had to manage before, and that two tasks she currently performs manually will be automated. It tells the warehouse team lead that pick sequencing will follow a different logic, that cycle counting will now be system-directed rather than supervisor-directed, and that his daily reports will come from a different screen with different data.

This level of specificity is only possible after the system has been configured and tested. Before testing, the change management team is working from design documents and process maps, which are useful but inherently theoretical. Testing is where theory meets the configured system, and the change impact assessment is the deliverable that captures what that collision reveals. It is the foundation for everything that follows in an effective change management program: targeted communications that tell each role exactly what is changing and why, training curricula that are built around actual system behavior rather than vendor demonstrations, benefits realization tracking that connects specific process changes to specific business outcomes, and readiness assessments that measure whether people genuinely understand and can perform their new responsibilities.

This creates a dependency that most project plans ignore. Effective change management depends on testing. You cannot develop effective training materials until the system is stable enough that what you train people on today will still be accurate when they use it next month. You cannot honestly answer the question "what does this mean for me?" until the system has been tested and the answer is known. You cannot track benefits realization until you know exactly which processes changed and how. When testing is compressed, the change impact assessment is either rushed or skipped entirely. And when it is rushed or skipped, every downstream change management activity is built on incomplete information. The communications are generic because nobody mapped the specific role-level impacts. The training is superficial because nobody confirmed how the system actually behaves for each user group. The readiness assessment produces misleading results because nobody defined what "ready" means at the task level. The organization does not just go live with an undertested system. It goes live with an underprepared workforce, because there was not enough time between testing and go-live to translate what was learned into effective change support.

This is one of the reasons the J-curve we discussed in the previous chapter is so much steeper for organizations that compress testing. It is not only that the system has more defects. It is that the people using the system have had less time to understand it, less time to practice, less time to work through their anxieties, and less time to receive the targeted support that only becomes possible once testing reveals exactly how their jobs will change.

The Compression

Here is how it typically unfolds. The project plan allocates, say, twelve weeks for testing. In theory, that is four weeks for integration testing, four weeks for UAT, two weeks for performance and regression testing, and two weeks for cutover rehearsals. It is a reasonable plan on paper.

Then reality intervenes. Configuration takes three weeks longer than planned because the business changed its requirements twice during the design phase. Integration development is delayed because a third-party vendor did not deliver their API on time. Data migration is behind because the source data was dirtier than anyone expected and the mapping logic had to be rewritten. By the time the project is ready for testing, the twelve-week window has become six weeks. Or four. Or, in the worst cases I have seen, two.

The go-live date does not move. The executives have committed to it. The board has been told. The organization has planned its operations around it. Moving the date would mean admitting that the project is behind, which nobody wants to do. So the testing window absorbs the delay.

What follows is a cascade of compromises. Integration testing is abbreviated. Instead of testing every business scenario, the team tests the "critical path" and hopes that the less common scenarios work as well. UAT is compressed from four weeks to two, or to one. Business users are pulled from their day jobs and asked to validate the system in a fraction of the time that was originally planned, while still doing their regular work. Performance testing is reduced to a single run, or skipped entirely. Cutover rehearsals are done once instead of three times, or not at all.

At one client, the situation was stark. The system integrator was pushing to go live despite defects that still existed. There were lots of unknowns. Testing had been rushed. The UAT that had been done needed to be redone because the data had been reconfigured after the test cycle. The go/no-go decision was April 29 for a May 6 go-live, and the organization no-goed. The SI partner immediately began pressuring them to set a new date no further than two weeks out.

Think about that dynamic. The organization made the right call. It looked at the testing results, recognized that the system was not ready, and said no. And the system integrator's response was to push for a go-live date two weeks later. Not because the defects would be resolved in two weeks. Because the SI needed to keep the project moving. Every week of delay is a week of additional cost for the SI, but more importantly, it is a week where the client might start asking uncomfortable questions about why the system was not ready in the first place.

The Defect Downgrade Game

There is a practice that occurs in ERP implementations that I consider one of the most dishonest and dangerous behaviors in the industry. It is not illegal. It is rarely discussed openly. And it has contributed to some of the most catastrophic go-live failures I have investigated.

It is called defect downgrading, and it works like this.

During testing, defects are identified and categorized by severity. A critical defect, sometimes called a "showstopper," is one that prevents a core business process from functioning. A high-severity defect is one that significantly impairs functionality. A medium or low defect is one that is inconvenient but workable. Most organizations establish go-live criteria that include some version of "no unresolved critical defects." The threshold is supposed to be a quality gate, a clear standard that must be met before the system is deployed to production.

The defect downgrade game circumvents this gate by changing the classification of the defect rather than fixing the defect itself. A critical defect is reclassified as high. A high defect is reclassified as medium. The defect has not been resolved. The system still has the same problem. But on the tracking spreadsheet, it no longer appears as a showstopper, which means it no longer triggers the quality gate that would delay go-live.

At Queensland Health, when defects were identified during testing, project managers frequently downgraded their severity ratings to circumvent quality gates and maintain project momentum. This manipulation of testing results created an artificial picture of system readiness that bore no resemblance to actual system quality. The lack of independent testing oversight meant that these practices continued unchecked until system deployment revealed their catastrophic consequences.

The result was a system that went live with over 2,000 known defects, including 14 that were genuinely critical. Over 35,000 healthcare workers were affected by payroll errors. Nurses could not pay their rent. Doctors had to take out loans. Some left the profession entirely. And the defects that caused all of this had been identified during testing. They were known. They were documented. They were simply reclassified so that the project could proceed on schedule.

Queensland Health is the extreme case, but the practice is not extreme. I see versions of it in nearly every implementation I review. The labels vary. Sometimes it is a formal reclassification. Sometimes it is a "risk acceptance" by the project team. Sometimes it is simply an agreement to "address it after go-live." But the effect is the same: known problems are carried into production because fixing them would delay the timeline, and the timeline is treated as more sacred than the quality of the system.

At MillerCoors, they had thousands of open items that they had to address at the time of go-live, and many of those defects were critical, things that were absolutely essential to ensure that operations could continue to run. But they still went live anyway. The result was a $100 million lawsuit against HCL, the system integrator.

When the Environments Lie

There is a technical dimension to testing failure that deserves attention, because it undermines the validity of even well-intentioned testing programs.

In any ERP implementation, there are multiple system environments: a development environment where configuration and code changes are made, a test or QA environment where those changes are validated, and a production environment where the live system runs. For testing to be meaningful, the test environment must accurately mirror the production environment. Same configuration. Same data. Same integrations. If the test environment is different from production, you are not really testing the system that will go live. You are testing something else.

At one company I investigated as an expert witness, the development, test, and production environments were not in sync. When the different environments are not kept in sync, it is impossible to validate exactly what is going into production. Testing becomes a fiction. You can run every test script perfectly in the QA environment, and it means nothing if the production environment has different configuration, different data, or different code.

One of the developers on that project admitted in a deposition that even when testing passed in the QA environment, he still expected problems because the QA environment did not simulate the production environment. He knew. The people closest to the system knew that the testing was not representative. But the project proceeded anyway.

In the final deployment, there were over 30 developers that had the ability to and were actively writing code in the production environment as late as hours before the go-live deadline. Thirty developers making changes directly in production, with no documentation, no testing of those changes, and no way of knowing how the new code would interact with everything else in the system. In my career, I have never heard of a project and cannot fathom a scenario where it would be appropriate to let this many developers have this level of unchecked access.

That case ended in litigation. Many do. But the underlying dynamic, environments that drift out of sync, last-minute changes that bypass the testing process, configuration that is pushed to production without proper validation, is far more common than the litigation statistics would suggest. It happens because the timeline is compressed, because the SI is under pressure to deliver, and because the rigor of environment management is invisible to the executives who are making the go/no-go decision.

UAT Theater

User acceptance testing is supposed to be the moment of truth. It is the point at which the people who will actually use the system confirm that it works for their business. In theory, UAT is the most important testing phase, because it is the one where the business takes ownership of the system and says, "Yes, this is ready."

In practice, UAT is often theater.

Business users are pulled into testing with minimal preparation. They are given test scripts that were written by the SI's technical team, not by people who understand the business process from the user's perspective. They are asked to execute transactions in a test environment that may or may not reflect the real production configuration. They click through the steps, see that the system produces a result, and check the box. Whether that result is correct, whether it matches what would happen in the real business, whether the scenario covers the edge cases that occur in daily operations: these questions are often not asked, because the users do not have the context, the time, or the confidence to ask them.

UAT is the last line of defense in detecting unacceptable defects and missing or misconstrued functionality. When it is done well, it catches problems that unit testing and integration testing missed, because it tests the system through the lens of real business operations rather than technical specifications. When it is done poorly, it provides a false sense of confidence that sends the organization into go-live with a system that has not been validated by the people who matter most.

At one implementation I reviewed, there were key processes that had not been fully delivered prior to the start of UAT. The system was not feature-complete, and yet the business was being asked to test and accept it. It is recommended that the system be 100 percent feature complete prior to the start of end-to-end testing and UAT. That recommendation should not need to be stated. But it does, because the pressure to maintain the timeline routinely overrides the logic of testing a complete system.

The result is that UAT becomes a formality. The business "signs off" on the system, not because they are confident it works, but because they have been told it is time to sign off. The go/no-go criteria, which were supposed to be objective quality gates, become subjective judgments made under pressure by people who do not have the information they need to make an informed decision.

The Go/No-Go Illusion

Every implementation has a go/no-go decision point. In theory, this is the moment when the organization's leadership reviews the testing results, assesses the readiness of the system and the organization, and makes an informed decision about whether to proceed to go-live.

In practice, the go/no-go decision is almost always go.

In my experience, there are often external factors, aside from mere system readiness, that figure into go-live decisions. External considerations are often present and may result in system deployment earlier than the client may prefer. In these cases, systems often go live with known defects that the client believes can be worked around until they are addressed.

The external factors are varied but predictable. The fiscal year is ending and the new system needs to be in place for the new period. The contract with the SI is structured around go-live milestones, and delaying means renegotiating payments. The board has been told a date and the executives do not want to report a delay. The old system's support contract is expiring. The organization has already scheduled the cutover with customers, suppliers, and partners and the logistics of postponement are daunting.

At one client, the teams felt pressure to go live before the system and the team were ready. The go-live criteria were ineffective in reducing risk. The guidance that the company would "learn more when the system went live" was not a quantifiable measure of readiness. They went live without a clear idea of whether their warehouse RF guns would be effective.

"We will learn more when the system goes live." I have heard versions of that statement in dozens of implementations, and it never ceases to alarm me. It is an admission that the testing was insufficient, dressed up as a statement of pragmatic confidence. It means: we do not know if this works, but we are going to find out by deploying it to production and seeing what happens. The people who will find out are the warehouse workers, the accounts payable clerks, the customer service representatives, and the customers themselves.

National Grid decided to go live a week after Hurricane Sandy hit a large portion of their customer base in the northeastern United States. They knew the hurricane had happened. They knew their operations were disrupted. They still decided to proceed with the implementation just days after the storm. When they went live with SAP, they were not able to pay their employees the proper amounts. They overpaid thousands of employees and underpaid thousands more. They had over 15,000 vendor invoices that they could not pay, creating credibility issues with their suppliers. They could not do the financial reporting they needed to maintain their credit facilities with their banks. National Grid had to spend $100 million in services to support the implementation after the fact. The company had been spending $30 million a month just to support the project while trying to get the product up and running.

One hundred million dollars in post-go-live remediation. Thirty million dollars a month in support. Because the go/no-go decision was go.

The Morning After

What happens after a poorly tested system goes live follows a depressingly predictable pattern.

At one client, PwC was the implementation partner, and the client believed they had missed a lot of things on configuration. They could not figure out how they had gotten to go-live. Issues should have come out during testing but did not. The client described the post-go-live experience as whack-a-mole. Bins would allow for negative inventory, causing people to go to bins without inventory. Throughput dropped to about half of what it had been. The company had been shipping $1 million per day and was now shipping $400,000 to $500,000.

Whack-a-mole. Fix one problem, another one appears. Fix that one, and two more surface. The project team is in firefighting mode, triaging defects, building workarounds, and trying to keep the business running while simultaneously diagnosing why the system is not doing what it was supposed to do. Meanwhile, the business is losing money, customers are being affected, and the employees who were already anxious about the new system are now being told that the system does not work and they should use manual workarounds until further notice.

To make matters worse, hypercare was cut back drastically. Hypercare is the post-go-live support period during which the SI provides additional resources to address issues as they emerge. It is supposed to be the safety net. In this case, the safety net had holes in it.

Revlon's SAP S/4HANA implementation was so disruptive that it shut down a core manufacturing facility in North Carolina, resulting in millions of dollars in lost sales and triggering multiple shareholder lawsuits when the company's stock fell nearly 7 percent within 24 hours of announcing the failure. The implementation ultimately contributed to the company's bankruptcy filing in 2022.

At another company I investigated, the go-live reduced daily shipping by approximately 70 percent. With only 30 percent shipping capacity, the company decided to roll back part of the solution to its legacy system just twelve days after going live. Twelve days. That is how quickly a poorly tested deployment can force an organization back to square one.

The Economics of Neglect

Why does this keep happening? The answer, as with so much in this book, comes back to the economics of the machine.

Testing does not sell software. No vendor ever closed a deal because of a rigorous testing methodology. Testing does not generate significant SI revenue relative to the configuration and development phases. It requires business users, not consultants, to do much of the work, which means the SI cannot staff it the same way it staffs the build phases. And testing, when done honestly, produces bad news. It surfaces defects. It reveals gaps. It creates pressure to delay go-live, which nobody in the machine wants.

The vendor wants the implementation to proceed because a successful go-live validates the product and generates case studies and references. The SI wants go-live because their contract milestones and revenue recognition are tied to it. The executives want go-live because they have made promises to the board.

Everyone in the room has an incentive to interpret the testing results favorably, to accept the reclassified defects, to believe the assurances that remaining issues will be addressed after go-live.

The only people who do not have this incentive are the ones who will be using the system on Monday morning. The warehouse worker. The accounts payable clerk. The customer who is waiting for a shipment. They are not in the go/no-go meeting. Their voices are not represented. And when the system fails, they are the ones who absorb the consequences.

One client's post-mortem recommended that for the next rollout, the organization should prioritize go-live decisions based on data quality, real-life testing success, and user understanding. It also recommended engaging an outside agent to objectively evaluate readiness to go live. That recommendation should not be remarkable. The fact that it had to be written down, after a failed go-live, tells you everything about how the machine handles testing.

Testing progress measured in scripts executed rather than end-to-end outcomes validated. Data migration described as "in progress" without reconciliation results and tolerance thresholds. These are the warning signs that testing has become a checkbox exercise rather than a genuine quality gate. When the steering committee is told that "85 percent of test scripts have passed" without being told what business scenarios those scripts represent, what defects were found and how they were classified, and whether the remaining 15 percent includes critical functionality, the committee is not making an informed decision. It is being managed.

The last line of defense only works if the organization is willing to act on what it finds. A testing program that identifies critical defects and then allows the project to proceed anyway is not a quality gate. It is a fig leaf. And the consequences of that fig leaf, measured in operational disruption, financial loss, employee suffering, and sometimes litigation, are borne entirely by the organization that chose not to listen to what its own testing was telling it.

The machine will always push for go-live. That is what it is built to do. The question is whether the organization has the discipline, the governance, and the courage to push back when the testing says it is not ready. In my experience, most do not. And most pay the price.

Chapter 8

Go-Live and the Morning After

Go-live day has a strange energy. There is a combination of relief, anxiety, and forced optimism that fills the room in a way that is unlike any other moment in the program. The project team has been working toward this date for a year or two, sometimes longer. The executives have committed to it publicly. The system integrator has built their entire engagement timeline around it. The cutover plan has been rehearsed, or at least discussed. The data has been migrated, or at least most of it. The switch is flipped. The old system goes dark. The new system goes live.

And then Monday morning arrives.

Monday morning is when the transformation stops being a project and starts being a reality. The warehouse workers log in and try to process receipts. The accounts payable team tries to run a payment batch. The customer service representatives try to look up an order. The plant manager tries to pull a production schedule. And in a disturbing number of cases, what they encounter is a system that does not do what they expected, does not work the way they were trained, and does not support the business processes they need to run the operation.

Of all companies in our study, 51 to 54 percent experienced a material operational disruption at the time of go-live. More than half. Not a minor inconvenience. A material disruption, meaning the business was measurably impaired in its ability to operate. The duration of these disruptions varies from a few weeks to several months. The costs of these disruptions increase the initial cost of the implementation by anywhere from 50 to 300 percent.

Let those numbers register. If you budgeted $20 million for your transformation, the post-go-live disruption could add another $10 million to $60 million in unplanned costs. If you budgeted $50 million, you might be looking at $25 million to $150 million in additional spending just to stabilize the system you already paid to implement. These are not edge cases. They represent the experience of the majority.

This chapter is about what happens after the switch is flipped. The morning after, the weeks after, the months after. It is the phase of the transformation that receives the least planning, the least budget, the least attention, and the least honesty. And it is the phase where many organizations discover that the real cost of the transformation has not yet been paid.

Whack-a-Mole

In the previous chapter, I described what happens when a poorly tested system is deployed to production. But even in implementations where testing was reasonably thorough, the post-go-live period produces a wave of issues that nobody anticipated.

At one client, PwC was the implementation partner, and the client described the post-go-live experience as whack-a-mole. Bins would allow for negative inventory, causing people to go to bins without inventory. Throughput dropped to about half of what it had been. The company had been shipping $1 million per day and was now shipping $400,000 to $500,000.

Whack-a-mole. It is the perfect description, and I have heard it from clients across industries, across geographies, across decades. You fix the inventory posting issue, and then the pick wave logic breaks. You fix the pick wave logic, and then the invoicing integration fails. You fix the invoicing integration, and then the warehouse RF guns lose connectivity to the server. Each fix reveals the next problem. Each resolution exposes the next gap. The project team, which was supposed to be transitioning to business-as-usual support, is instead operating in perpetual crisis mode, triaging a queue of issues that grows faster than it shrinks.

The whack-a-mole phenomenon occurs because enterprise systems are not linear. They are interconnected webs of processes, data flows, integrations, and business rules that interact in ways that are difficult to predict in a test environment. Testing catches the defects that can be anticipated. Go-live reveals the ones that could not be. The volume of transactions, the diversity of real-world scenarios, the timing dependencies between processes that run simultaneously in production but sequentially in testing, all of these factors conspire to surface problems that were invisible during the testing phase.

This is normal. Every experienced implementation professional knows that go-live will produce unexpected issues. The question is not whether problems will surface. The question is whether the organization has planned for them, budgeted for them, and built the support structure to resolve them before they compound into a crisis.

In my experience, most have not.

The Stabilization Period Nobody Budgeted For

There is a concept in implementation methodology called "stabilization." It is the period between go-live and the point at which the system is operating reliably and the organization has adapted to the new way of working. Depending on the complexity of the implementation, stabilization can take anywhere from a few weeks to six months or longer.

In theory, every project plan accounts for stabilization. In practice, it is one of the most consistently underfunded and underplanned phases of the entire program.

The reason is structural. The project budget was built during the sales cycle or the planning phase, typically twelve to eighteen months before go-live. At that point, the focus was on getting to go-live: licensing, configuration, integration, testing, training, cutover.

Post-go-live stabilization was treated as a minor line item, a few weeks of "hypercare" from the SI, a small contingency reserve, and the assumption that the internal IT team would absorb the rest.

By the time go-live arrives, the budget is often already exhausted. The project ran over during the build phase. Testing was compressed rather than extended, which saved money in the short term but pushed costs into the post-go-live period. The contingency reserve, if it existed, was consumed by change orders during implementation.

And the stabilization phase, which was supposed to be a controlled wind-down, becomes instead the most expensive phase of the entire program, because it is the phase where all the shortcuts, all the deferred decisions, and all the undertested scenarios come due.

National Grid had to spend $100 million in services to support the implementation after the fact. The company had been spending $30 million a month just to support the project while trying to get the product up and running. One hundred million dollars. After go-live. For a system that was supposed to be operational. That is not stabilization. That is an emergency room.

The timing of National Grid's go-live made an already dangerous situation catastrophic. The system went live just one week after Hurricane Sandy struck the northeastern United States. The company was simultaneously managing one of the largest natural disaster responses in its history and cutting over to a new enterprise system. The predictable result: thousands of employees were overpaid or underpaid, over 15,000 vendor invoices went unprocessed, and the operational disruption compounded the disaster recovery effort. National Grid ultimately sued its system integrator for $75 million. The decision to go live during a natural disaster response is an extreme example, but the underlying dynamic is common: organizations commit to go-live dates that do not account for the real-world conditions in which the go-live will occur, because changing the date would mean admitting the timeline was wrong.

National Grid is an extreme case, but the pattern it illustrates is not extreme. In the majority of implementations I have been involved with, the post-go-live costs significantly exceed what was planned. Organizations that budgeted three months of hypercare discover they need six. Organizations that planned for a small defect resolution team discover they need a war room with twenty consultants working around the clock. Organizations that expected their internal IT team to manage the transition discover that their internal team does not have the skills, the system knowledge, or the bandwidth to handle the volume of issues.

The budget surprise is compounded by a staffing surprise. During the build and testing phases, the SI had a large team on site. After go-live, the contract typically calls for a rapid drawdown of that team. The SI's best consultants are already being lined up for their next engagement. The project manager who knew every workaround and every configuration decision is being transitioned off. The functional consultants who built the system are being replaced by a smaller support team that may not have the same depth of knowledge.

The organization is left trying to stabilize a complex system with fewer resources, less expertise, and a shrinking budget. It is like pulling the scaffolding off a building before the mortar has dried.

Hypercare vs. Abandonment

The industry term for post-go-live support is "hypercare." It is supposed to denote a period of heightened attention, elevated support, and rapid response to issues. The word itself implies something beyond normal care, something exceptional, something that recognizes that the organization is in a vulnerable state and needs extra protection.

The reality of hypercare often falls far short of the name.

At one client, hypercare was cut back drastically. The SI reduced its post-go-live support faster than the organization could absorb the transition. The client was still in crisis mode, still dealing with the whack-a-mole defects, still trying to get throughput back to acceptable levels, and the safety net was being pulled away.

This is not unusual. In fact, it is the norm. The SI's contract defines a hypercare period, typically two to four weeks, during which a specified number of consultants remain on site to address post-go-live issues. After that period, the SI's contractual obligation is fulfilled. The team draws down. The consultants move on. The client is expected to manage on its own.

The problem is that two to four weeks of hypercare is almost never sufficient for a major ERP implementation. The first two weeks after go-live are consumed by firefighting, addressing the immediate, urgent issues that prevent the business from operating. The deeper, more systemic problems, the ones that affect reporting accuracy, month-end close, intercompany transactions, and long-running business processes that only execute periodically, do not surface until weeks three, four, five, and beyond. By the time these problems appear, the hypercare team is gone.

What remains is the SI's ongoing support contract, which is typically a managed services agreement with defined service levels, ticket queues, and response times. This is a fundamentally different model from having consultants on site who know the system intimately because they built it. A managed services team may be staffed by different people than the implementation team. They may be located offshore. They may not have the context to understand why a particular configuration decision was made or how a specific workaround was designed.

The institutional knowledge that the implementation team accumulated over twelve to eighteen months of build walks out the door, and the organization is left explaining its own system to people who have never seen it before.

This is the "Day 2" problem, and it is one of the least discussed and most consequential dynamics in digital transformation. Day 1 is go-live. Day 2 is when the organization realizes it is alone.

The Knowledge Transfer That Never Happens

Every SI contract includes a section on knowledge transfer. It typically says something about ensuring that the client's internal team is equipped to operate and maintain the system after the SI's engagement concludes. It sounds responsible and thorough.

In practice, knowledge transfer is one of the most consistently broken promises in the industry.

The reasons are both structural and economic. Structurally, the implementation team is building the system under time pressure for the entirety of the engagement. There is no natural pause in the work where the team can stop, document everything they know, and teach it to the client's internal resources. Knowledge transfer is supposed to happen alongside the build, but in reality, it is always the activity that gets deferred when the timeline is tight. And the timeline is always tight.

Economically, the SI has no incentive to transfer knowledge effectively. If the client can operate the system independently, the client does not need the SI's managed services contract. If the client's internal team understands every configuration decision and every custom development, the client does not need to call the SI when something breaks. Effective knowledge transfer reduces the SI's post-go-live revenue. The machine is not designed to make itself unnecessary.

The result is that organizations emerge from implementation dependent on a system integrator they may no longer trust, may no longer be able to afford, and may no longer want. The system's configuration logic lives in the heads of consultants who have moved on to other projects. The custom code is documented in technical specifications that the internal team cannot interpret. The integration architecture is understood by the middleware specialists who built it, none of whom work for the client.

I have worked with organizations that were still paying the SI millions of dollars per year, three and four years after go-live, because they could not operate their own system. Not because the system was too complex for their internal team to learn. Because the knowledge transfer never happened, and the internal team was never given the opportunity, the documentation, or the training to become self-sufficient. The dependency was not inevitable. It was the predictable result of a business model that profits from it.

When Data Destroys the Business: Target Canada

If there is one case study that captures the full catastrophe of post-go-live failure, it is Target Canada. Not because the technology itself was fundamentally flawed, but because every failure that should have been caught before go-live was instead discovered afterward, in the most punishing way possible.

Target Canada represents the most extreme example of a digital transformation contributing directly to a business exit. The company's 2013 expansion into Canada, supported by a new SAP implementation, resulted in approximately $7 billion in losses and the closure of all 133 Canadian stores by 2015.

Seven billion dollars. One hundred and thirty-three stores. Approximately 17,600 employees who lost their jobs. The largest corporate withdrawal in Canadian retail history.

The failure was driven by catastrophic data quality issues. Product information migrated from acquired Zellers stores into Target's SAP system was riddled with errors: incorrect dimensions, wrong costs, missing product attributes, and broken supplier links that made accurate replenishment impossible.

The data problems were not subtle. They were visible on the shelves. Stores opened with empty aisles because the replenishment system could not order the right products in the right quantities to the right locations. Customers who walked into a Target Canada expecting the same experience they had in the United States found a disorganized, understocked store that bore little resemblance to the brand they trusted.

Target's internal data accuracy was found to be approximately 30 percent. Industry standards typically require 98 to 99 percent accuracy for effective supply chain operations. Thirty percent. In a retail operation, where every product must be accurately described, correctly priced, properly dimensioned, and linked to the right supplier, data accuracy of 30 percent means that seven out of ten items in the system contain errors. The supply chain does not function. The stores cannot be stocked. The business cannot operate.

The data migration failures at Target Canada were not a technology problem. They were a governance problem and a testing problem. The data should have been validated before go-live. The accuracy gaps should have been identified and remediated. The go/no-go decision should have flagged data quality as a showstopper. But the pressure to open stores on schedule, to hit the market entry timeline that the board had committed to, overrode every quality gate that might have prevented the disaster.

Target Canada spent the months after launch in a desperate remediation effort, trying to fix data records one by one while simultaneously trying to run a retail operation. But the damage was done. First impressions in retail are difficult to reverse, and Target

Canada's first impression was empty shelves and incorrect pricing. Customers who were disappointed by their initial experience did not come back. The business never recovered.

The Target Canada case is instructive not because it is unique but because it demonstrates what happens when post-go-live remediation becomes the primary activity of the organization. When the morning after is not a transition period but a survival exercise, the business stops transforming and starts firefighting. And the longer the firefighting lasts, the less likely it is that the transformation will ever deliver the benefits it promised.

When the System Lies to You: Nike

Nike's implementation of i2 Technologies' demand-planning software in 2000 resulted in over $100 million in lost sales, a 20 percent stock price decline, and multiple class-action lawsuits.

The Nike failure is a different species from Target Canada, but equally devastating. Where Target's problems were rooted in data migration, Nike's were rooted in a demand-planning system that produced inaccurate forecasts, causing the company to manufacture the wrong products in the wrong quantities.

The system generated inaccurate demand forecasts due to a combination of software bugs, data integration problems, and inadequate testing of the planning algorithms under real-world conditions. The system ordered too many of the shoes that nobody wanted and too few of the shoes that everyone wanted.

Too many of the shoes nobody wanted. Too few of the shoes everyone wanted. In a demand-driven business like athletic footwear, where trends move quickly and inventory decisions are made months before the selling season, inaccurate forecasting is catastrophic. Nike found itself with warehouses full of unsaleable inventory and empty shelves where the bestsellers should have been.

The demand-planning system had been tested. It had been configured. It had been deployed. But it had not been validated against the real-world complexity of Nike's supply chain, which involved thousands of products across multiple geographies with highly variable demand patterns. The algorithms that worked in the test environment, with a limited dataset and simplified scenarios, broke down when exposed to the full volume and variability of production data.

Nike's CFO at the time told analysts that the company had placed "ichiban on this issue," using a Japanese word meaning "first" or "number one priority." But by the time the company acknowledged the problem publicly, the damage was already done. The wrong shoes had been manufactured. The right shoes had not. The supply chain had been distorted in ways that would take quarters to unwind.

What the Nike case demonstrates is that post-go-live failure is not always visible immediately. Target Canada's empty shelves were obvious. Nike's forecasting errors were hidden inside the system, producing decisions that looked rational on screen but were based on inaccurate data. The system was not crashing. It was not throwing errors. It was quietly generating bad forecasts that the organization was acting on, trusting the technology to do what it was supposed to do. By the time the mismatch between forecast and reality became apparent in the physical supply chain, the damage had already propagated through the entire manufacturing and distribution process.

This is one of the most dangerous categories of post-go-live failure: the system that does not obviously fail but silently produces incorrect outputs. When a system crashes, you know something is wrong. When a system produces data that looks plausible but is wrong, you make decisions based on that data and only discover the error when the consequences become visible in the real world. The delay between the system error and the business impact can be weeks or months, and during that delay, the damage compounds.

The Long Tail of Transformation

There is a fundamental misunderstanding in the industry about when a transformation is complete. The common assumption, reinforced by every project plan and every SI engagement model, is that the transformation is complete when the system goes live. Go-live is the finish line. Champagne is poured. The project team takes a photo. The SI sends a congratulatory email. The program is declared a success.

This is a fantasy.

Go-live is not the finish line. It is the starting line. It is the point at which the organization begins the real work of transformation: absorbing the new system, adapting the new processes, building the new capabilities, and realizing the business benefits that justified the investment. That work takes months, often years. And the industry, for the most part, has no model, no methodology, and no economic incentive to support it.

Benefits realization is the term used for the process of tracking whether the expected business outcomes from a transformation are actually being achieved. In theory, every transformation has a benefits realization plan. In practice, benefits realization is the workstream that dies first after go-live.

The reasons are predictable. The benefits were defined in the business case, which was written during the sales cycle, often by the vendor, and which used projections that were optimistic by design. After go-live, the organization is consumed by stabilization. The project team is disbanding. The executives who championed the business case have moved on to other priorities. Nobody wants to go back and measure actual performance against projections that everyone suspects were inflated, because the measurement will confirm what everyone already knows: the benefits are not materializing as promised.

Even in implementations that are technically successful, the full realization of business benefits typically takes two to three years beyond go-live. Process improvements that depend on people changing how they work take time. Reporting capabilities that depend on data quality take time to produce accurate outputs. Efficiency gains that depend on workflow optimization only emerge after the organization has moved past the learning curve and is operating the new system at proficiency.

The machine has no patience for this timeline. The vendor declared success at go-live and has moved on to the next deal. The SI's contract ended, or transitioned to a managed services engagement with different economics and different people. The advisory firm, if one was engaged, has completed its scope and closed its workstream. The organization is left alone to harvest benefits from a field that has barely been planted, using tools that are still being calibrated, operated by people who are still learning.

This is the long tail of transformation, and it is where the real value is either captured or lost. The organizations that succeed in this phase are the ones that plan for it from the beginning. They build internal capability during the implementation, not after. They fund a dedicated benefits realization team that persists beyond go-live. They track adoption metrics, process compliance, and business outcomes with the same rigor they applied to the implementation timeline. They treat go-live as a milestone, not a destination.

The organizations that fail in this phase are the ones that treated go-live as the goal. They spent everything getting to the finish line and had nothing left for the race that begins on the other side. They are the ones who, twelve months after go-live, are running the new system the same way they ran the old one, with spreadsheets alongside the ERP, workarounds that bypass the standard process, and a benefits case that sits in a drawer unexamined.

The Morning After Is Not a Phase. It Is the Transformation.

I want to close this chapter by challenging the most fundamental assumption that the machine imposes on every organization it processes: that the transformation is the implementation, and the implementation ends at go-live.

The transformation is what happens after go-live. The implementation is just the setup. The technology is just the infrastructure. The real transformation, the one that justifies the investment, the one that changes how the organization operates, the one that delivers the business outcomes the board was promised, that transformation happens in the months and years following go-live, when the organization learns to work differently, when the new processes become the default, when the data starts to flow cleanly, when the workforce moves from compliance to proficiency to mastery.

The machine is not designed to support this phase. The machine is designed to sell software, configure systems, and get to go-live. Everything that happens afterward is someone else's problem. And that someone else is you.

The organizations that understand this build their budgets, their timelines, and their expectations around the full lifecycle of transformation, not just the implementation phase. They negotiate contracts that include meaningful post-go-live support. They invest in internal capability development throughout the implementation so that when the SI leaves, the organization can stand on its own. They set realistic expectations with the board about when benefits will materialize and what it will take to realize them.

The organizations that do not understand this wake up on the morning after go-live and discover that the hardest part of their transformation has just begun, and they are facing it alone, underfunded, understaffed, and unprepared.

Target Canada learned this lesson at a cost of $7 billion. Nike learned it at a cost of $100 million and a 20 percent drop in its stock price. National Grid learned it at a cost of $100 million in post-go-live remediation and $30 million a month in ongoing support. These are the cases that became public. For every one of them, there are hundreds of organizations learning the same lesson in private, absorbing the same costs in silence, and discovering that the morning after is the part of the transformation that the machine never told them about.

The morning after is when the machine moves on. It is when you discover what was really built, how well it works, and whether your organization has what it takes to make it deliver on its promise. It is the most honest moment in the entire transformation, because it is the moment when the vendor's sales pitch, the SI's methodology, the executive's town hall optimism, and the project plan's confident milestones all collide with reality.

In the next chapter, we will examine what happens when that collision is so devastating, so costly, and so impossible to absorb that the only remaining option is a courtroom. But for most organizations, the morning after does not end in litigation. It ends in a long, quiet struggle to extract value from a system that cost far more than anyone expected and delivered far less than anyone was promised. That struggle is the true price of the machine. And it is a price that is paid long after the project team has disbanded, the consultants have left, and the vendor has cashed the check.

Chapter 9

The Litigation Aftermath

There comes a point in some digital transformations where the accumulated failures become so severe, so costly, and so impossible to ignore that the only remaining option is a courtroom. The executives who approved the program are looking for someone to blame. The board is demanding answers. The vendor and the system integrator are pointing fingers at each other and at the client. Tens of millions of dollars, sometimes hundreds of millions, have been spent with nothing to show for it. And a lawyer picks up the phone.

My team and I have analyzed over 50 implementations that ended in litigation. In each case, we dug into how decisions were made, how projects were managed, how failures originated. We reviewed internal documents, emails between executives, sales presentations, deposition transcripts, and post-mortem reports. We traced the failures backward from the courtroom to the conference room where they began.

What we found, across all of those cases, was a remarkably consistent set of patterns. The same mistakes. The same misaligned incentives. The same breakdowns in governance and accountability. The same failures in testing, change management, and process design. Different industries, different vendors, different consulting firms, different decades. The same machine, producing the same outcomes.

But there is something new. The machine has always been dangerous. What has changed is the speed at which it operates and the distance it now travels from the organizations trying to keep up with it. Technology is advancing at an exponential pace. Cloud platforms, artificial intelligence, robotic process automation, and the emerging demands of Industry 5.0 are compressing innovation cycles that once spanned decades into years, and years into months. The vendors selling these capabilities are racing to market with products whose full implications neither they nor their customers fully understand. And the organizations attempting to implement them are working with the same fundamental change capacity they have always had -- human beings who need time to learn, adapt, and absorb disruption.

That gap -- between the exponential velocity of technology and the largely linear capacity of organizations to change -- is widening. It is not a temporary condition. It is a structural feature of the current era. And it is making the machine more dangerous than it has ever been. The litigation cases I examine in this chapter are not just cautionary tales from the past. They are early signals of a future in which the gap between what technology promises and what organizations can absorb will continue to produce failures of increasing scale and frequency.

This chapter is about what litigation reveals. Not just about individual failures, but about the systemic dysfunction that makes those failures inevitable -- and about why that dysfunction is becoming harder, not easier, to escape.

What Triggers a Lawsuit

ERP lawsuits are not filed lightly. Litigation is expensive, slow, and reputationally damaging for everyone involved. Most organizations that experience a failed transformation do not sue. They absorb the loss, renegotiate with the vendor or SI, and try to salvage what they can. The cases that do reach court represent the extreme end of the failure spectrum, situations where the damage is so great and the behavior so egregious that the client sees no alternative.

In my experience, the triggers fall into a few recurring categories.

The first is sales cycle fraud and misrepresentation. This is when the vendor or the system integrator made promises during the sales process that they knew, or should have known, they could not keep. Inflated ROI projections. Claims about product capabilities that did not exist. Demonstrations that were scripted to conceal limitations. Timelines that bore no relationship to reality.

The second is contract compliance failures. The vendor or SI did not deliver what was specified in the contract. The system does not perform as described. The milestones were not met. The deliverables are incomplete or defective. The scope expanded without authorization, or the client was billed for work that was not performed.

The third is consultant errors and negligence. The system integrator staffed the project with unqualified resources, made configuration errors that caused system failures, failed to follow established implementation methodologies, or provided advice that was demonstrably wrong.

The fourth is budget overages and scope disputes. The project cost multiples of what was originally quoted, and the client believes the overages resulted from the vendor or SI's mismanagement, underestimation, or deliberate lowballing during the sales cycle.

But it would be dishonest to suggest that lawsuits are triggered exclusively by vendor and consultant behavior. In many of the cases I have analyzed, the client's own organizational failures played a significant and sometimes decisive role in creating the conditions that led to litigation. These patterns do not excuse vendor misconduct, but they are essential to understanding why transformations collapse badly enough to end up in court.

The fifth trigger, and one that is rarely discussed openly, is the client's failure to provide adequate internal resources. Digital transformation is not something that can be outsourced entirely to a vendor and an SI. It requires deep engagement from subject matter experts, process owners, and decision-makers across the organization. In case after case, I have seen clients assign their least available people to the most critical project of the decade. The A-team stays focused on daily operations while the B-team is expected to define requirements, validate configurations, and make decisions that will shape the organization for the next twenty years. When the project fails, the vendor and SI bear responsibility for the technical outcome, but the client's unwillingness to commit its best people made that outcome far more likely.

The sixth is slow and indecisive decision-making. Transformation projects operate on timelines that assume decisions will be made within days or weeks, not months. When a client organization cannot align its stakeholders, cannot resolve internal disagreements about process design, or cannot approve critical deliverables on schedule, the project timeline stretches, costs escalate, and the SI's team sits idle or moves on to other engagements. The vendor and SI often get blamed for the resulting budget overruns, but in many cases the delays originated inside the client organization.

The seventh is lack of internal alignment. In some of the most contentious cases I have investigated, the client's own leadership was fundamentally divided about the goals, scope, and priorities of the transformation. Different business units wanted different things. The CFO's priorities conflicted with the COO's. Regional leaders resisted a global template. When there is no unified vision inside the client organization, the SI is left trying to satisfy contradictory requirements, and the project becomes a political battlefield rather than a technology implementation. The failure that follows is predictable, but it did not originate with the vendor or the consultant.

The eighth is unrealistic internal expectations. Some clients enter a transformation expecting the new system to solve problems that are fundamentally organizational, not technological. They expect the ERP to fix broken processes, resolve departmental conflicts, or compensate for years of underinvestment in data quality. When the system goes live and these problems persist, the client's disappointment becomes anger, and that anger gets directed at the vendor and SI. But the expectation was never realistic to begin with, and no amount of software could have delivered what the client was hoping for.

Underlying all eight of these triggers is a ninth force that is accelerating every one of them: the pace of technological change itself. When the technology being sold is evolving faster than any organization can evaluate, implement, or absorb it, every trigger intensifies. Vendors make bolder promises because the capabilities they are selling are genuinely new and untested at scale. Consultants overestimate their own readiness because the platforms they are implementing have changed since their last project. Clients set unrealistic expectations because the marketing around cloud, AI, and automation makes transformation sound frictionless. And the gap between what the technology can theoretically do and what the organization can practically adopt grows wider with every product release, every feature update, every new module bolted onto a platform that was already more complex than the client could manage. The acceleration of technology does not just create new opportunities. It creates new categories of failure -- and new grounds for litigation.

In practice, most lawsuits involve some combination of these factors -- vendor, consultant, and client failures interacting in ways that amplify each other. The vendor's unrealistic promises collide with the client's unrealistic expectations. The SI's underqualified team meets a client organization that cannot make decisions or free up its best people. Each party's weaknesses expose and worsen the others. This is what makes attribution so difficult in litigation, and why the courtroom rarely produces a clean narrative of blame.

The Sales Presentation That Becomes Exhibit A

Of all the dynamics that trigger litigation, sales cycle misrepresentation is the one that most clearly illustrates how the machine operates.

During the sales process, the vendor's goal is to close the deal. The sales team is compensated on bookings, not on implementation success. They are measured on whether the contract gets signed, not on whether the system works two years later. This creates an incentive structure where optimism is rewarded and honesty is punished. The sales team that presents a realistic timeline, an honest assessment of limitations, and a conservative ROI projection will lose the deal to the team that promises more, faster, cheaper.

The Waste Management case brought this dynamic into sharp public view. SAP had promised that Waste Management could achieve $106 million to $220 million in annual benefits from a consolidated ERP system that could be implemented in 18 months. The contract was awarded based on claims that the solution was out-of-the-box, adapted to U.S. standards, and could fulfill the company's goals with minimal customization.

Waste Management said they were part of a fraudulent sales scheme on the part of SAP, whereas SAP turned the tables and pointed the finger at Waste Management, saying that they did not make key business decisions and define requirements in a timely manner and did not provide the right knowledgeable resources to support the project.

This mutual blame is characteristic of nearly every ERP lawsuit I have analyzed. The vendor says the client was unprepared. The client says the vendor oversold. The truth, in virtually every case, involves failures on both sides. But the imbalance of information is what makes the vendor's behavior more troubling. The vendor knows what its product can and cannot do. The vendor has implemented this software hundreds of times. The vendor knows what a realistic timeline looks like. The client, often going through this for the first time, is relying on the vendor's representations to make a multi-million dollar decision. When those representations are inflated, the client is making that decision based on information that the vendor knows is inaccurate.

Waste Management filed a $100 million lawsuit against SAP in 2008, later raising that amount to $500 million before settling out of court in 2010. Waste Management sued SAP for over $1 billion in damages and from their financial records showed that they had realized gains of $77 million as a result of their settlement. They recovered some money. They lost far more than they recovered. And the years of litigation extracted their own toll in executive attention, organizational distraction, and reputational damage.

In a case I investigated involving a manufacturing software vendor in Australia, the sales dynamics were even more brazen. The vendor's sales team over-promised and exaggerated solution benefits that their own solution team could not back up with results. A configurator they claimed was 80 percent built did not work and was slower than the legacy system. They promised 25 to 50 percent efficiency gains. Not only did those gains fail to materialize, but there is a good argument that there would have been problems even with ideal execution.

The vendor's sales lead told the client words to the effect of "I'm very confident that we can deliver the project. All the work's done. We've already built 80 percent of the system" and "let's just get this thing done, don't worry about the legal mechanics as it's going to sit in a bottom drawer anyway." Do not worry about the legal mechanics. It is going to sit in a bottom drawer. That is what the vendor told the client about the contract that was supposed to protect them. It did not sit in a bottom drawer. It ended up in a courtroom.

The Corrupted Selection

Sometimes the failure begins before the project starts, in the process by which the system integrator is selected.

In one case I investigated as an expert witness, the client's project executive was paid over $50,000 by the system integrator during the period when bidding for the next phase of the project was taking place. This fact was never disclosed to anyone else at the client organization. This conflict of interest is highly unusual in a bidding process and is a red flag early on regarding the fairness and objectivity of the SI selection.

It got worse. The project executive was paid more than $1 million between 2015 and 2018, which includes the time period during which he was responsible for managing the SI on behalf of the client. There was nothing showing that these payments were ever disclosed to the client. The person who was supposed to be protecting the client's interests was being paid by the system integrator he was supposed to be overseeing.

The project executive had access to competitor proposals and shared them with the preferred SI. A witness recalled seeing a spreadsheet where the SI had all the competitor information laid out side by side. Emails showed that the project executive had sent a competing firm's proposal directly to the SI.

On at least one occasion, the project executive instructed the EDI team to fake the testing and process it manually so a key customer would not know.

This implementation failed on many levels. The project executive demanded control of the project and was a consistent bottleneck, hiding key information, downplaying failures, and orchestrating this failure from the inside, all while receiving over $1 million from the system integrator.

This case is extreme in its specifics. One million dollars in undisclosed payments is not typical. But the broader dynamic, an SI selection process that is influenced by relationships, financial incentives, and information asymmetry rather than by an objective assessment of capability, is far more common than the industry would like to admit. I will address this in much greater detail in Part III of this book, when we examine the consultant's side of the machine.

When the Government Gets Defrauded

The Queensland Health case, which I have referenced several times in this book for its testing and human impact dimensions, also produced one of the most damning findings about vendor behavior in the history of the industry.

The official inquiry found that IBM had acted improperly and corruptly in forming and submitting its tender to the government. Key IBM staff had been provided confidential information by government executives relating to the available budget, and the company used its pre-existing system access from other projects to retrieve internal government documents related to the tender.

Additionally, IBM staff improperly accessed the proposals of its competitors. The inquiry concluded that had the government been aware of these failures, IBM would have been automatically excluded from the procurement process.

IBM knew the government's budget. IBM had read its competitors' proposals. IBM used information obtained through prior government engagements to gain an unfair advantage in the tender process. And the government, which trusted IBM as a reputable global technology firm, had no idea any of this was happening until the official inquiry exposed it.

The result was a $1.25 billion disaster that affected over 80,000 healthcare workers. The technical failures were severe. The human cost was devastating. But the root cause was not a configuration error or a testing shortfall. It was a procurement process that was corrupted from the beginning by a vendor that prioritized winning the deal over serving the client.

The Contract That Does Not Protect You

One of the patterns that emerges consistently across the litigation cases I have analyzed is that the contract between the client and the vendor or SI, the document that is supposed to define obligations, allocate risk, and provide recourse when things go wrong, is almost always written to favor the vendor.

This should not be surprising. The vendor writes the first draft. The vendor has a legal team that has negotiated hundreds of these contracts. The client, often going through this for the first time, may not fully understand the implications of the terms it is agreeing to.

Subscription license agreements can be problematic as they frequently massively favor the service provider at the expense of the client. Availability warranties are often weak, partial availability not covered, assignment rights and novation not mentioned, performance guarantees missing, and all with poor indemnities for data protection violations and cyber-risks.

Contracts are another minefield for the unwary, and even with expert review by legal counsel, onerous terms can sometimes slip through.

The most common contractual traps I see include limitation of liability clauses that cap the vendor's exposure at a fraction of the total project cost, binding arbitration clauses that prevent the dispute from reaching a public courtroom, and intellectual property provisions that give the vendor ownership of customizations that the client paid to build.

By the time the client realizes the contract does not protect them, they are already deep into an implementation that is going sideways, and the contract they signed gives them almost no leverage.

But the most insidious contractual traps are not the headline clauses. They are the assumption schedules -- the pages of one-line statements buried in appendices that no one reads carefully until the project is in crisis. These assumptions are written in plain, neutral language that appears entirely reasonable at first glance. "Client shall be responsible for data cleansing and migration." "Client shall be responsible for training end users." "Client shall ensure availability of subject matter experts throughout the implementation." Each sentence looks like a sensible allocation of responsibility. Each sentence, in practice, can represent millions of dollars in unscoped, unbudgeted work.

Data cleansing and migration is one of the most consistently underestimated activities in any transformation. Organizations often have decades of dirty, inconsistent, incomplete data living across legacy systems, spreadsheets, and manual processes. The work of extracting, cleaning, mapping, and validating that data before it can be loaded into a new system frequently costs as much as the implementation itself -- sometimes more. The vendor and SI know this. They have seen it hundreds of times.

And yet the assumption schedule contains one sentence: "Client shall be responsible for data cleansing and migration." The client signs. The project begins. The reality of what that sentence actually means does not become apparent until months into the project, when the data work falls catastrophically behind schedule and the budget is already exhausted.

Training end users is another. A single assumption line -- "Client shall be responsible for training end employees" -- transfers responsibility for one of the most complex and consequential activities of the entire transformation. How many users need to be trained? On which processes? In which languages? With what documentation? Over what timeline? None of these questions are answered in the assumption schedule. The answers, when they emerge, routinely add hundreds of thousands or millions of dollars to project costs that the client never anticipated, budgeted for, or approved.

The assumption schedule is not an accident. It is a legal instrument designed to allocate risk to the party least equipped to understand that risk at the time of signing. By the time the client understands what those one-line assumptions really mean, the project is too far along to renegotiate and too far behind to recover.

The risk approach to procuring an implementation ranges from time and materials at one end to shared rewards at the other. In a T&M contract, the client takes full accountability for the implementation. The supplier is providing resources, not outcomes. It is surprisingly common that an organization will feel the supplier is accountable for successfully implementing the solution, even when on a T&M contract.

This disconnect between perceived accountability and actual accountability is at the heart of many disputes. The client believes the SI is responsible for a successful outcome. The contract says the SI is responsible for providing qualified resources for a specified number of hours. When the outcome is failure, the client discovers that the contract they signed does not give them the recourse they assumed they had.

The Blame Game

When an ERP lawsuit reaches the discovery phase, a predictable pattern emerges in the depositions and document exchanges. Each party constructs a narrative that places the blame on the others.

The vendor says the software works and the failure was caused by the SI's implementation errors and the client's lack of readiness.

The SI says the software had limitations and the client did not provide adequate resources, make timely decisions, or manage its own organizational change. The client says the vendor oversold the product and the SI was underqualified, overstaffed, and unresponsive to escalated risks.

At MillerCoors, HCL's public response to the $100 million lawsuit was somewhat flippant. Their reaction was that it was just one client and that they had several other reference clients available for every one client that had something bad to say about them. HCL also counter-sued MillerCoors, saying that management dysfunction was the real reason the project failed.

This mutual recrimination is not just a legal tactic. It is a genuine reflection of how failure works in the machine. Because in most cases, all three parties did contribute to the failure. The vendor did oversell. The SI was underqualified. And the client was unprepared. The machine is designed so that each party's failures amplify the others. The vendor's unrealistic promises set the SI up for an impossible timeline. The SI's underqualified staff leaves the client without the guidance it needs. The client's lack of readiness means the organization cannot absorb the changes being pushed onto it. Each gear of the machine fails in a way that makes the other gears fail harder.

What is absent from every deposition, every brief, and every negotiated settlement is an honest acknowledgment of the most perverse dimension of the machine: in virtually every failed transformation, all three parties -- the vendor, the SI, and the consulting firm -- are made whole. The vendor received its license fees. The SI billed its hours. The consultants collected their retainers. The only party that is almost guaranteed not to benefit from the project is the one that paid for it.

This is not a flaw in the machine. It is a feature. The incentive structures of the enterprise technology industry are designed so that profit is decoupled from outcome. The vendor is paid when the software is licensed, not when it delivers the promised ROI. The SI is paid when its consultants show up, not when the system works. The consulting firm is paid when it completes its engagement, not when the client succeeds. All three parties can -- and frequently do -- collect every dollar they were owed from a project that ends in complete failure, that produces nothing the client can use, and that leaves the organization worse off than before it began. The client is left holding the full weight of a catastrophe that everyone else has already been paid to deliver.

This is perhaps the most perverse element of the machine, and the one the industry is least willing to discuss. Failure is profitable -- for everyone except the client. A failed project does not destroy the vendor's business model. It generates a follow-on engagement to remediate the failure. It produces a renegotiation that generates new licensing revenue. It may even produce a settlement that the vendor funds out of a reserve it has already set aside precisely for this purpose. For the SI, a failed project means more hours billed in remediation, not fewer. For every consultant who was on the disastrous implementation, there is another engagement opportunity in the aftermath. The machine is not designed to succeed. It is designed to continue.

This is why litigation, while sometimes necessary, is rarely satisfying for the client. Even when they win, the recovery is typically a fraction of the damage. National Grid sued their system integrator for $75 million and were awarded a large share of that. But the company had spent $100 million in post-go-live remediation and was burning $30 million a month at the peak of the crisis. The lawsuit recovered money. It did not recover the years of disruption, the damage to employee morale, or the strategic opportunities that were lost while the organization was consumed by the failure.

MillerCoors provides another instructive example of the litigation dynamic. The company was attempting to consolidate seven separate SAP instances into a unified platform -- a technically ambitious but strategically sound objective. The implementation went live with thousands of open critical items. The operational disruption was severe enough that MillerCoors sued its system integrator, HCL Technologies, for $100 million. HCL countersued, blaming MillerCoors' management for the failure. The finger-pointing was textbook: the SI blamed the client's readiness, the client blamed the SI's delivery, and the truth -- as usual -- involved failures on both sides that the engagement model was structurally designed to produce.

LeasePlan, one of the world's largest fleet management companies, tells a different kind of cautionary tale -- one that ended not in court but in abandonment. The company invested €92 million in an SAP implementation that was ultimately declared "unfit for purpose." After years of effort, LeasePlan scrapped the entire implementation, salvaged approximately €14 million of value from the wreckage, and moved to a best-of-breed approach. No lawsuit. No settlement. Just €78 million lost and a lesson learned the most expensive way possible. LeasePlan's case illustrates that the absence of litigation does not mean the absence of catastrophic failure. For every case that ends in court, there are dozens that end in quiet abandonment, with the losses absorbed in silence.

What the Courts See That the Industry Ignores

One of the most valuable things about litigation, from an analytical perspective, is that it forces transparency. During discovery, the internal documents come out. The emails that were never meant to be read by anyone outside the project team. The status reports that were sanitized before being presented to the steering committee. The sales presentations that made promises the implementation team knew were impossible. The deposition transcripts where consultants and executives are compelled to describe, under oath, what actually happened versus what was reported.

Courts do not ask whether the system "went live." They ask whether professional standards were met and whether leaders acted reasonably given what they knew at the time. An ERP can technically run and still represent a governance failure if it cannot produce intended outcomes, if risks were concealed or minimized, or if decisions were made without evidence.

In recoveries and disputes, leaders are evaluated on process, not on whether the project was hard, not on whether the vendor promised best practices, and not on whether the integrator worked long hours. Reasonableness, transparency, and documented decision-making are the currency of defensibility.

This is an important insight for any executive leading a transformation. The legal standard is not whether the project succeeded. It is whether the decisions along the way were reasonable, informed, and documented. Did you conduct adequate due diligence before selecting the vendor? Did you maintain independent oversight of the SI? Did you act on the findings of your testing program? Did you make the go/no-go decision based on objective criteria? If the answers to these questions are no, the organization is exposed, not just to operational failure, but to legal liability.

Silent failure is where liability accumulates. During silent failure, schedules slip but get rebaselined. Scope expands but is normalized. Risk logs exist but are unmanaged. Dashboards stay green while the business experiences red. This is the territory between "things are not going well" and "things have failed." It is the period during which the warning signs are visible but no one acts on them. And it is the period that, in litigation, becomes the focus of the plaintiff's case. You knew. The documents show you knew. And you did not act.

The Cases That Never Reach Court

For every ERP lawsuit that is filed, there are dozens, perhaps hundreds, of failures that never see the inside of a courtroom. The reasons are varied, but they share a common thread: the machine is designed to suppress transparency.

Some organizations do not sue because they are embarrassed. A failed digital transformation is a visible, expensive, deeply personal failure for the executives who championed it. Filing a lawsuit makes that failure public. The board, the shareholders, the employees, the competitors, and the media all learn the details. Many executives would rather absorb the loss quietly than endure the public scrutiny of litigation.

Some do not sue because they are exhausted. By the time a transformation fails catastrophically enough to warrant litigation, the organization has been through years of disruption, internal conflict, and financial strain. The prospect of another two to four years of legal proceedings, with all the depositions, document production, and executive distraction that entails, is more than many organizations can stomach.

Some do not sue because the contract does not let them. Binding arbitration clauses keep the dispute out of public courts and into private proceedings where the outcomes are confidential. Limitation of liability caps mean that even a successful claim would recover only a fraction of the losses. Non-disclosure agreements, signed as part of the original contract or negotiated during settlement discussions, prevent the client from speaking publicly about what happened.

And some do not sue because the vendor offers just enough to make litigation unattractive. A discount on future licensing. Additional consulting hours at no charge. An extension of the support period. These concessions cost the vendor a fraction of what a lawsuit would cost, and they buy silence. The failure disappears from public view. The next customer walks in with no knowledge of what happened to the last one.

There is one more reason that cases never reach court, and it is the one that the industry works hardest to ensure. Independent, objective voices -- advisors with no financial stake in the software being sold or the hours being billed -- are rarely welcomed into the machine. Firms like ours at Third Stage Consulting have spent years providing clients with unbiased assessments of vendor capabilities, SI performance, and project health. We are not compensated by software vendors. We do not have referral relationships with system integrators. Our only obligation is to the client. And precisely because of that independence, we are frequently excluded, marginalized, or actively discouraged from participating in transformation projects.

The reason is straightforward: an objective, independent voice is dangerous to the machine. It asks questions the vendor does not want answered. It examines project health reports the SI would prefer to keep internal. It gives the client an honest assessment of what the contract actually says and what the project is actually delivering. The vendor and SI benefit enormously from an environment in which the client has no independent frame of reference -- no outside expert telling them that the go-live timeline is unrealistic, that the testing coverage is inadequate, that the assumption schedule they signed transfers millions in unbudgeted risk onto their organization. The client, navigating this experience for the first time, has no way to know what it does not know. And the machine, which has done this hundreds of times, prefers it that way.

When independent advisors are engaged, the dynamic shifts. Risks are identified earlier. Contracts are negotiated more carefully. Go/no-go decisions are based on actual readiness rather than vendor pressure. The litigation cases in my portfolio that involved independent oversight are, almost without exception, the ones that produced better outcomes -- or caught the warning signs early enough to avoid the courtroom entirely. The cases that never involved independent oversight are the ones that ended in the full catastrophe: the nine-figure losses, the regulatory investigations, the executive terminations, the lawsuits that settled under NDA and disappeared from public view. The machine does not fear litigation. It fears transparency.

When we see an uptick in expert witness engagements, we know this is a leading indicator of broader failures in the market. Lawsuits represent just the tip of the iceberg, representing just the most extreme examples of failure. When this sample increases, it is reasonable to assume that more moderate and less publicized failures are on the rise as well.

The trajectory is not encouraging. As cloud migrations replace on-premise implementations, as AI capabilities are layered onto ERP platforms that organizations have not yet mastered, as the pressure to adopt accelerates while the organizational capacity to absorb remains flat, the conditions that produce catastrophic failure are becoming more common, not less. The technology is moving faster. The sales cycles are more aggressive. The promises are bigger. And the organizations buying those promises are no better equipped to evaluate them than they were a decade ago.

This is the most insidious aspect of the litigation landscape. The cases that reach court are the ones where the failure was so extreme, the behavior so egregious, or the client so determined that litigation became unavoidable. The vast majority of failures are resolved privately, quietly, and in ways that ensure the market never learns from them. The same vendor that oversold one client goes on to oversell the next. The same SI that understaffed one project goes on to understaff another. The machine processes the failure, absorbs it, and continues operating without interruption.

What Litigation Teaches

I have spent a significant portion of my career inside these cases, and the experience has shaped my understanding of the machine more than anything else. When you read the internal documents, when you trace the decisions backward from the catastrophe to the conference room where they were made, you see the entire system in operation. The optimistic sales pitch. The unrealistic timeline. The underqualified SI team. The compressed testing. The defect downgrade. The go/no-go meeting where everyone knew the system was not ready but no one was willing to say so. The go-live. The crisis. The blame.

Every chapter of Part I is visible in every case. The burning platform that was not burning. The leadership vacuum that let the SI drive the agenda. The cow paths that got paved at enormous expense. The human firewall that nobody prepared for. The testing that got compressed. And finally, the courtroom, where all of it is laid bare under oath.

Most ERP failures do not happen because the software is bad. They happen because leadership abandons governance, because strategy is confused with vendor selection, and because organizational change is treated as an afterthought. That finding comes not from a consulting framework or an academic study. It comes from the evidence, the internal emails and deposition transcripts and project documents that surface when a transformation fails badly enough to end up in court.

There is one more lesson that the litigation cases teach, and it may be the most important one for the years ahead. The pace of technological change is accelerating in ways that the machine was never designed to handle. Cloud computing has eliminated the capital expenditure barrier that once slowed adoption, making it easier than ever to launch a transformation and harder than ever to control one. Artificial intelligence is being embedded into every major ERP and CRM platform, often before the vendors themselves fully understand how it will behave in production environments. Robotic process automation promises to eliminate manual work, but the organizational redesign required to support it is rarely scoped or funded. And the emerging paradigm of Industry 5.0 -- with its emphasis on human-machine collaboration, sustainability, and resilience -- is adding layers of complexity that most implementation methodologies have not even begun to address.

The technology is growing exponentially. The human capacity to absorb change is not. This is not a metaphor. It is a measurable, observable reality that is visible in every case I have analyzed. The projects that fail most catastrophically are not the ones using the oldest technology. They are the ones attempting to implement the newest technology inside organizations whose decision-making speed, change management maturity, and internal alignment have not meaningfully improved in twenty years. The gap between what the technology demands and what the organization can deliver is the single most reliable predictor of the severity of failure. And that gap is widening.

This is why the number of litigation cases is increasing, not decreasing, despite decades of supposed lessons learned. The industry is not getting better at implementation. The technology is getting harder to implement. Every new wave -- cloud, AI, machine learning, advanced analytics, IoT -- adds capability that the market demands and complexity that organizations cannot absorb at the pace required. The machine feeds on this gap. It sells the capability, bills for the complexity, and leaves the client to absorb the consequences when the organization cannot keep up.

The litigation cases confirm what the rest of this book argues: that digital transformation failure is systemic, not incidental. It is the predictable output of a machine that is designed to sell software, bill hours, and go live on schedule, regardless of whether the organization or the system is ready. The clients who end up in court are not uniquely unlucky. They are the ones whose experience of the machine was so damaging that they refused to stay silent.

The machine counts on silence. It counts on NDAs and settlements and the embarrassment that keeps failed organizations from telling their stories. Every case that does reach court is a crack in that silence, a rare moment of forced transparency in an industry that depends on opacity.

Part I of this book has examined the transformation from the client's perspective: why organizations enter the machine, how leadership failures enable it, how legacy processes and human resistance sustain it, how testing is sacrificed to it, and what happens when the consequences become severe enough to require a legal reckoning. The client bears real responsibility. But the client is also operating inside a system that is designed to exploit every weakness, amplify every failure, and obscure every lesson.

In Part II, we turn to the technology itself, the engine of the machine, and examine how the business models, products, and practices of the vendors who build enterprise software have shaped the system that consumes their customers. We will also examine how the exponential acceleration of technology -- cloud, AI, robotics, and beyond -- is widening the gap between what is sold and what organizations can absorb, and why this widening gap means the machine is not winding down. It is speeding up.

Part II: THE TECHNOLOGY

The Engine of the Machine

"The technology works. The problem is everything around it."

Chapter 10

The Money Machine

In Part I of this book, I described how organizations feed themselves into the machine. Leadership vacuums, cultural dysfunction, process rigidity, inadequate testing, catastrophic go-lives, and the courtroom reckonings that follow. In each case, the organization bore real responsibility for its own failure. The conventional wisdom says that is where the story ends. Clients fail because they were not ready.

But the conventional wisdom conveniently ignores the engine that powers the machine. The engine is not the software itself. The technology, by and large, works. The engine is the business model surrounding the technology, a business model that has been deliberately redesigned over the past decade to serve one constituency above all others: investors.

This chapter is about money. Not the money you spend on your transformation, which we covered in Part I. This chapter is about the money that drives the decisions of the vendors, the consultants, and the analyst firms who shape the market you are buying from. It is about how the economics of cloud computing created the most powerful set of aligned financial incentives in the history of enterprise technology, and how those incentives have systematically diverged from the interests of the organizations they are supposed to serve.

If you want to understand why the machine behaves the way it does, follow the money. It will take you straight to the cloud.

The Cloud Tipping Point

There was a time, not long ago, when I believed that on-premise enterprise software would coexist with cloud for the foreseeable future. I believed the market would sort itself out, that some organizations would move to the cloud because it made sense for them, and others would stay on-premise because that made sense for them. Customer choice would prevail. The technology would be a means to an end, not an end in itself.

I was wrong. The reason for my change of heart is simple: money favors cloud ERP. Investors simply love the cloud business model too much. The recurring revenue, higher profit margins, and high customer switching costs make cloud ERP vendors an investor's dream.

To understand why, you need to understand the economics that changed everything.

In the old world of enterprise software, the business model was built on perpetual licenses. A company paid a large upfront fee to license the software, then paid annual maintenance, typically around 18 to 22 percent of the license cost, for access to updates and support. The vendor's revenue was lumpy: big license deals in good quarters, smaller ones in bad quarters. Maintenance revenue was recurring, but the margins were moderate and the growth was slow. Wall Street valued these companies, but not extravagantly. The economics were solid but unspectacular.

Cloud changed everything. In the cloud model, the perpetual license disappears. In its place is a subscription, a recurring fee paid monthly or annually for access to the software, the infrastructure, and the support. The customer never owns the software. They rent it. And the rent never stops.

For investors, this is extraordinary. Investors and shareholders are investing billions in cloud-friendly software companies because the economics are almost irrationally attractive. Subscription revenue is predictable. It compounds. It creates a baseline of recurring cash flow that grows as new customers are added and rarely shrinks, because the switching costs are enormous. Once an organization has migrated its entire operation to a cloud ERP platform, the cost and complexity of moving to a competitor is so prohibitive that most customers never leave. They renew. They expand. They pay whatever the vendor charges at renewal, because the alternative is a multi-year, multi-million-dollar reimplementation.

The gross margins on subscription revenue are staggering. In a mature SaaS business, subscription gross margins typically run 75 to 80 percent or higher. Compare that to professional services, which run 20 to 35 percent. Every dollar a vendor can convert from services revenue to subscription revenue drops dramatically more profit to the bottom line. And because the revenue is recurring, the market assigns dramatically higher valuation multiples to subscription revenue than to any other kind.

This is not abstract financial theory. It is the engine that is driving every major decision in the enterprise software industry today.

The Numbers Do Not Lie

Consider SAP, the largest enterprise software company in the world and the one whose products touch more global business processes than any other. In 2021, SAP's market capitalization was approximately $164 billion. By the end of 2024, it had risen to $283 billion, an increase of more than 70 percent in three years. By mid-2025, it peaked at approximately $355 billion. What happened between 2021 and 2025 to nearly double the value of a company that has been selling enterprise software for fifty years?

Cloud happened.

SAP's 2025 annual report tells the story in a single number: cloud revenue reached €21 billion, surpassing every other revenue stream to become the company's largest source of income. Total revenue was €36.8 billion. Operating profit grew to €9.6 billion. Free cash flow hit €8.2 billion.

The market was not rewarding SAP for selling better software. It was rewarding SAP for converting its customer base from perpetual licenses to recurring cloud subscriptions. Every customer who moved from ECC to S/4HANA Cloud was not just a migration. They were a conversion from low-multiple revenue to high-multiple revenue. They were, in the language of Wall Street, a recurring revenue asset.

SAP's own analysts have articulated the math explicitly: the company believes it can convert €1 of on-premise revenue into €5 or more of cloud revenue through end-to-end value chain transformation. Read that number again. Five times the revenue from the same customer, for what is in many cases a functionally similar product delivered through a different model. That is not a technology strategy. That is a financial engineering strategy. And the market loves it.

Oracle tells a parallel story. In September 2025, Oracle reported that its remaining performance obligations, the most popular measure of booked revenue, had jumped 359 percent to $455 billion. Cloud revenue grew 28 percent to $7.2 billion in a single quarter. Oracle's stock rose 27 percent in a single day on the back of that earnings report. The company's CEO projected cloud infrastructure revenue would grow from $18 billion to $144 billion over the next five years. Oracle's market capitalization, which stood at roughly $524 billion in early 2026, has been driven almost entirely by the market's enthusiasm for its cloud transition.

Microsoft's Dynamics 365 follows the same trajectory, as does virtually every other major enterprise software vendor. The message from Wall Street is unambiguous: convert customers to the cloud, and we will reward you with a higher stock price. Keep them on-premise, and we will punish you. The market has spoken, and it has spoken in the only language that public companies understand: valuation.

The Incentive Cascade

Here is what most technology buyers do not understand: the investor pressure at the top of the pyramid creates a cascade of economic incentives that flows through every level of the industry, and at every level, those incentives conflict with the interests of the customer.

At the top, investors drive stock prices up for vendors that convert more customers to the cloud. The faster you migrate your installed base, the higher your stock goes. The higher your stock goes, the more your executives are worth, because executive compensation at these companies is heavily weighted toward equity. Stock options, restricted stock units, performance shares tied to cloud revenue targets -- the C-suite at every major enterprise software vendor has a direct, personal financial interest in moving every customer to the cloud as fast as possible, regardless of whether each individual customer is ready for or would benefit from the move.

Below the C-suite, the incentives continue. Sales representatives earn higher commissions on cloud subscriptions than they ever did on on-premise deals. This is by design. The vendors have restructured their compensation plans to reward cloud sales disproportionately, because cloud sales are what the market rewards. A sales rep who convinces you to sign a multi-year cloud subscription is more valuable to the vendor than a sales rep who closes a perpetual license deal of the same size, because the subscription generates recurring revenue that the market values at a higher multiple. The sales rep knows this. Their quota knows this. Their commission check knows this.

The result is a cloud and AI arms race that the technology vendors are on, which is not a bad thing on the surface, but when you look under the hood, you find that the technology vendors now have a conflicting self-interest that conflicts with the interests of customers. Not every customer needs to go to the cloud right now.

Not every customer needs to be using AI right now. A lot of customers have not even gotten their house in order to be able to leverage these technologies even if they wanted to.

But the incentive cascade does not ask whether the customer is ready. It asks whether the deal is closed. It asks whether the subscription is booked. It asks whether the cloud revenue number will hit the target that triggers the bonus, the promotion, the stock option vesting. The customer's readiness is someone else's problem. The customer's success is someone else's metric. The only metric that matters, from the investor to the board to the CEO to the VP of Sales to the account executive sitting across from your CIO, is conversion.

This is the money machine. And your transformation is its fuel.

The Ecosystem Falls in Line

With investors and vendors both investing heavily in cloud, the rest of the ERP ecosystem falls into line. Consultants and system integrators, paid by the vendors, reinforce the vendors' pro-cloud philosophy. Industry analysts, who are also paid by the vendors, have been touting the death of on-premise for years. The industry has built a fully integrated ecosystem that is crushing on-premise into oblivion.

Let me unpack how this works, because the alignment is more complete and more deliberate than most people realize.

Start with the system integrators. The big system integrators have hundreds of thousands of consultants that they need to keep staffed. Deloitte, Accenture, KPMG, PwC, Infosys, Wipro -- these firms have built enormous practice areas around specific vendor platforms. They have SAP practices, Oracle practices, Microsoft practices. Their revenue depends on implementations, and their implementation pipeline depends on the vendor's ability to generate demand. When SAP announces a forced migration deadline, the system integrators do not object. They celebrate. Thirty thousand organizations that must migrate means thirty thousand potential implementation engagements. The bigger and more complex the migration, the more billable hours it generates.

The system integrators are not independent advisors to the customer. They are, in economic terms, an extension of the vendor's sales channel. Many of them earn commissions on software deals they help close. Many of them receive referral fees, co-marketing funds, and preferential access to vendor resources in exchange for steering customers toward the vendor's preferred products. When a system integrator recommends that you move to the cloud, that recommendation is not purely -- or even primarily -- based on what is best for your business. It is based on what generates revenue for their practice, what satisfies their vendor partnership obligations, and what keeps their consultants staffed.

You have a whole ecosystem of implementation partners, system integrators, resellers, technical consultants that focus on SAP. The big four, for example, all focus pretty heavily on S/4HANA. So Deloitte, Accenture, KPMG, PwC -- all those big consulting firms have big SAP practices, and their goal is to get you to implement SAP and go to S/4HANA Cloud using their services.

Now consider the analyst firms. Gartner, Forrester, IDC -- the organizations whose research reports and Magic Quadrant rankings heavily influence buying decisions. These firms are paid by the vendors they evaluate. Not exclusively, but significantly. Vendor sponsorships, analyst access programs, and paid consulting engagements create a financial relationship between the analyst and the vendor that is not always visible to the buyer reading the report. When an analyst firm publishes a report declaring that on-premise is dead and every organization should be planning its cloud migration, the buyer assumes this is independent research. It may be. But the financial relationship between the analyst and the vendor introduces a bias that is structural, not incidental.

The ecosystem alignment is circular and self-reinforcing. The vendor creates the product. The analyst validates it. The system integrator recommends it. The vendor pays the analyst. The vendor pays the system integrator. The customer pays everyone. And the message that reaches the customer, from every direction, is the same: go to the cloud. Do it now. Your competitors already have. You cannot afford to wait.

There are recent studies that show that 80 to 85 percent of people distrust big organizations, and they distrust big technology providers at an even higher rate. The irony is that the organizations making the biggest technology decisions of their lives are relying on an information ecosystem that is funded by the companies trying to sell them something. The buyer's trust is already low. The ecosystem does nothing to earn it.

The Lock-In Machine

If the incentive cascade gets you into the cloud, the lock-in mechanisms keep you there. This is by design, and it is one of the most important dynamics for any technology buyer to understand.

In the on-premise world, you owned your software. You controlled your data. You ran your own infrastructure. If you decided to switch vendors, it was expensive and painful, but it was architecturally possible. Your data was in your data center. Your customizations were yours. The switching costs were high but not insurmountable.

In the cloud world, the vendor controls everything. SAP controls your infrastructure. They control your SLAs, your service level agreements. They control your renewal terms. They control your commercial bundling and a host of other factors. Your data lives on the vendor's infrastructure. Your integrations run through the vendor's middleware. Your customizations, if you are even permitted to make them, exist within the vendor's extensibility framework. You are not a software owner. You are a tenant. And like any tenant, your leverage decreases the longer you stay.

What RISE does is lock you in. You are more locked in than ever in an S/4HANA environment than you might have been in an ECC environment. Switching costs are going to be a lot higher when you decide someday potentially to move from S/4HANA to something else.

The lock-in operates at multiple levels. At the data level, migrating your data out of a vendor's cloud platform and into a competitor's is a massive, expensive, and risky undertaking. At the process level, your business processes have been configured to the vendor's platform, and reconfiguring them for a different platform means repeating a substantial portion of the implementation.

At the integration level, your third-party systems are connected through the vendor's APIs and middleware, and those connections must be rebuilt. At the contractual level, multi-year subscription agreements, auto-renewal clauses, and steep early termination penalties create financial barriers to exit that are separate from and additional to the technical barriers.

This is why investors love the cloud model. The switching costs are not a bug. They are the feature. They are what makes the revenue truly recurring. They are what justifies the premium valuation multiples. When Wall Street values a cloud ERP company at 10 or 15 times revenue, they are not valuing the technology. They are valuing the lock-in. They are valuing the fact that once a customer is on the platform, the customer is unlikely to leave -- and therefore the revenue stream is, for all practical purposes, permanent.

From the vendor's perspective, this is brilliant business strategy. From the customer's perspective, it means that the decision to move to a particular cloud platform is not a software selection. It is a marriage with no prenuptial agreement and a very expensive divorce.

There is a useful framework for understanding just how thoroughly the cloud model has tilted the playing field in the vendor's favor.

Michael Porter's Five Forces Model, developed at Harvard Business School decades ago, analyzes the competitive dynamics of an industry across five dimensions: the threat of new entrants, the threat of substitutes, the bargaining power of buyers, the bargaining power of suppliers, and the rivalry among existing competitors. Applied to the enterprise software industry, every single force favors the vendor.

Vendor lock reduces the bargaining power of buyers, reduces the threat of substitutes, reduces the threat of new entrants, and diminishes rivalry among competitors. The cloud subscription model with its long-term contracts, high switching costs, and mandatory infrastructure dependency has created an industry structure that is, by any objective analysis, a vendor's utopia. The barriers to entry for a new ERP vendor are enormous -- no startup is going to displace SAP's hold on the Fortune 500 anytime soon. The substitutes are limited -- once you are on a cloud platform, the cost of switching to an alternative exceeds the cost of staying. The buyer's negotiating leverage is minimal -- have you ever tried to negotiate with SAP or Oracle as a mid-market company? And the rivalry among existing vendors, while real, is constrained by the fact that each vendor's installed base is effectively captive.

Underlying all of this is money. Investors are driving up stock prices, rewarding software vendors for their ability to lock customers in, tie them to long-term subscription costs, and create high switching costs. The software vendors that are doing the best are the ones doing the best job of migrating customers to the cloud. Porter's model explains why the machine behaves the way it does: the industry structure makes it rational. Every actor in the ecosystem is responding to incentives that the structure creates. The vendor locks in the customer because the market rewards lock-in. The SI supports the lock-in because their revenue depends on the vendor's platform. The analyst validates the lock-in because their business model depends on the vendor's sponsorship. The structure is self-reinforcing, and the only party whose interests are not served by it is the customer.

What I have just described is a protection racket. The vendor's lawyers would prefer I not call it that. But the economic structure is identical. The vendor has engineered a situation where the cost of non-compliance -- losing support, losing upgrades, losing access to AI capabilities -- is calibrated to slightly exceed the cost of compliance. The "choice" to migrate is economically coerced rather than freely made. Nice business you have there. Shame if your SAP support ran out in 2030.

The Double Pay

There is a particularly cynical dimension to the current cloud transition that deserves its own examination, because it affects tens of thousands of organizations worldwide and represents one of the most audacious revenue strategies in the history of enterprise technology.

Consider the position of a company running SAP ECC. They licensed the software years ago. They paid for the implementation. They have been paying annual maintenance fees, typically 18 to 22 percent of the original license cost, every year since. They have invested millions, sometimes hundreds of millions, in a system that works. And now SAP is telling them that the system is going away. Mainstream support ends in 2027. Extended support is available through 2030, at an additional cost. After that, they are on their own.

The customer's options are: migrate to S/4HANA, which will cost tens of millions of dollars in a new implementation; continue paying maintenance on a system with a diminishing support horizon; or switch to a competitor, which will cost even more than migrating within the SAP ecosystem.

SAP is convincing customers to pay twice for the same software they have always had, with the dream of potentially having S/4HANA within their operations someday in the future. Through programs like RISE with SAP, customers can begin paying cloud subscription fees while still running their ECC systems, effectively paying maintenance on the old system and subscription fees on the new system simultaneously. It is, as one commentator noted, brilliant sales and marketing. It is also a strategy that extracts maximum revenue from a customer base that has limited alternatives.

There is a related tactic that starts even earlier: over-licensing. Vendors frequently ask customers to purchase more licenses or modules than they currently need, positioning it as a volume discount or future-proofing strategy. The pitch sounds reasonable: "Buy now at a discount and you will have the capacity when you need it." But many clients who accept that offer end up with software they never deploy -- licenses sitting unused, subscription fees accruing monthly, for capabilities that were never part of the business case and never made it onto the implementation plan. The over-licensing tactic turns the vendor's sales quota into the client's recurring cost.

There is a structural fix for this, but it would require the vendors to change their compensation model -- which is why it has not happened. Many vendors compensate their sales teams primarily for closing deals, often with large upfront payments, regardless of whether the customer ultimately succeeds with the product. If vendor compensation were tied to customer success -- to adoption rates, to realized business value, to measurable outcomes after go-live -- the sales behavior would change overnight. The vendor would stop selling modules the customer does not need, because unsold modules do not generate success metrics. But no major vendor has adopted this model voluntarily, because the current model is too profitable. The machine rewards the sale, not the outcome.

I have yet to see a single customer that is on ECC that has been able to prove a positive business case to move to S/4HANA. Especially when you incorporate the realistic time and cost associated with the implementation.

That is a remarkable statement, and I want to make sure it lands. After twenty-five years of working with organizations on their digital transformations, after having evaluated more implementations than I can count, I have not encountered a single ECC customer who has been able to demonstrate, with rigorous analysis, that the migration to S/4HANA will generate a positive return on investment when all realistic costs are included. Not one.

And yet it was recently revealed in a study that 40 percent of SAP customers have not yet started their journey to S/4HANA. Despite years of strong-arm tactics and incentives, the RISE program, the discontinuation of maintenance and support in 2030, despite all these tactics, 40 percent of customers still have not even started. That 40 percent is not evidence of laziness or ignorance. It is evidence of customers who have done the math and cannot make it work. It is a market that is being dragged, not led.

Some are refusing altogether. There is a big company called Kingfisher that is a global company with thousands of locations, and they are on SAP ECC. They had long considered an upgrade to S/4HANA, but they came out and said they are not moving to S/4HANA because it is going to cost them what they say to be twenty times more. Instead, they deployed third-party AI tools on top of their existing ECC system and found a way to innovate without migrating. They rejected the premise that innovation requires a platform change. They rejected the machine.

The R&D Starvation Strategy

If the economic incentives and the lock-in mechanisms are the machine's carrots, the R&D starvation strategy is its stick.

Because money and the ecosystem favor cloud ERP, vendors are going to keep doubling down and upping the ante on their cloud investments. Since R&D money is a finite resource, on-premise systems will receive a declining share of R&D dollars until there are no future enhancements.

This is the quiet weapon. It does not make headlines. There is no announcement that says "we are deliberately starving our on-premise product of innovation to force you to the cloud." But that is precisely what is happening. Every dollar invested in S/4HANA Cloud is a dollar not invested in ECC. Every new feature, every AI capability, every integration enhancement is built for the cloud product. The on-premise product does not get worse in absolute terms, but it gets worse in relative terms, and in a competitive market, relative is all that matters.

Over time, the on-premise customer finds themselves running a system that works today but is falling behind tomorrow. Their competitors who migrated to the cloud have access to new features. The vendor's support staff is increasingly trained on the cloud product and decreasingly familiar with the on-premise version. The ecosystem of third-party integrations and extensions migrates to the cloud, leaving the on-premise customer with a shrinking marketplace of compatible tools.

The customer is not forced out. They are starved out. The distinction matters, because it allows the vendor to claim that the customer always has a choice. And technically, they do. They can stay on-premise. They can pay for extended support. They can run their system without vendor innovation for as long as they like. But each year, the gap between what the cloud product can do and what the on-premise product can do grows wider, and the customer's competitive position erodes incrementally. The choice is technically real but practically illusory. It is the difference between choosing not to eat and choosing between a feast and an empty plate.

The Regulatory Reckoning

The lock-in strategy has not gone entirely unnoticed. Regulatory bodies, particularly in Europe, have begun to examine whether the forced migration tactics and anti-competitive bundling practices of major enterprise software vendors cross legal lines.

The European Union is investigating SAP for potential and alleged antitrust behavior. SAP has made it extremely difficult for customers to use third-party options for maintenance. The investigation centers on whether SAP has leveraged its dominant market position to restrict competition, particularly in the areas of third-party maintenance and complementary software.

SAP has made it nearly impossible for companies like Rimini Street and others to provide alternative maintenance services. In some cases, SAP has also made it impossible for third-party software providers to connect to SAP systems. One business process mining company found that SAP had effectively blocked their software from integrating with SAP environments, steering customers instead toward SAP's own competing product.

Whether these investigations result in meaningful enforcement remains to be seen. The regulatory process is slow, and the technology industry has historically been adept at navigating antitrust scrutiny without fundamental changes to its business practices. But the fact that regulators are looking is significant. It suggests that the lock-in strategy, which the market rewards as a competitive advantage, is beginning to be recognized by at least some institutions as what it also is: an exercise of market power at the expense of customer choice.

This whole forced migration is causing SAP to lose a lot of goodwill in the industry. So much so that a lot of legacy customers are actually questioning their decision to be on SAP and are secondguessing that decision and evaluating other options. Only 30 percent of people who commented on SAP across our channels are saying anything positive. Another 30 percent spoke negatively, and the remaining 40 percent were neutral. When only three in ten of your customers have something positive to say about you, and you are simultaneously posting record revenues and record stock prices, the divergence between market performance and customer satisfaction tells you everything you need to know about whose interests the money machine is designed to serve.

What Happened to Customer Choice?

Cloud ERP systems generally still cost more than on-premise in the long run, after years five or seven. The products are relatively immature compared to more established on-premise systems. Missing functionality is more likely to require point solutions to address, increasing technical complexity. Cloud ERP systems are less flexible than on-premise. And once you are on a cloud ERP platform, it can be harder to switch vendors in the future.

These are not arguments against the cloud. Cloud deployment has genuine advantages: lower upfront capital expenditure, automatic upgrades, reduced infrastructure management burden, and the ability to scale compute resources on demand. For many organizations, particularly mid-market companies without large IT departments, cloud is the right choice.

But "right for many" is not the same as "right for all." And the money machine does not make that distinction. The money machine needs every customer on the cloud, because every customer on the cloud is a recurring revenue stream that justifies the stock price. The distinction between organizations that would genuinely benefit from cloud migration and organizations that would be better served by a different approach is economically inconvenient. So it is ignored.

The market is beginning to push back, in small ways. Buyers are pushing back on forced migrations, proprietary extension models, and take-it-all platform bundles. RFPs increasingly demand data portability, exit rights, transparent pricing, open standards, and proof of interoperability with competitors. Some organizations are adopting composable approaches, assembling capabilities module by module rather than committing to a single monolithic platform. This approach lowers switching costs, reduces program risk, and allows innovation to move at the speed of the business rather than the pace of a single vendor's roadmap.

But these are still exceptions. The overwhelming majority of organizations continue to navigate a market in which every voice they hear, the vendor, the system integrator, the analyst, the conference keynote speaker, is telling them the same thing: cloud, cloud, cloud. Now, now, now. The dissenting voices, the organizations that chose differently and succeeded, the analysts who question the conventional wisdom, the advisors who suggest that maybe not every company needs to migrate right now, those voices are drowned out by a chorus that has trillions of dollars of financial incentive behind it.

The Money Machine and Your Transformation

Here is what all of this means for you, the person reading this book because you are about to undertake, or are in the middle of, or are recovering from a digital transformation.

Every vendor who pitches you is operating under incentives that may not align with your interests. The salesperson across the table has a compensation plan that rewards them for selling you cloud subscriptions, not for ensuring your implementation succeeds. The account executive who promises that the migration will take eighteen months and cost $20 million is quoting numbers that are designed to close the deal, not numbers that reflect what your specific organization will actually experience.

Every system integrator who proposes to implement your transformation is operating under a business model that profits from complexity, duration, and staffing volume. Their vendor partnership means they walked into your building with a predetermined recommendation, and their incentive is to make the project as large as possible, because larger projects generate more revenue.

Every analyst report you read was produced within an ecosystem where the vendors being evaluated are also paying customers of the analyst firm. The rankings and recommendations are not necessarily wrong, but they are produced within a financial relationship that you should understand and account for.

None of this means that the cloud is bad, that the vendors are evil, or that the system integrators and analysts are deliberately trying to harm you. Most of the individuals within these organizations are talented, well-intentioned professionals doing their jobs within the system they operate in. The problem is not the people. The problem is the system. The incentives are misaligned. The information is asymmetric. And the money, the extraordinary, unprecedented, cascading wall of money that flows through the enterprise technology ecosystem, pushes every decision in the direction that serves the machine, whether or not it serves you.

It might look good for them right now. It is driving their stock value higher, their overall valuation higher. They are profitable and doing great as companies right now. But I have been around long enough to know that the incumbents at the top do not stay there very long.

The money machine is powerful. But it is not invincible. The organizations that understand how it works, that see the incentive cascade for what it is, that demand transparency and independence in their advisory relationships, that make technology decisions based on their own business case rather than the vendor's financial engineering, those organizations can navigate the machine without being consumed by it.

Understanding the money is the first step. In the next chapter, we will examine the specific tactics the vendors use to win your deal -- the playbook that turns the money machine's incentives into the pitch that lands on your conference room table.

Chapter 11

The Vendor Playbook

In the previous chapter, I described the money machine: the economic engine that drives the enterprise software industry's behavior. Investor pressure, executive compensation, sales commissions, ecosystem alignment -- a cascade of financial incentives that has very little to do with whether your specific implementation succeeds or fails. That chapter was about why the machine behaves the way it does. This chapter is about how.

Every major enterprise software vendor operates from a playbook. The playbook is not written down in a single document. It does not have a title or a table of contents. But it is real, it is consistent, and it is remarkably similar across vendors, from SAP to Oracle to Microsoft to Infor and beyond. The playbook has been refined over decades, tested against thousands of buyers, and optimized for one outcome: closing the deal.

Notice what the playbook is not optimized for. It is not optimized for successful implementation. It is not optimized for business outcomes. It is not optimized for the long-term satisfaction of the customer. It is optimized for the moment the contract is signed. Everything that happens after that moment is, structurally and economically, someone else's problem.

This chapter will walk you through the playbook, tactic by tactic. Not because every vendor is dishonest, because most are not. But because the system within which vendors operate produces behaviors that are systematically misleading, even when the individuals involved believe they are acting in good faith. Understanding the playbook is your first line of defense.

The Demo That Sells the Dream

The software demonstration is the centerpiece of the vendor's sales process. It is also, in most cases, a carefully choreographed performance that bears only a passing resemblance to what the software will look like when it is actually deployed in your environment.

Vendors will have their demo environments, websites, and web videos set up to show all the bells and whistles functioning at a high level. Again, they are selling. Remember that most ERP software does not come out of the box looking or operating like that.

The demo environment is purpose-built. It runs on optimized infrastructure with clean data, pre-configured workflows, and a scripted scenario that highlights the product's strengths while carefully avoiding its weaknesses. The demo operator, who is typically a sales engineer rather than an implementation consultant, knows exactly which screens to show, which buttons to click, and which questions to deflect. They have rehearsed this presentation dozens if not hundreds of times. They know where the product shines and where it stumbles, and the demo script is designed to keep you firmly in the shining zone.

What you see in the demo is the product's ceiling: its best possible performance, under ideal conditions, with perfect data, running a simplified version of your business processes. What you will experience in your implementation is the product's floor: its actual performance, in your environment, with your messy data, running the full complexity of your real-world operations. The gap between the demo and the deployment is where most of the disappointment in enterprise software lives.

I have sat through hundreds of vendor demonstrations over my career. The good ones are genuinely impressive. The dashboards are beautiful. The workflows are seamless. The analytics are powerful. The integrations appear effortless. And every time, I watch the client's team lean forward in their seats, their eyes widening, their skepticism dissolving. The demo is doing exactly what it is designed to do: it is selling the dream.

I have a story that illustrates this dynamic more vividly than any abstract description can. Early in my independent consulting career, we were helping a Fortune 500 consumer products company evaluate ERP systems. Based on our analysis, we recommended Oracle as the best fit for their specific needs -- their flexibility requirements, their integration landscape, and their functional depth all pointed in that direction. The client was receptive to the recommendation. Then SAP and a large system integrator came in for their presentation.

At the front of the room, they had set up two easels, each covered with a sheet. They delivered their pitch -- polished, confident, compelling. And then, at the end of the presentation, they had this big dramatic finish. They pulled the sheets off the easels. Underneath was a mock-up of an advertising campaign: "SAP Runs [Client Name]." They had created a custom advertisement showing the client's brand alongside SAP's, as if the partnership were already a fait accompli.

I still remember the oohs and ahs from the executive team. The room lit up. The executives were not evaluating software anymore. They were imagining their company's name on that advertisement. They were feeling what it would be like to be an SAP customer, to join the club, to run with the big brands. It was pure emotion, expertly manufactured. The client went with SAP, against our recommendation. The decision was not made on functionality, fit, or total cost of ownership. It was made on a feeling -- a feeling that a sales team engineered in the final sixty seconds of a presentation.

This is the demo at its most effective and its most dangerous. It bypasses the rational evaluation entirely. The executives who approved the decision could not have told you which system scored better on their requirements matrix. They could tell you which presentation made them feel something. And that feeling, not the analysis, drove a decision worth tens of millions of dollars.

The problem is that nobody in the room during the demo will be the one who has to make the dream a reality. The sales engineer who just showed you that seamless workflow will not be on the implementation team. The account executive who nodded confidently when you asked about that integration will not be the one building it. The people who will actually configure your system, migrate your data, and test your processes have often never seen the demo and would have significant reservations about several of the claims that were made during it.

What you see is not always what you get. Ask if the functionality shown is out-of-the-box or if it requires customization. This is one of the most important questions you can ask during a vendor demonstration, and it is one of the most commonly neglected. When the vendor shows you a capability, is that capability standard in the product? Or does it require configuration, customization, third-party add-ons, or development work that is not included in the license price? The vendor is not going to volunteer this distinction. You have to demand it.

Ask the vendor to include a solution architect and professional services or delivery team resource in the demonstration if possible. This will keep the sales team honest. When the person who will actually build the system is sitting in the same room as the person selling it, the claims tend to become more modest. The solution architect knows what is realistic. The sales engineer knows what looks good on screen. The tension between those two perspectives is informative, and it is a tension the vendor would prefer you never see.

Shelfware: The Licenses Nobody Uses

One of the least discussed and most expensive vendor tactics is the sale of software that the customer will never use. In the industry, this is called shelfware: licenses purchased as part of a bundle or a platform deal that sit on the shelf, unused, generating subscription revenue for the vendor and zero value for the customer.

Shelfware happens because of how enterprise software deals are structured. The vendor's incentive is to maximize the size of the deal, because larger deals generate more revenue, more commission, and more recurring subscription income. The easiest way to increase deal size is to bundle additional products into the agreement. The sales team pitches this as a "platform play": rather than buying a standalone ERP system, you buy the entire platform -- ERP, CRM, human capital management, supply chain planning, analytics, procurement, and whatever else the vendor can attach to the deal.

The pitch is compelling. The bundled price is lower per module than buying each product individually. The vendor frames it as future-proofing: you may not need all of these capabilities today, but you will eventually, and it is cheaper to license them now than to add them later. The CIO nods. The procurement team sees the discount. The contract is signed.

And then reality sets in. The implementation focuses on the core ERP modules, because that is where the business need is most urgent. The ancillary products, the CRM module, the planning tools, the analytics platform, sit dormant. The organization does not have the bandwidth, the budget, or the organizational will to implement them. They were never part of the original business case. Nobody defined the requirements for them. Nobody planned the change management for them. They exist as line items on a subscription invoice, generating recurring revenue for the vendor every month, providing exactly nothing in return.

SAP sells it as though it is one complete solution that can solve all the world's problems, but it is actually a collection of best-of-breed products -- Ariba, SuccessFactors, Concur, and others -- that SAP has acquired and bundled together. Each of those products was originally a standalone application built by a different company with a different architecture, a different user experience, and a different integration model. The integration between them is not seamless. It requires configuration, middleware, and often custom development. The "platform" is less a unified system than a portfolio of products wearing the same logo.

The shelfware problem is compounded by the cloud subscription model. In the old perpetual license world, shelfware was a sunk cost. You paid for the license once and wrote it off. In the cloud world, shelfware is a recurring cost. You pay for it every month, every year, for the duration of your subscription agreement. And because the subscription bundles are often structured with significant discounts that are contingent on maintaining the full bundle, dropping the unused modules can actually increase your per-unit cost on the modules you do use. The vendor has designed the pricing to make it more expensive to use less. That is not an accident.

There is another dimension to the shelfware problem that is worth calling out explicitly: timing. Vendors want you to start paying for all modules and subscriptions on day one of the contract, the moment the ink is dry. But your implementation will not go live for twelve, eighteen, or twenty-four months. Some modules will not be deployed for years, if they are deployed at all. You are paying full subscription fees for software that is sitting in a cloud environment that nobody in your organization is using, generating zero business value, while the vendor collects recurring revenue from the moment the contract is signed.

This is not an oversight in the contract structure. It is the contract structure. The vendor's incentive is to start the revenue clock as early as possible and to bundle as many modules into that initial contract as they can, because every month of subscription revenue that accrues before you even go live is pure profit with zero delivery obligation.

The Platform Play

The shelfware tactic is a subset of a larger strategic move that every major vendor is making: the platform play. The platform play is the vendor's attempt to become the single technology provider for your entire enterprise, replacing not just your ERP system but every adjacent system -- CRM, HCM, procurement, analytics, integration, and increasingly, AI -- with their own products.

The platform play serves the vendor's interests in three ways. First, it maximizes deal size, as discussed above. Second, it deepens lock-in, because the more of your technology stack that runs on a single vendor's platform, the harder it is to leave. And third, it eliminates competition, because once you are committed to a vendor's platform, the vendor's own products have an inherent advantage over third-party alternatives in every subsequent purchasing decision.

The platform play is marketed as simplicity: one vendor, one platform, one support contract, one integration architecture. And there is some truth to this. Managing a single-vendor environment is, in theory, simpler than managing a multi-vendor environment. But the theory breaks down in practice for several reasons.

First, no vendor is best-in-class at everything. SAP's core ERP may be strong, but their CRM may not compete with Salesforce. Oracle's database may be unmatched, but their HCM may not compete with Workday. Microsoft's productivity tools are ubiquitous, but their manufacturing capabilities may not match a dedicated industry solution. When you commit to a platform, you are accepting the vendor's entire portfolio, including the products where they are second or third best, in exchange for the convenience of a single relationship.

Second, the "integration" between products on the same platform is often less seamless than advertised. As I mentioned, many of these product suites were assembled through acquisitions rather than built from scratch. The products may share a logo and a login page, but underneath they may have different data models, different architectures, and different upgrade cycles. The integration work required to make them function as a unified system can be substantial -- and it is work that the customer pays for, not the vendor.

Third, the platform play creates a form of vendor dependency that goes beyond traditional lock-in. When your ERP, your CRM, your HCM, your analytics, and your integration middleware all run on one vendor's platform, the vendor is not just your software provider. They are your infrastructure. Leaving becomes not a migration but a complete architectural rebuild. The switching costs are not just high. They are existential.

Roadmap Selling: Buying Tomorrow's Features Today

Of all the tactics in the vendor playbook, roadmap selling may be the most insidious, because it asks you to make a purchasing decision today based on features that do not yet exist.

Here is how it works. During the sales process, the vendor shows you their product as it exists today. Inevitably, there are gaps. Features your business needs that the product does not currently support. Integrations that are not yet built. Industry-specific capabilities that are still in development. In an honest evaluation, these gaps would be documented, weighted, and factored into the decision.

Instead, the vendor shows you the roadmap. They pull up a slide that shows the product's planned development over the next twelve to twenty-four months. The missing features are on the roadmap. The integrations are planned for the next release. The industry capabilities are in beta and will be generally available by the time you go live. The message is: yes, the product does not do this today, but it will by the time you need it.

Understand if what they are selling and showing is what will be deployed on your go-live date. This is critical, and it is routinely ignored. A feature on a roadmap is a promise, not a product. Roadmaps change. Priorities shift. Development timelines slip. The feature that was promised for Q3 gets pushed to Q4, then to the next fiscal year, then quietly deprioritized as the vendor's strategic focus evolves. And by the time you discover that the feature you were counting on is not going to materialize, you have already signed the contract, started the implementation, and committed your organization to a platform that cannot do what you were told it would do.

I have seen this pattern play out dozens of times. A manufacturing company selects a cloud ERP vendor based in part on a promised shop floor execution module that is on the roadmap. Twelve months into the implementation, the module has not materialized. The company is forced to either build a custom solution, integrate a third-party product, or redesign their processes to work without the capability they were promised. In every case, the cost and complexity increase, the timeline extends, and the vendor points to the fine print in the contract that says roadmap items are not guaranteed.

The fine print is the point. Vendor contracts are carefully written to ensure that roadmap commitments are not legally binding. The salesperson can promise the moon during the sales cycle, and the contract protects the vendor when the moon does not arrive. This asymmetry between the sales message and the contractual obligation is one of the most consistently damaging dynamics in the industry.

Nowhere is roadmap selling more prevalent today than in artificial intelligence. Every major vendor is racing to embed AI into their platform, and the sales pitch has evolved accordingly. SAP claims thousands of AI agents built into its platform. Oracle touts AI-powered automation across its cloud suite. Microsoft positions Copilot as the intelligence layer that will transform every business process. The demos are dazzling. An AI agent that automatically resolves supply chain exceptions. A copilot that generates financial forecasts from natural language prompts. Intelligent automation that eliminates manual data entry across procurement workflows.

But ask the hard questions and the picture changes. How many of these AI agents have been successfully deployed at actual customer sites, in production, at scale? How many customers are using them today -- not piloting them, not testing them in a sandbox, but running their business on them? The answer, in most cases, is very few. The AI capabilities being sold today are, for the vast majority of enterprise customers, roadmap features dressed in a production demo. They are real enough to demonstrate. They are not mature enough to rely on.

There is also a cost dimension to AI that vendors are not eager to discuss during the sales cycle. Today's AI capabilities may be bundled into the subscription or offered at a promotional price to encourage adoption. But AI consumes compute resources -- processing power, data storage, API calls -- that scale with usage. As your adoption of these AI capabilities grows, so will the cost.

And because the vendor controls the infrastructure in a cloud model, they control the pricing. The introductory rate that looked attractive when you signed the contract may bear little resemblance to what you are paying three years from now, once you are dependent on capabilities that the vendor can price however they choose. AI is the next frontier of vendor lock-in, and the pricing model is being designed with the same long-term extraction strategy that made the cloud subscription model so profitable for investors.

The Sales Team vs. the Delivery Team

There is a structural divide within every major technology vendor that buyers need to understand, because it is the source of some of the most painful surprises in enterprise software.

The sales team and the delivery team are two different organizations. They have different goals, different incentives, different knowledge, and in many cases, different levels of honesty about what the product can do. The sales team's job is to win the deal. The delivery team's job is to implement what the sales team promised. These two objectives are frequently in conflict.

There is evidence of sales teams bypassing their own development teams' warnings about product-fit limitations. Read that sentence carefully. The vendor's own technical people told the sales team that the product could not do what the prospect needed. The sales team sold it anyway. This is not a hypothetical scenario I am constructing for dramatic effect. This is a documented pattern that has surfaced in litigation, in post-implementation reviews, and in my own advisory work.

There may be claims made in the sales process that simply cannot be fulfilled by the professional services team. The sales engineer demonstrates a capability. The account executive confirms it in writing. The statement of work references it. And then the implementation team arrives, reviews the requirements, and discovers that what was sold does not match what the product can deliver. The implementation team is now in an impossible position: they must either find a workaround for a capability that does not exist, or go back to the client and explain that the sales team over-promised.

In my experience, the implementation team almost never goes back to the client with that admission. Instead, they try to engineer a solution, which adds cost and complexity. Or they redefine the requirement, convincing the client that they did not really need what they asked for. Or they push the issue to a later phase, deferring the problem rather than resolving it. The sales team, having closed the deal and collected their commission, has moved on to the next prospect. The gap between what was sold and what can be delivered becomes the implementation team's problem, and ultimately, the client's.

There is a specific variant of this dynamic that surfaces with alarming frequency: the demo-contract mismatch. During the sales cycle, the vendor demonstrates specific software versions, features, or modules. The client sees a capability. The client is impressed by the capability. The client decides to buy based on what they saw. And then the contract arrives -- and the contract does not include what was demonstrated. The feature was part of a newer version that has not been released yet. The module was a premium add-on that requires a separate license. The capability exists in the demo environment but is not available in the standard product the contract covers. The gap between the demo and the contract is the gap where buyer disappointment begins, and where, in extreme cases, the litigation begins.

The Waste Management case is the most publicly documented example of this dynamic. SAP had promised that the company could achieve $106 million to $220 million in annual benefits from a consolidated ERP system that could be implemented in 18 months. The contract was awarded based on claims that the solution was out-of-the-box, adapted to U.S. standards, and could fulfill the company's goals with minimal customization. However, Waste Management found these claims to be false.

One hundred to two hundred and twenty million dollars in annual benefits. Eighteen months. Out-of-the-box. Minimal customization. For the largest waste services company in North America, with one of the most complex operational footprints in any industry. These claims were not merely optimistic. They were, in Waste Management's view, fraudulent. Waste Management was unable to glean any benefit from the software and filed a $100 million lawsuit against SAP, later raising that amount to $500 million before settling out of court.

Waste Management is an extreme case. But the dynamic it illustrates, a sales team making promises that the delivery team cannot keep, is not extreme. It is ordinary. It happens in some form in the majority of enterprise software sales cycles I have observed.

The severity varies, but the pattern is constant: the incentive to close the deal overrides the obligation to be accurate about what the product can do.

If the structure sounds familiar, it should. What I have described across this chapter -- the lowball proposal, the scripted demo, the roadmap promises, the sales-delivery gap -- is the enterprise software industry's version of a shakedown. The initial proposal is the price of entry: the made offer you cannot refuse, because every competing proposal uses the same playbook. Once you have accepted and the project is underway, the real price is established, one envelope at a time -- change orders, scope additions, licensing true-ups, premium support tiers -- in a sequence designed to extract maximum revenue from a client who cannot walk away. Each demand is reasonable on its own terms. The cumulative effect is that you pay two or three times what was quoted. The difference between this and what happens in a back room in a Scorsese film is that the vendor sends a statement of work instead of a man in a tracksuit.

The RFP Theater

Most large organizations use a Request for Proposal process to evaluate and select enterprise software. The RFP is supposed to be a structured, objective mechanism for comparing vendors against a defined set of requirements. In practice, it is often a piece of theater in which both the buyer and the vendor are performing roles that have little to do with finding the best fit.

The vendor's RFP response is written by the sales team, not the delivery team. It is crafted to check as many boxes as possible, because the evaluation is typically scored on how many requirements the vendor can claim to meet. The word "claim" is doing a lot of work in that sentence. A vendor can claim to meet a requirement through standard functionality, through configuration, through customization, through a third-party add-on, through a partner product, or through a feature on the roadmap. All of these are different things, with vastly different implications for cost, complexity, and risk. But in many RFP scoring models, they all count the same: the box is checked.

I have reviewed vendor RFP responses where over 90 percent of requirements were marked as "supported." When we dug into the details, we found that a significant percentage of those were supported only through customization, through third-party products, or through features that did not yet exist. The headline score looked impressive. The reality was far more qualified.

The buyer contributes to the theater as well. Many organizations develop RFPs with hundreds or even thousands of requirements, the majority of which are not true business requirements but wish lists, legacy process descriptions, or change resistance dressed up in the language of system specifications. In Chapter 5, I described the phenomenon of 1,800 requirements that should have been 400. The bloated requirement set makes the RFP process longer, more expensive, and less discriminating, because the signal of genuine business need gets buried in the noise of organizational politics.

The RFP process also creates a false sense of objectivity. Because the evaluation is structured and scored, participants believe the outcome is data-driven. In reality, the scoring is only as good as the questions, and the questions are only as good as the organization's ability to define what it actually needs. When the requirements are vague, the scoring is meaningless. When the requirements are specific, the vendor's response may still be misleading. The RFP process gives the organization the comfort of having followed a rigorous process, which makes it harder to question the outcome even when the outcome is wrong.

There is a deeper problem with the RFP model that goes beyond the theater of the process itself: the format assumes that software evaluation is a binary exercise. Can the system do this? Yes or no. Check or no check. But enterprise software does not work that way. The truth almost always lies in the gray area between yes and no, and it is in that gray area where the real differences between solutions live. One vendor may support a capability natively with a mature, well-tested feature. Another may support the same capability through a workaround that technically functions but requires significant configuration and ongoing maintenance. A third may claim support through a partner add-on that introduces a separate licensing relationship and an integration dependency. In the RFP scoring model, all three responses look the same: supported. In reality, they represent fundamentally different levels of cost, risk, and long-term viability. The nuance is everything, and the standard RFP process is designed to eliminate nuance.

This is why objective data from independent third parties can be so valuable during the evaluation. An independent advisor who has seen these products implemented across dozens of organizations can tell you what the vendor's RFP response actually means in practice. They can distinguish between a capability that works reliably out of the box and one that requires six months of custom development to approximate what was demonstrated. They can identify the gaps that the vendor's response obscures and quantify the risk that the scoring model ignores. Without that independent perspective, you are evaluating marketing materials with a spreadsheet and calling it due diligence.

There is also a strategic error that most organizations make in how they structure their evaluation criteria. They try to evaluate everything. Every process, every function, every workflow gets documented as a requirement and scored against every vendor. The result is an evaluation that treats accounts payable processing with the same weight as the unique manufacturing workflow that is your organization's competitive advantage. But these are not equivalent. Accounts payable is vanilla. It is a commodity process that every major ERP system handles competently. You do not need to spend weeks evaluating whether SAP, Oracle, or Microsoft can process an invoice, because they all can, and the differences between them on that dimension are negligible. The evaluation should focus on two things: the must-haves that are non-negotiable for your business, and the true differentiators -- the processes and capabilities where the solutions genuinely diverge and where your organization's competitive advantages live. A distribution company whose edge comes from a proprietary fulfillment process should spend 80 percent of its evaluation time on how each vendor handles that process, not on whether the general ledger works. An honest evaluation is not comprehensive. It is focused. It identifies the twenty percent of requirements that will determine eighty percent of the outcome, and it evaluates those requirements with a depth and rigor that the standard RFP process cannot provide.

The Vendor-Specific Dynamics

Every vendor has its own version of the playbook, shaped by its product architecture, its market position, and its specific economic incentives. Understanding these vendor-specific dynamics is important, because the risks they create are different, even though the underlying patterns are the same.

SAP: Rigidity Shock

SAP's product rigidity forces a painful trade-off: customize the system, incurring technical debt and upgrade risk, or force the business to adapt to the software, generating resistance and organizational disruption. This is the fundamental tension at the heart of every SAP implementation, and the sales team will almost never frame it this honestly.

The sales pitch for SAP emphasizes best practices. The system is designed around industry-standard processes. By adopting these processes, your organization will be more efficient, more standardized, and more scalable. This sounds compelling in a sales presentation. In practice, it means that the software will require your organization to change the way it operates, sometimes dramatically, and the degree of change required is almost always underestimated during the sales cycle.

SAP's integration cascading risk means that one configuration change can ripple across the entire system. The tightly integrated architecture that SAP markets as a strength is also a source of fragility. A change to the pricing logic affects the billing logic. A change to the billing logic affects the revenue recognition logic. A change to the revenue recognition logic affects the financial reporting. In a system this tightly coupled, the implementation team must understand the downstream impact of every configuration decision, and in many cases, they do not.

S/4HANA is a rewrite of ECC and is still a work in progress. The acquired tools -- Ariba, Concur, SuccessFactors -- add integration seams that create additional complexity and risk. The sales team presents S/4HANA as the next generation of SAP's proven platform. The reality is that it is a fundamentally new product, built on a different database architecture, with a different user experience, and with integration points to acquired products that were never designed to work together natively. The maturity of S/4HANA is not equivalent to the maturity of ECC, and organizations that assume otherwise are in for a surprise.

The core dynamic of SAP implementations: rigidity forces change, which generates organizational resistance, which drives budget and timeline overruns.

Oracle: Complexity Overwhelm

Oracle's playbook is different from SAP's, but no less challenging for the buyer. Where SAP's risk is rigidity, Oracle's is complexity.

Oracle's multi-product architecture requires sophisticated in-house IT capabilities and solution architects. Oracle's product portfolio was built through decades of acquisitions: JD Edwards, PeopleSoft, Hyperion, Siebel, and many others. Each acquisition brought a different product, a different architecture, and a different customer base. Oracle Cloud ERP is an attempt to unify these capabilities into a single cloud platform, but the complexity of the underlying architecture remains.

The complexity creates a specific risk during the sales cycle: the vendor oversells. There is evidence of Oracle sales teams bypassing their own development teams' warnings about product-fit limitations. Because Oracle's portfolio is so broad, the sales team can claim a capability for almost any requirement. The question is whether that capability works as advertised, integrates with the other modules in the way the demo suggested, and can be implemented within the timeline and budget the sales team quoted. The answer, in too many cases, is no.

Oracle Cloud ERP lags its own on-premise JD Edwards in manufacturing and complex supply chain capabilities. For manufacturing organizations, this is a critical gap. The sales team may position Oracle Cloud ERP as the successor to JD Edwards, but the cloud product has not yet achieved functional parity with the on-premise product it is meant to replace. Organizations that select Oracle Cloud for manufacturing based on the JD Edwards pedigree may find themselves implementing a product that cannot support their most critical processes.

The core dynamic of Oracle implementations: complexity absorbs all available bandwidth, leaving insufficient resources for people and process considerations, resulting in cost overruns and poor adoption.

Microsoft Dynamics 365: The Flexibility Trap

Microsoft's playbook is the most subtle of the three, because it exploits something that most people would consider a virtue: flexibility.

Dynamics 365's flexibility allows organizations to over-customize, automating legacy processes rather than transforming them. Where SAP forces you to change (sometimes painfully), Microsoft lets you stay the same (sometimes dangerously). The platform is highly configurable, with a robust ecosystem of independent software vendors who build extensions, add-ons, and customizations that can make D365 do almost anything. This flexibility is marketed as a strength, and for organizations with the discipline to use it wisely, it can be.

But most organizations do not have that discipline. When the system can be customized to match your existing processes, the path of least resistance is to customize it to match your existing processes. This is the flexibility trap: the technology enables you to avoid the hard work of business process transformation by giving you a sophisticated way to replicate what you already have. The result is NS + OP = EOP -- new software plus old processes equals expensive old processes -- delivered with a friendly Microsoft interface.

The familiar Microsoft user interface creates a false sense of ease. Organizations assume that because D365 looks like Office, it should be easy to implement, leading to under-budgeted and under-staffed projects. I have seen this assumption destroy more mid-market implementations than I can count. The IT team looks at D365 and sees Microsoft. They know Microsoft. They use Microsoft every day. How hard can it be? The answer is: very hard. An enterprise ERP implementation is an enterprise ERP implementation, regardless of the vendor. The user interface may be familiar, but the configuration, the data migration, the integration, the change management, and the organizational transformation are every bit as complex as they would be with SAP or Oracle.

Microsoft probably has the least amount of control and oversight of their reseller network, and that is a big problem. Unlike SAP and Oracle, which rely on a relatively concentrated set of large system integrators, Microsoft's implementation ecosystem is fragmented across thousands of Value-Added Resellers of varying size, capability, and quality. Some are excellent. Many are not. The quality of your D365 implementation depends heavily on which partner you select, and the selection process is complicated by the fact that many of these partners are small firms with limited track records and no independent quality oversight.

Once you are dependent on a specific ISV's customization, you are locked into that one specific ISV or solution provider because they are the only ones that know how that software works. This is a form of lock-in that is unique to the D365 ecosystem. In the SAP and Oracle worlds, lock-in is primarily to the vendor. In the D365 world, lock-in can be to the reseller, the ISV, or the specific consultant who built your customizations. Your data is in Microsoft's cloud, but your configuration knowledge may live in the head of a developer at a fifty-person consulting shop in Kansas City. If that relationship sours, you may find yourself unable to maintain your own system.

The core dynamic of D365 implementations: flexibility avoids change, which enables over-customization, which creates technical debt and scope creep.

Salesforce: The Platform Identity Crisis

Salesforce occupies a unique and increasingly complicated position in the enterprise software landscape. Most people know Salesforce as a CRM system, which it is. But over the past decade, Salesforce has quietly evolved into something much broader. Through its Force.com platform, Salesforce has enabled third-party developers and its own customers to build applications that extend far beyond CRM, into financials, operations, manufacturing, and other capabilities that look and feel like ERP. Products like FinancialForce and Rootstock are built entirely on the Salesforce platform and provide legitimate enterprise capabilities. The result is that Salesforce has become, for some organizations, a de facto ERP platform assembled from components rather than delivered as a unified system.

The sales pitch emphasizes flexibility and ecosystem. Rather than buying a monolithic ERP suite, you buy the Salesforce platform and bolt on the specific capabilities you need, when you need them. You start with CRM, add financials later, bolt on manufacturing when you are ready. It is the best-of-breed promise delivered through a single platform login.

The reality is more complicated. Each bolt-on application, whether built by Salesforce, a third-party ISV, or your own development team, introduces an integration point, a separate data model, and a dependency on a vendor or developer who may or may not be around in five years. The flexibility that makes the platform attractive is also the source of its greatest risk: complexity. Bidirectional integrations between Salesforce and an external ERP system are technically challenging and require proven implementation experience. Customer master reconciliation across systems is, in the words of one of our assessments, a "tricky area" that requires careful data governance. And the more applications you layer onto the platform, the more pressure you place on your IT department to maintain, integrate, and upgrade a system that nobody fully understands end to end.

There is also a broader cautionary statistic worth noting. A Forrester Research study found that fewer than 40 percent of CRM implementations achieve their stated objectives, with user adoption being the primary factor distinguishing success from failure. Salesforce is the dominant CRM platform in the market. The failure rate is not about the technology. It is about the same organizational and change management challenges that plague every enterprise system -- challenges that the Salesforce sales cycle, with its emphasis on platform flexibility and rapid deployment, tends to minimize.

The core dynamic of Salesforce implementations: platform flexibility attracts bolt-on complexity, which creates integration risk, IT dependency, and a system whose total architecture lives in the heads of developers rather than in documentation.

Workday: The HR Giant Stretching Beyond Its Core

Workday is one of the most respected names in human capital management software, and for good reason. In the HCM space, Workday is a proven, mature, well-regarded platform. When organizations are evaluating HR systems, Workday is almost always on the shortlist, and it frequently wins.

The challenge arises when Workday is positioned as more than an HCM system. In recent years, Workday has invested heavily in expanding its ERP capabilities, adding financial management, supply chain, and planning modules to its portfolio. The company has made substantial strides, and its financials product has gained meaningful market traction. But there is a gap between where Workday is and where SAP and Oracle are in core ERP functionality, and the sales cycle does not always make that gap visible.

Workday is a sure bet in the HR space, but it is a greater stretch when asked to provide a comprehensive, fully working mature solution across financials, supply chain, and operations. In one evaluation we conducted for a life sciences company, we ultimately recommended Oracle over Workday because Workday required several third-party products to provide a cohesive solution -- including tools for invoice automation that Oracle included natively -- and because the functional depth in areas like FIFO inventory management was not yet at parity. Workday was slightly more expensive and represented a higher-risk path for the client's full scope of needs.

There is also an implementation ecosystem concern that buyers should take seriously. We are seeing an increasing number of Workday failures in the marketplace. It seems that the company has grown very quickly and that its implementation capabilities have not kept up with the software itself. The pool of experienced Workday implementation partners is smaller than what exists for SAP, Oracle, or Microsoft. Workday does not have the geographical reach or depth in its system integrator community, particularly for finance implementations, that the larger vendors enjoy. This means that the quality of available implementation talent is more variable, and the risk of being assigned an under-resourced or under-qualified team is higher.

In one Workday implementation I analyzed as an expert witness, the system integrator stopped work with the project only 56 percent complete. The client had paid over $800,000 in consulting fees. Activities were unaligned with Workday's own implementation methodology. The SI's team was under-resourced in critical functional areas. Configuration changes were made on the fly with no documentation. The financial lead billed 160 hours in a month with no recorded activity. Four different engagement managers were cycled through the project. End-to-end testing was zero percent complete when the relationship collapsed. The client estimated it would cost an additional $300,000 just to hire a new partner and rebuild what had been done incorrectly.

The core dynamic of Workday implementations: a mature, reliable HCM platform that is still proving itself as a full ERP solution, supported by a growing but still limited implementation ecosystem where quality varies significantly and the consequences of a bad partner selection are severe.

The Universal Truth

I want to close this chapter with a finding that may surprise you, given everything I have just written about vendor-specific dynamics.

The vendor selected has very little statistical impact on outcomes. The risks described in this chapter dominate regardless of which platform is chosen.

Let that sink in. After all the demos, all the RFP responses, all the reference checks, all the analyst reports, all the internal debates about SAP versus Oracle versus Microsoft, the choice of vendor is not the primary determinant of whether your transformation will succeed or fail. The primary determinants are the organizational factors we discussed in Part I -- leadership, culture, accountability, change management -- and the systemic dynamics we are discussing in Part II -- misaligned incentives, information asymmetry, and consultant conflicts.

The vendor playbook is designed to make you believe that the technology choice is the most important decision you will make. It is not. It is an important decision, and making it badly can certainly compound your problems. But making it well will not save you from the organizational dysfunction, the cultural resistance, or the consultant conflicts that are the true drivers of failure.

The vendors do not want you to know this, because if you knew it, you would spend less time evaluating their products and more time preparing your organization. You would invest less in licensing and more in change management. You would worry less about which vendor has the best demo and more about whether your people are ready for what is coming. And that shift in attention and investment would be better for your transformation but worse for the vendor's deal size.

The playbook works because it keeps your eyes on the technology. The most important thing you can do is look past it.

What an Honest Evaluation Looks Like

If the standard vendor evaluation process is theater, what does an honest process look like? Based on twenty-five years of facilitating software selections, here are the principles that separate a genuine evaluation from a performance.

First, define your requirements from your business outcomes, not from your current processes. The goal is not to find software that does what you already do. The goal is to find software that supports what you need to become. This means doing the hard work of business process redesign before the evaluation, not after.

Second, keep the requirement set focused. Four hundred well-defined, outcome-driven requirements will give you a better evaluation than 1,800 process descriptions. More requirements do not mean more rigor. They mean more noise.

Third, insist on seeing the product in your context, not the vendor's. Request demonstrations that use your data, your scenarios, your processes. A vendor who cannot or will not demonstrate their product against your real-world requirements is telling you something important about the gap between the demo and the deployment.

Fourth, separate the sales team from the delivery team in your evaluation. Talk to the people who will actually implement the system. Ask them the hard questions. Ask them what goes wrong. Ask them what the sales team promises that they cannot deliver. If the vendor will not let you talk to the delivery team, walk away.

Fifth, validate every roadmap claim independently. Do not accept a roadmap slide as a commitment. If a feature is critical to your business case, require it to be contractually guaranteed with specific delivery dates and financial remedies if the dates are missed. If the vendor will not put it in the contract, it is not a commitment. It is a suggestion.

Sixth, check references honestly. Do not accept the vendor's curated list of happy clients. Ask for references from organizations similar to yours in size, industry, and complexity. Ask the references what went wrong, not just what went right. Ask them what they wish they had known before they started. The answers will be more valuable than anything the vendor tells you.

Seventh, engage independent advisory support. Not a firm that partners with the vendor. Not a system integrator that will bid on the implementation. An independent advisor whose only interest is helping you make the best decision for your organization. The cost of independent advisory is a fraction of the cost of selecting the wrong vendor, and it is the single most effective countermeasure to the vendor playbook.

The sticker price is not the real price. Enterprise software pricing is negotiable, often dramatically so. We have seen most of the Tier 1 and Tier 2 ERP vendors come down by over 30 percent on the list price. But be careful about how the discount is structured. Vendors frequently offer aggressive short-term discounts to secure your signature on a long-term contract. The first two or three years may look attractive. Years four through seven, when the introductory pricing expires and the renewal terms kick in, may look very different. The total cost of ownership over the life of the contract is what matters, not the first-year price. Insist on modeling the full lifecycle cost, including renewal escalation clauses, consumption-based pricing for AI and analytics, and the cost of modules you may never deploy. Vendors have fiscal year-end dates when they are most incentivized to close deals -- Oracle's is May 31, Microsoft's is June 30, Infor's is April 30. Understanding the vendor's financial calendar and using it to your advantage is not gamesmanship. It is basic procurement discipline. The vendor uses every informational advantage they have. You should too.

The vendor playbook is powerful because it is practiced, polished, and backed by the full weight of the money machine. But it is not invincible. Buyers who understand the tactics, who ask the right questions, who demand transparency, and who invest in independent guidance can level the playing field. The playbook works best in the dark. Your job is to turn on the lights.

In the next chapter, we will look at what happens when the technology moves from the sales cycle to the implementation -- specifically, at the integration and data migration challenges that are the most consistently underestimated dimensions of every transformation.

Chapter 12

The Integration Nightmare

In the previous two chapters, I described the money that drives the machine and the playbook the machine uses to close the deal. But there is a moment in every digital transformation when the sales cycle ends and reality begins. The vendor has been selected. The contract has been signed. The system integrator has mobilized. The project plan has been posted on the wall. And somewhere in the middle of that project plan, buried beneath the more visible workstreams of configuration and process design and change management, is the workstream that will quietly become the most dangerous element of the entire program.

Integration and data migration.

I have been involved in more than a thousand digital transformations. If I had to identify the single most consistently underestimated dimension of these programs, it would be this one. Not change management, though that is chronically underfunded. Not testing, though that is chronically compressed. Integration and data migration. The invisible architecture that connects the new system to everything else in the enterprise, and the painstaking work of moving decades of accumulated data from the old world to the new.

These workstreams do not make it into the vendor's sales presentation. They do not appear in the demo. They are not the subject of the executive steering committee's monthly review, at least not until they are in crisis. They are the plumbing of the transformation: unglamorous, essential, and catastrophically expensive when they fail.

This chapter is about what happens when the plumbing breaks.

The Invisible Architecture

Every enterprise runs on integrations. Not one system, but dozens, sometimes hundreds, connected through a web of data flows that most people in the organization have never seen and do not understand. The ERP talks to the warehouse management system. The warehouse management system talks to the shipping carriers. The shipping carriers talk to the customer portal. The customer portal talks to the CRM. The CRM talks to the marketing platform. The marketing platform talks to the data warehouse. The data warehouse talks to the financial reporting system. The financial reporting system talks to the general ledger inside the ERP.

And that is a simplified version. In a mid-sized enterprise, the integration landscape typically includes fifty to a hundred distinct interfaces. In a large enterprise, it can be several hundred. Each interface is a connection between two systems, carrying data in one or both directions, on a schedule or in real time, through a file transfer or an API call or an EDI transaction or a middleware platform. Each interface has its own logic, its own data mapping, its own error handling, and its own set of assumptions about the format, timing, and completeness of the data it carries.

Most of this architecture is undocumented. It was built over years, sometimes decades, by different teams, using different technologies, to solve different problems at different times. The person who built the integration between the legacy ERP and the warehouse management system may have left the company ten years ago. The logic that governs how purchase orders flow from procurement to the supplier's EDI gateway may live in a script that nobody has touched since it was written. The middleware platform that routes messages between systems may be running a version of software that the vendor no longer supports.

When you replace the ERP at the center of this web, you are not just swapping out one system. You are severing and rebuilding every connection that touches it. Every interface must be redesigned, rebuilt, tested, and validated against the new system's data model, APIs, and processing logic. And every interface that is missed, misunderstood, or incorrectly rebuilt becomes a defect that will surface at go-live, when transactions start flowing through the system at production volume and the gaps become impossible to hide.

This is why integration complexity is consistently underestimated. The sales cycle focuses on the ERP. The project plan focuses on configuration and process design. The budget focuses on licensing and consulting hours. But the integration landscape, the invisible architecture that makes the ERP useful by connecting it to the rest of the enterprise, is treated as a secondary workstream. It receives less attention, less budget, less senior talent, and less testing than any other dimension of the program. And it repays this neglect with a disproportionate share of the defects, delays, and post-go-live crises that derail transformations.

Bidirectional Integrations and the Complexity Multiplier

Not all integrations are created equal. A one-way integration that pushes data from System A to System B is relatively straightforward. The data flows in one direction, the mapping is defined, and the error handling is simple: if the data does not arrive, you resend it.

A bidirectional integration, where data flows from A to B and from B back to A, is an order of magnitude more complex. Now you have two data flows, two sets of mapping logic, two sets of error handling, and a synchronization challenge: if System A updates a record at the same time System B updates the same record, which version wins? How do you detect the conflict? How do you resolve it? What happens to the downstream processes that depend on the accuracy of that record?

Bidirectional integrations are common in enterprise environments. The ERP sends a sales order to the warehouse management system. The warehouse management system sends back a shipment confirmation. The ERP sends an invoice to the customer. The customer sends back a payment through the bank integration. The ERP sends a purchase order to the supplier. The supplier sends back an advanced shipping notice through EDI. Each of these is a bidirectional data flow with its own timing, its own validation rules, and its own failure modes.

EDI, the Electronic Data Interchange standard that governs transactions between trading partners, deserves special mention because it is one of the oldest and most brittle integration technologies still in widespread use. EDI transactions follow rigid formatting standards, and the implementation of those standards varies significantly between trading partners. A company with five hundred suppliers may have five hundred slightly different EDI configurations, each with its own mapping, its own test requirements, and its own history of workarounds that someone built years ago to handle a partner's non-standard behavior. Migrating EDI integrations to a new ERP is one of the most tedious and error-prone tasks in any implementation, and it is one of the tasks most likely to be underestimated in the project plan.

The complexity multiplier is real and measurable. In my experience, the number of integrations in an enterprise transformation is typically two to three times higher than what was identified during the sales cycle. The vendor's proposal assumed thirty interfaces. The actual count is seventy-five. The project plan budgeted six months for integration development. The actual work takes twelve. The testing plan allocated two weeks for integration testing. The actual testing requires six, because every interface must be validated not only individually but in combination with every other interface it touches, in a sequence that replicates the actual flow of business transactions through the enterprise.

The Middleware Mirage

The industry's answer to integration complexity is middleware: integration platforms like MuleSoft, Dell Boomi, SAP Integration Suite, Microsoft Azure Integration Services, and others that promise to simplify the connection between systems by providing a centralized layer through which all data flows.

The promise is compelling. Instead of building point-to-point connections between every pair of systems, you build connections from each system to the middleware platform. The middleware handles the routing, the transformation, the error handling, and the monitoring. When you replace one system, you only need to rebuild the connections from that system to the middleware, not from that system to every other system in the landscape.

In practice, middleware introduces its own layer of complexity. The platform must be licensed, implemented, configured, and maintained. It requires specialized skills that may not exist within the organization. It creates a single point of failure: if the middleware platform goes down, every integration that runs through it goes down. It adds latency to data flows that may be time-sensitive. And it creates a new vendor dependency, because the organization is now reliant on the middleware vendor for support, upgrades, and pricing, in addition to the ERP vendor, the WMS vendor, the CRM vendor, and every other vendor in the landscape.

The middleware mirage is the belief that a technology solution can eliminate integration complexity. It cannot. It can manage complexity, organize it, make it more visible and more maintainable. But it cannot make the fundamental challenge of connecting disparate systems with different data models, different processing logic, and different timing requirements go away. The complexity is inherent in the enterprise's architecture. Middleware moves it from one place to another. It does not reduce it.

Organizations that adopt middleware expecting simplicity often find that they have added another system to manage, another vendor to negotiate with, another set of skills to hire for, and another budget line that was not in the original plan. The integration workstream does not get simpler. It gets more organized. Those are different things, and the difference matters when you are trying to hit a go-live date.

Data Migration: The Most Exposed Workstream

If integration is the most underestimated dimension of a transformation, data migration is the most dangerous. Integration complexity can cause delays. Data migration failures can destroy a business.

Data migration is the most exposed workstream in enterprise transformation, consistently comprising 20 percent or more of all overdue risk items. In one active engagement our team is overseeing, data migration accounts for 59 overdue action items out of 263 total -- 22 percent of the entire program's risk backlog, making it the single largest source of overdue items by a wide margin. This is not an outlier. It is the pattern. Across every program I have worked on, data migration is the workstream most likely to be behind schedule, most likely to have unresolved issues, and most likely to be operating in reactive mode rather than executing against a controlled plan.

The reasons are structural. Data migration sits at the intersection of every other workstream. You cannot migrate data until the target system's configuration is complete, because the data model defines how the data must be structured. You cannot validate migrated data until the business processes are designed, because the processes define what "correct" data looks like in the new system. You cannot fully test the migrated data until the integrations are built, because the integrations determine how the data flows between systems after migration. Data migration is dependent on everything and nothing is dependent on data migration until the very end, when everything is dependent on it at once.

This dependency structure means that data migration absorbs the delays of every other workstream. When configuration runs late, data migration starts late. When process design changes, the data mapping changes. When integrations are delivered late, data validation is delayed. The migration team is perpetually waiting for upstream deliverables that are perpetually behind schedule, and then they are blamed when the migration itself is not ready on time.

The work itself is grueling and unglamorous. Data must be extracted from legacy systems that may be decades old, running on technologies that the current IT team did not build and may not fully understand. The extracted data must be cleansed: duplicates removed, formats standardized, missing fields populated, invalid values corrected.

The cleansed data must be transformed: mapped from the legacy system's data model to the target system's data model, which requires understanding both systems at a level of detail that is rarely documented and often exists only in the heads of people who are already overloaded with their day jobs. The transformed data must be loaded into the target system, validated against business rules, and reconciled against the source to ensure nothing was lost or corrupted in transit.

Every one of these steps is harder than it sounds. The extraction is complicated by legacy systems that lack modern export capabilities. The cleansing is complicated by data quality problems that have accumulated over years of inconsistent entry and lax governance. The transformation is complicated by differences in data models that require business decisions, not just technical mapping: when the legacy system has fifteen statuses for a customer account and the new system has five, someone must decide how to map the other ten, and that someone is usually a business user who is already struggling to keep up with their normal responsibilities while simultaneously participating in a transformation they did not ask for.

And nobody owns data migration. In most organizations, there is no standing team whose job is to manage enterprise data quality. The data was created by hundreds of people over many years, each following their own conventions, their own shortcuts, their own interpretations of what a field means. There are no data owners, or the data owners exist on paper but have never been asked to exercise their ownership.

The data governance framework, if one exists, was created for a different purpose and does not address the specific challenges of migration. The result is that data migration becomes a workstream with no natural owner, no established authority, and no existing infrastructure to support it. It must be built from scratch, staffed from scratch, and governed from scratch, all while the rest of the program is consuming the organization's attention and resources.

When Data Destroys the Business: Target Canada

If you want to understand what happens when data migration goes catastrophically wrong, study Target Canada. The case was introduced in Chapter 8, but it deserves deeper examination here because it illustrates the specific mechanisms by which data failures propagate through an enterprise and destroy its ability to operate.

Target Canada represents the most extreme example of a digital transformation contributing directly to a business exit. The company's 2013 expansion into Canada, supported by a new SAP implementation, resulted in approximately $7 billion in losses and the closure of all 133 Canadian stores by 2015.

The conventional assumption was that this would be a relatively straightforward implementation. Target Canada was a new entity. There was no legacy system to replace. They were starting from scratch, which should have been an advantage. They could define their processes cleanly, build their data model correctly, and stand up a system without the burden of technical debt.

That is not what happened.

The failure was driven by catastrophic data quality issues. Product information migrated from acquired Zellers stores into Target's SAP system was riddled with errors: incorrect dimensions, wrong costs, missing product attributes, and broken supplier links that made accurate replenishment impossible.

Even though Target Canada had no legacy ERP to migrate from, they still needed to create master data -- product data, supplier data, location data, pricing data -- to stand up the system. Some of this data was sourced from the Zellers stores that Target had acquired. Some was created from scratch. In both cases, the data quality was abysmal. Target's internal data accuracy was found to be approximately 30 percent. Industry standards typically require 98 to 99 percent accuracy for effective supply chain operations.

Thirty percent. Seven out of ten data records contained errors. In a retail supply chain, where every product must be accurately described, correctly priced, properly dimensioned, and linked to the right supplier, data accuracy of 30 percent means the supply chain cannot function. The replenishment system cannot order the right products. The distribution centers cannot route inventory to the right stores. The stores cannot price merchandise correctly. The entire operation, from supplier to shelf, is running on data that is wrong more often than it is right.

The consequences were visible on the shelves. Stores opened with empty aisles. Products that customers expected to find were not there. Products that were there were priced incorrectly. The replenishment algorithms, which depended on accurate product dimensions and supplier lead times, were generating orders that made no sense. Trucks arrived at stores with the wrong merchandise. Warehouses were stacked with inventory that nobody had ordered and nobody could use.

Target Canada spent the months after launch in a desperate remediation effort, trying to fix data records one by one while simultaneously trying to run a retail operation. But in retail, first impressions are nearly impossible to reverse. Customers who walked into a Target Canada expecting the American Target experience and found empty, disorganized shelves did not come back. The business never recovered. Within two years, all 133 stores were closed. Approximately 17,600 employees lost their jobs. The total losses were approximately $7 billion.

The Target Canada failure was not a technology failure. SAP works. The system was configured. The infrastructure was operational. The failure was a data failure, pure and simple. The data that was loaded into the system was wrong, and because the data was wrong, everything the system did with that data was wrong. The technology amplified the data errors at the speed and scale of an automated supply chain, turning thousands of individual data quality problems into a systemic operational collapse.

This is the lesson of Target Canada: in an enterprise system, the data is the foundation. If the foundation is rotten, nothing built on top of it will stand.

Testing the Invisible

Integration and data migration failures share a common enabler: inadequate testing. In Chapter 7, I discussed the broader dynamics of testing compression and the political pressure to downgrade defects to maintain the go-live date. Here I want to focus specifically on integration testing, because it has unique characteristics that make it more difficult and more important than other forms of testing.

Integration testing requires an environment that replicates the full landscape of connected systems. It is not enough to test the ERP in isolation. You must test the ERP connected to the WMS, connected to the shipping carriers, connected to the CRM, connected to the banks, connected to the EDI partners, connected to the data warehouse, all running simultaneously, all processing transactions in the sequence and at the volume they will encounter in production.

Building this environment is expensive, time-consuming, and often incomplete. Third-party systems may not provide test environments. Trading partners may not participate in integration testing. Banks may not provide sandbox environments for payment processing. The result is that integration testing is frequently conducted with simulated connections, stubbed-out interfaces, and assumptions about how the production environment will behave that may or may not be accurate.

The defects that integration testing reveals are also uniquely difficult to diagnose and resolve. When a unit test fails, the problem is in the unit. When an integration test fails, the problem could be in System A, System B, the interface between them, the middleware, the data, the timing, or some combination of all of these. Diagnosing the root cause requires expertise across multiple systems, which means assembling a cross-functional team that includes the ERP consultants, the WMS specialists, the middleware team, the data migration analysts, and the business users who understand the process. Getting all of those people in a room, focused on the same defect, at the same time, is a logistical challenge that compounds the technical one.

I have worked with organizations where integration testing revealed fundamental architectural flaws two weeks before go-live. Not minor defects. Fundamental flaws in how the systems were connected, flaws that required redesigning the integration approach, rebuilding interfaces, and retesting the entire data flow from end to end. In one case, a wholesale distributor discovered during integration testing that the bidirectional interface between the new ERP and their warehouse management system was dropping transactions under load. The interface worked fine in unit testing, where transactions were processed one at a time. In integration testing, where hundreds of transactions were processed simultaneously, the interface could not keep up. The root cause was an architectural decision made months earlier that nobody had validated against production volumes. Fixing it required redesigning the interface, which pushed the go-live date by three months and cost over a million dollars in additional consulting fees.

The lesson is simple but consistently ignored: integration testing is not a phase you compress when the timeline gets tight. It is the phase that tells you whether your transformation actually works. Every other form of testing validates individual components. Integration testing validates the system as a whole. If you compress it, you are not saving time. You are deferring the discovery of defects from the test environment, where they can be fixed in a controlled manner, to the production environment, where they will be discovered by your employees, your customers, and your supply chain partners, at full volume, with real money on the line.

The Composable Paradox

In Chapter 16, we will discuss the emergence of composable ERP as a market response to vendor lock-in and monolithic platform risk. The promise of composable architecture is that organizations can assemble their technology stack module by module, selecting best-of-breed solutions for each capability and connecting them through APIs and integration platforms. It is a compelling vision: flexibility, interoperability, and the ability to swap out any component without replacing the entire system.

But composable architecture has a consequence that its proponents often understate: more components means more integration points. A monolithic ERP suite from a single vendor may have poor integration between its own modules, but at least those modules share a common data model, a common database, and a common vendor responsible for making them work together. A composable architecture, by design, does not have any of those things. Every component is a separate system, built by a separate vendor, with a separate data model and a separate API. Every connection between components is an integration that must be designed, built, tested, maintained, and upgraded over the life of the system.

Instead of multi-year, big-bang migrations to a monolithic suite, organizations assemble capabilities module by module, connected by clean APIs and shared data products. This approach lowers switching costs, reduces program risk, and allows innovation to move at the speed of the business rather than the pace of a single vendor's roadmap.

The benefits are real. Composable approaches do lower switching costs for individual components. They do reduce the blast radius of any single vendor's failure. They do allow organizations to innovate incrementally rather than transforming all at once. But they also multiply the integration surface area of the enterprise. An organization running a composable stack with fifteen best-of-breed components may have more integrations to manage than an organization running a monolithic ERP suite. The integrations may be cleaner, more modern, more API-driven. But they are still integrations, and they still require design, development, testing, monitoring, and maintenance.

The composable paradox is this: the architecture that liberates you from vendor lock-in simultaneously chains you to integration complexity. You trade one form of dependency for another. The question is not which is better in the abstract. The question is which set of trade-offs your organization is equipped to manage, given your IT capabilities, your budget, your staffing, and your appetite for ongoing architectural complexity.

Organizations with strong internal IT teams, mature integration capabilities, and a disciplined approach to data governance can thrive with composable architectures. Organizations that lack those capabilities, which is the majority, may find that the composable vision creates a complexity burden they are not prepared to carry. The integration nightmare does not go away in a composable world. It changes shape.

The Data Governance Deficit

Underlying every integration failure and every data migration disaster is a deficit that almost no organization addresses until it is too late: the absence of enterprise data governance.

Data governance is the set of policies, processes, roles, and standards that define how data is created, maintained, stored, and used across the organization. It includes data ownership: who is responsible for the accuracy and completeness of customer data, product data, vendor data, financial data? It includes data quality standards: what are the rules for how a customer name is formatted, how a product is classified, how a location is coded? It includes data stewardship: who monitors data quality over time and remediates issues when they arise?

In most organizations, the answer to all of these questions is nobody. Or more precisely, everybody and nobody. Data is created by hundreds of people across the organization, each following their own conventions, or no conventions at all. There are no enforced standards for how data is entered. There are no automated checks for data quality. There are no designated data owners who are accountable for the accuracy of their domain. The data accumulates over years, each record a small monument to the priorities, shortcuts, and misunderstandings of the person who created it.

This deficit is invisible in normal operations, because the people who use the data have learned to work around its flaws. The warehouse manager knows that the product dimensions in the system are wrong and compensates by eyeballing the bin assignments. The accounts payable clerk knows that the vendor master has duplicates and searches by tax ID instead of vendor name. The supply chain planner knows that the lead times in the system are stale and maintains their own spreadsheet with the real numbers. The organization functions not because the data is accurate, but because the people have developed workarounds that compensate for its inaccuracy.

A new ERP system eliminates those workarounds. The system does not know that the product dimensions are wrong. It does not know to search by tax ID instead of vendor name. It does not maintain a side spreadsheet with the real lead times. The system trusts the data, and it processes the data at scale, at speed, and without the human judgment that compensated for its flaws. The inaccuracies that were manageable in the old world, because people knew about them and worked around them, become catastrophic in the new world, because the system does not know and cannot compensate.

This is why data governance is not a nice-to-have for organizations embarking on a digital transformation. It is a prerequisite. And it is a prerequisite that must be established before the transformation begins, not during and certainly not after. Organizations that wait until the data migration phase to address data quality are already too late. They are trying to clean decades of accumulated data debt under the pressure of a project timeline, with resources that are already overcommitted, against standards that have not been defined. The result is predictable: data that is "good enough" for migration but not good enough for the business processes that depend on it, leading to the defects, workarounds, and operational disruptions that characterize the post-go-live period.

There is a dimension to data governance that has become dramatically more important in recent years, and it is one that most organizations have not yet reckoned with: artificial intelligence has made clean data more valuable -- and more consequential -- than at any point in the history of enterprise technology.

Consider what has happened to the technology landscape. Cloud ERP systems are increasingly commoditized. The same software, running in the same multi-tenant cloud environment, configured according to the same best practices, is deployed at thousands of organizations worldwide. The processes are standardized. The workflows are vanilla. The functionality is, by design, the same for everyone. In this world, the technology is no longer a differentiator. Your competitors are running the same software you are, configured in largely the same way, on the same vendor's infrastructure. The last remaining piece of intellectual property, the last source of competitive advantage that an organization still maintains within its enterprise systems, is its data. Your customer data. Your pricing data. Your supply chain data. Your demand patterns. Your operational history. This is the secret sauce that AI models need to generate insights, predictions, and recommendations that are specific to your business. Without clean, governed, proprietary data, AI is just a general-purpose engine running on generic inputs. With it, AI becomes a genuine competitive advantage. Data is no longer just the foundation of your ERP system. It is the foundation of your AI strategy. And if the foundation is dirty, incomplete, or ungoverned, your AI will produce outputs that are not just useless but actively misleading -- bad recommendations at machine speed.

But here is the part that should genuinely alarm you. Tens of thousands of organizations throughout the world have opted in to allow their ERP vendors to use their data to train and improve the vendor's AI models. Read that again. Your proprietary operational data -- the data that represents decades of accumulated business intelligence, the data that differentiates your supply chain from your competitor's -- is being fed into AI models that benefit every other customer on the same platform, including your direct competitors. The vendor benefits because their AI gets smarter with every customer's data. Your competitors benefit because the AI trained on your data improves the recommendations they receive. And you benefit... how, exactly? The promise is that you get access to better AI capabilities in return. But the trade-off is that the very data that made your operations unique is being homogenized into a shared model that levels the playing field between you and everyone else on the platform. In a world where cloud ERP has already commoditized the technology, opting in to shared AI models risks commoditizing the one asset you had left. This is a strategic decision that most organizations are making by clicking "accept" on a terms of service update without understanding its implications. Data governance is no longer just about migration accuracy. It is about protecting the intellectual property that will define your competitive position in an AI-driven future.

Some organizations are beginning to recognize this risk and are responding accordingly. Rather than relying on their ERP vendor's embedded AI -- which is trained on pooled data from thousands of customers and returns homogenized insights -- they are going outside the core ERP system to find independent AI toolsets that operate exclusively on their own proprietary data. This is the same logic that drove the Kingfisher decision we discussed in Chapter 10: the global retailer that refused to migrate to S/4HANA and instead deployed third-party AI tools on top of their existing ECC system. These organizations are making a calculated bet that the competitive value of keeping their data proprietary and their AI models unique outweighs the convenience of the vendor's bundled AI offering. They are choosing differentiation over commoditization. It is a strategy that requires more technical sophistication, more integration work, and more internal capability than simply turning on the vendor's AI switch. But it preserves the one asset that the cloud has not yet commoditized. As more organizations recognize that their ERP vendor's AI strategy is designed to benefit the vendor's ecosystem rather than any individual customer's competitive position, expect this trend to accelerate. The companies that treat their data as intellectual property to be protected, rather than as a resource to be shared, will be the ones best positioned to compete in a world where the technology itself is identical across competitors.

The data governance deficit is not a technology problem. It is an organizational problem. The technology to enforce data quality exists. The challenge is getting the organization to invest in it, to define the standards, to assign the ownership, to fund the remediation, and to maintain the discipline over time. The machine does not sell data governance. There is no vendor pitching a data governance platform at the annual conference with the same energy that they pitch AI agents and cloud migration. Data governance is boring. It is also the difference between a system that works and a system that lies to you.

What Nobody Tells You About Integration

I want to close this chapter with a list of truths about integration and data migration that you will not hear during the sales cycle, will not see in the vendor's proposal, and will not find in the system integrator's project plan. These are the things that every experienced implementation professional knows but that the machine has no incentive to tell you.

First, the number of integrations will be higher than anyone estimated. The sales cycle identifies the obvious ones. The implementation discovers the rest. Budget accordingly.

Second, data migration will take longer and cost more than planned. It always does. Build a data migration team early, fund it properly, and give it the authority to hold other workstreams accountable for the dependencies they create.

Third, your data is worse than you think. Every organization believes their data is "pretty good." It is not. Start a data quality assessment before the implementation begins, and plan for remediation that will take months, not weeks.

Fourth, integration testing cannot be compressed. It is the last major quality gate before go-live, and it is the one that reveals problems that no other form of testing can detect. Give it the time, the budget, and the environment it requires.

Fifth, middleware is not a silver bullet. It is a tool that, when properly implemented, can make integration more manageable. It does not reduce the number of integrations, the complexity of the data mapping, or the need for thorough testing. It adds a layer of organization. It also adds a layer of cost, skill requirements, and vendor dependency.

Sixth, the people who understand your integrations are your most valuable resource. They are usually the most overloaded people on the project, because their knowledge is needed everywhere. Protect their time, prioritize their work, and do not let the project plan treat integration as a secondary workstream that can be staffed with junior resources.

Seventh, data governance is not a phase. It is a permanent organizational capability that must be established before the transformation and maintained long after. If you do not invest in it, you will pay for its absence every day the new system is in production.

The integration nightmare is not inevitable. It is the predictable consequence of underestimating complexity, underfunding critical workstreams, and treating the invisible architecture of the enterprise as an afterthought. Organizations that take integration and data migration seriously -- that staff them properly, test them thoroughly, and govern the data that flows through them -- can avoid the nightmare. The machine, which profits from complexity and benefits from your unpreparedness, is not going to tell you any of this. Consider yourself told.

In the next chapter, we will examine the customization paradox: the tension between implementing a system as the vendor designed it and modifying it to fit the way your business actually works. It is a tension that has no clean resolution, and it is the source of some of the most expensive decisions in any transformation.

Chapter 13

The Customization Paradox

In the previous chapter, I described the integration and data migration challenges that sit beneath the surface of every transformation. This chapter addresses a challenge that sits right on the surface, visible to everyone, debated endlessly, and almost never resolved well: the question of customization.

Should you change the software to fit your business? Or should you change your business to fit the software?

This is the question at the heart of every enterprise software implementation, and it is the question that generates more conflict, more cost overruns, and more post-go-live dysfunction than almost any other. It is also the question that has no clean answer, which is why I call it a paradox. Both extremes are dangerous. Too much customization creates technical debt, upgrade risk, and a system that is impossible to maintain. Too little customization forces the organization to abandon processes that may be genuine competitive advantages, replacing them with generic workflows that serve no one particularly well. The right answer is somewhere in the middle, and finding it requires a level of organizational self-awareness that most companies do not possess and the machine has no incentive to develop.

The Spectrum

Every ERP implementation sits somewhere on a spectrum between two extremes.

At one end is the vanilla implementation: the system is deployed exactly as the vendor designed it, with no modifications, no custom code, no extensions. The organization adapts its processes to match the software's standard workflows. This is the approach that vendors advocate, system integrators prefer, and industry analysts recommend. It is faster to implement, cheaper to maintain, and easier to upgrade. It is also, in many cases, brutally difficult for the organization to absorb, because it requires people to abandon workflows they have used for years and adopt new ones that may not align with how the business actually operates.

At the other end is the heavily customized implementation: the software is modified extensively to replicate the organization's existing processes. Custom code is written. Standard workflows are overridden. The system is bent and shaped until it does exactly what the legacy system did, with a new interface and a new database underneath. This approach is familiar to the organization, minimizes the change management burden in the short term, and satisfies the business users who want the new system to work the way the old one did. It is also a recipe for long-term disaster, because every customization creates a maintenance obligation, an upgrade obstacle, and a point of fragility that will haunt the organization for years.

The paradox is that neither extreme works. Vanilla implementations fail because organizations cannot absorb the degree of change required. Heavily customized implementations fail because the technical debt becomes unmanageable. And the middle ground, where most implementations try to land, is a political minefield where every process, every workflow, and every exception becomes a negotiation between what the software can do and what the business wants it to do.

Fit-to-Standard: Philosophically Right, Practically Brutal

The industry's current orthodoxy is fit-to-standard. The term means what it sounds like: implement the software according to the vendor's standard design and fit your business processes to the standard the software provides. Do not customize. Do not extend. Do not replicate your legacy processes. Accept the vendor's best practices as your own and move on.

SAP has been particularly aggressive in promoting this approach. SAP pushes hard for a clean core because they have the Business Technology Platform that allows extensions and customizations outside the core S/4HANA system. The message is clear: keep the core system vanilla, and if you need something the standard product does not provide, build it as an extension on BTP rather than modifying the core. This protects the system's upgrade path, reduces maintenance complexity, and keeps the customer on a version of the product that SAP can support efficiently.

From the vendor's perspective, fit-to-standard is ideal. It reduces support costs. It simplifies the upgrade cycle. It ensures that every customer is running a version of the product that the vendor's support organization understands. And it aligns with the cloud model, where multi-tenant architectures require a degree of standardization that on-premise systems never demanded.

From the customer's perspective, fit-to-standard is often brutal. It means telling the warehouse manager who has been running operations his way for twenty years that his way is about to change. It means telling the finance team that the month-end close process they have refined over a decade will be replaced by the vendor's standard workflow, which may not accommodate the specific reporting requirements of their industry or their board. It means telling the manufacturing plant that the scheduling logic they have developed to handle their unique production constraints will be replaced by a generic planning algorithm that was designed for the average manufacturer, not for them.

Organizations that relied more on "best practices" and off-the-shelf software functionality to drive their transformations actually experienced the most difficulties.

Read that finding carefully. It runs counter to the industry's prevailing wisdom. The organizations that did what the vendors told them to do -- accept the standard, adopt the best practice, minimize customization -- actually struggled more than those that took a more nuanced approach. Why? Because "best practice" is a misnomer. It implies that there is a single best way to run a given process, and that the vendor's standard workflow represents that way. In reality, best practices are generic practices. They are designed to work adequately across a wide range of industries, geographies, and business models. They are nobody's best practice. They are everybody's adequate practice. And for organizations whose competitive advantage depends on doing something differently -- a unique fulfillment model, a proprietary pricing algorithm, a specialized quality control process -- adopting the generic practice means abandoning the thing that makes them successful.

This is the cruel irony of fit-to-standard: it works best for organizations that have the least to lose from standardization, and it hurts most the organizations that have the most to protect.

When Customization Is Change Resistance in Disguise

If fit-to-standard is not the answer, does that mean customization is? Absolutely not. Because the majority of customization requests in any implementation are not driven by genuine business need. They are driven by change resistance.

In my experience, approximately 60 percent of the "requirements" that surface during the discovery phase of an ERP implementation are not true business requirements. They are descriptions of how the organization currently operates, presented as demands that the new system must replicate. "We need the system to allow negative inventory." Why? Because the legacy system allowed negative inventory, and we have built our warehouse processes around that capability. "We need twelve approval levels on a purchase order." Why? Because we have always had twelve approval levels, and removing any of them would require someone to make a decision about who actually needs to approve what.

These are not requirements. They are habits. They are the accumulated sediment of decades of workarounds, exceptions, and organizational compromises, codified into a list and handed to the system integrator as though they were immutable laws of nature. And the system integrator, who is paid by the hour and benefits from every additional customization, has no incentive to challenge them.

I have sat in discovery workshops where the requirements list grew to 1,800 items. Eighteen hundred requirements for a mid-market manufacturer. When we audited the list, fewer than 400 were legitimate business needs that could not be met by the standard software. The other 1,400 were a combination of legacy process descriptions, user preferences, edge cases that occurred once a year, and outright change resistance expressed in the language of system specifications.

There is a practical leading indicator that can help you detect when customization requests are being driven by resistance rather than genuine need: volume. If you see a sudden spike in customization requests during design workshops -- particularly in workstreams where the standard software should be adequate -- pause and investigate. High customization volume is often a signal that the organization is trying to preserve the old way of working through the project budget. The customization request becomes the mechanism through which change resistance expresses itself in the language of system specifications. Before approving any batch of customization requests, ask: are we customizing because the software genuinely cannot do what we need, or are we customizing because we have not yet done the change management work that would make the standard process acceptable?

The distinction between a legitimate customization and change resistance in disguise is one of the most important judgments in any implementation. But I want to be very clear about something, because the industry's rhetoric on this topic has swung so far toward "all customization is bad" that an equally dangerous message has taken hold: the idea that every modification to the standard software is technical debt to be avoided.

It is not. That remaining 40 percent -- the requirements that survived our audit, the ones that were not habits or preferences or change resistance -- represents real business value. These are the customizations that serve your customers better than the generic process could. The inventory logic that lets you promise next-day delivery when your competitors cannot. The pricing engine that accommodates the complex rebate structures your distributors depend on. The quality control workflow that catches defects at a rate your industry peers cannot match. The production scheduling algorithm that your plant managers spent years refining to squeeze efficiency out of a constraint that is unique to your operation. These are not technical debt. These are intellectual property. They are the codified expression of decades of operational learning, and they represent competitive advantages that are genuinely difficult for others to replicate.

This is the part of the customization conversation that vendors do not want to have. When a vendor tells you that your customizations are technical debt, what they are really telling you is that your customizations are inconvenient for their business model. A clean core is cheaper for the vendor to support. A standardized customer base is easier for the vendor to upgrade. A vanilla implementation is faster for the system integrator to deliver. Every one of those benefits accrues to the vendor and the SI, not to you.

The label "technical debt" is being applied indiscriminately to modifications that are genuinely harmful -- the twelve approval levels, the negative inventory workaround -- and modifications that are genuinely valuable -- the fulfillment logic that wins you customers, the supplier integration that saves you millions. The vendor does not distinguish between the two, because the vendor's incentive is to eliminate both.

I have worked with organizations that were pressured by their vendor and their system integrator to abandon customizations that were directly responsible for their market position. A distributor was told that their proprietary order routing logic was "not standard" and should be replaced with the vendor's default allocation engine. That routing logic was the reason their fill rates were fifteen points higher than their nearest competitor. A manufacturer was told that their custom shop floor scheduling module was "legacy technical debt" that should not be carried forward. That scheduling module was the reason they could deliver complex configured products two weeks faster than anyone else in their industry. In both cases, the vendor and the SI were not wrong that the customization created maintenance obligations. They were wrong that the maintenance obligation outweighed the business value.

The honest conversation about customization is not "customize or don't customize." It is "which customizations deliver value that exceeds their cost, and which ones don't?" The 60 percent that represents change resistance should be eliminated. The 40 percent that represents genuine competitive advantage should be preserved, invested in, and carried forward -- even if the vendor would prefer you didn't, even if the SI would rather not deal with it, and even if someone labels it technical debt to make you feel guilty about protecting the things that make your business work.

There is a competitive dimension to this that most organizations have not considered. Think about the most successful organizations in the world -- the ones that have become dominant players in their industries. They did not do it by implementing a public cloud environment that anyone else has access to. In most cases, they did it by creating something unique, some secret sauce embedded within their technology and their operations. When a vendor pushes you toward a multi-tenant public cloud model with minimal customization, they are asking you to run your business on the same software, configured the same way, as every other company on that platform -- including your direct competitors. Your competitor can go buy the same software, implement the same best practices, and replicate capabilities that you spent decades building. The barriers to entry in your own industry drop. The competitive advantages you built through years of operational learning are erased by a standardized implementation that anyone with a subscription can access.

The vendor will tell you that standardization is a good thing, that you want a clean core, that you should follow best practices. That is a narrative invented by software vendors to make standardization sound appealing. What it actually does is dilute any competitive advantage you might have had in your systems. There may be parts of your business where commodity processes and vanilla configurations are perfectly appropriate -- accounts payable, basic general ledger, standard HR transactions. But the processes that make you who you are, the ones that your customers value and your competitors cannot easily replicate, those are not commodity processes. And surrendering them to a standardized platform because a vendor told you they were "technical debt" is not modernization. It is competitive disarmament.

Too much software customization was determined to be a symptom of poor organizational change management rather than a root cause in and of itself. This is a critical insight. Over-customization is not a technology problem. It is an organizational problem. When the organization does not have the leadership commitment, the change management infrastructure, or the cultural readiness to adopt new processes, the path of least resistance is to customize the system to avoid the change. The customization becomes a pressure valve that releases the organizational tension that should have been addressed through change management. The project stays on schedule because nobody has to change. The system goes live because nobody had to fight. And five years later, the organization is running a system so heavily customized that it cannot be upgraded, cannot be supported, and cannot be maintained without the consultants who built it.

The Technical Debt Spiral

Every customization creates technical debt. Not in the abstract, metaphorical sense. In the concrete, measurable, financially devastating sense.

Technical debt is the accumulated cost of shortcuts, workarounds, and non-standard modifications that must eventually be paid through additional maintenance, rework, or replacement. In the context of an ERP implementation, every piece of custom code, every modified workflow, every overridden standard process adds to the technical debt. And like financial debt, technical debt compounds over time.

Here is how the spiral works. During the implementation, the organization customizes the system to meet what it believes are critical requirements. The customizations work. The system goes live. The immediate crisis is averted.

Then the vendor releases an update. In a vanilla implementation, the update is applied with minimal effort. The standard workflows absorb the update because they were designed to. In a customized implementation, the update must be tested against every customization to ensure compatibility. Custom code that interacts with modified workflows may break. Extensions that depend on specific database structures may fail. The update that was supposed to take a week takes three months, costs hundreds of thousands of dollars, and requires the organization to choose between applying the update and maintaining the customizations.

I have worked with manufacturers whose customizations were so extensive that they could not apply vendor updates for a decade. Ten years without a single update, because the risk of breaking the customizations was too high and the cost of testing was prohibitive. These organizations were running software that was functionally frozen in time, missing a decade of security patches, feature enhancements, and regulatory compliance updates. They had built a prison out of their own customizations, and they could not escape without rebuilding the system from scratch.

In the cloud world, the technical debt spiral has an additional dimension. Cloud vendors release updates continuously, sometimes monthly or quarterly. These updates are mandatory. You cannot defer them the way you could defer on-premise patches. If your customizations are incompatible with a mandatory cloud update, you have a crisis. The vendor is going to apply the update whether you are ready or not. Your customizations must be compatible, or they will break. The cloud model that was supposed to free you from upgrade cycles has instead created a treadmill: you must continuously validate your customizations against a continuously evolving platform, at a pace dictated by the vendor, not by you.

SAP's response to this problem is the Business Technology Platform, which allows customers to build extensions outside the core system. The theory is that by keeping the core clean and building extensions on a separate platform, the customer can absorb core updates without disrupting their customizations. In practice, the extensions still interact with the core through APIs and data flows, and any change to the core's APIs or data model can still break the extensions. The BTP model reduces the problem. It does not eliminate it.

The Lidl Catastrophe

In 2018, Lidl, one of the largest discount grocery chains in the world, walked away from seven years and approximately €500 million worth of investment in an SAP implementation. They had insisted on replicating their existing pricing and inventory processes within SAP rather than adapting to the software's standard capabilities, and the gap proved unbridgeable.

Seven years. Half a billion euros. And in the end, the German retailer simply reverted to their legacy systems and started over.

The Lidl case is the customization paradox taken to its logical extreme. Lidl is a company with a distinctive operating model. Their pricing logic, their inventory management, their supplier relationships are all built around a specific approach to discount retail that has made them one of the most successful grocery chains in the world. When they attempted to implement SAP, they were unwilling to abandon the processes that had made them successful. They wanted SAP to accommodate the way they worked, not the other way around.

The specific functional mismatch that doomed the Lidl implementation was deceptively simple: inventory valuation. SAP's standard product valued inventory at cost. Lidl's entire pricing model -- the model that had made them one of the most successful discount retailers in the world -- required inventory to be valued at the retail price. This was not a configurable setting. It was a fundamental architectural difference between how SAP's system worked and how Lidl's business worked. No amount of customization could bridge the gap without rebuilding a core element of SAP's financial logic. The €500 million failure was not caused by organizational resistance or poor change management. It was caused by a genuine, irreducible mismatch between what the software did and what the business needed. This is the customization paradox at its most unforgiving: sometimes the gap between the software and the business is real, and no amount of process change or system modification can close it.

This is not an unreasonable position. Lidl's processes were not arbitrary. They were competitive advantages. The pricing logic that SAP's standard product could not accommodate was the pricing logic that had enabled Lidl to offer lower prices than its competitors. Asking Lidl to abandon that logic in favor of SAP's standard approach was asking them to abandon a core element of their business model.

But the customizations required to make SAP accommodate Lidl's processes were so extensive, so complex, and so fundamentally at odds with the system's architecture that after seven years of effort, the gap could not be closed. The project consumed half a billion euros and delivered nothing. Lidl walked away, went back to their old systems, and their business continued to thrive -- because the processes they were trying to preserve were, in fact, worth preserving.

The Lidl case does not prove that customization is wrong. It proves that the gap between what the software can do and what the business needs it to do must be assessed honestly, early, and with a clear-eyed understanding of the cost of bridging it. If the gap is small, fit-to-standard is the right approach. If the gap is large but the process is not a competitive differentiator, the organization should change. If the gap is large and the process is a genuine competitive advantage, the organization must either find software that fits better or accept the cost and risk of extensive customization. What it must not do is embark on a seven-year, half-billion-euro project hoping the gap will close itself.

The Vendor-Specific Customization Trap

The customization paradox manifests differently depending on which vendor you have selected, and understanding the vendor-specific dynamics is important because the risks are not symmetric.

SAP is painful to customize and painful not to customize. The system's rigidity means that adapting to the standard requires significant organizational change. But the system's architecture means that customizing it is expensive, fragile, and creates long-term maintenance burdens. SAP customers face a two-front war: fight the organization to accept the standard, or fight the technology to accept the customization. Neither fight is easy, and most implementations end up fighting both simultaneously.

When you compare S/4HANA to more flexible products in the tech space, it is clear that S/4HANA is just not as flexible. For some that is not a bad thing because they want to standardize their operations. However, that can lead to a lot of pain organizationally and operationally because you are forced to change to accommodate the way the software was built.

Microsoft Dynamics 365 presents the opposite problem. Its flexibility makes it easy to customize, and the discipline required to stop customizing is precisely the discipline that most organizations lack. The D365 ecosystem, with its thousands of ISVs building extensions and add-ons, makes it trivially easy to bolt on additional functionality. The result is that D365 implementations often accumulate customizations gradually, each one small and reasonable on its own, until the cumulative weight of modifications creates a system that is as customized as any legacy platform -- but without the decades of testing that made the legacy platform stable.

The D365 flexibility trap is particularly insidious because it feels like success. The business users are happy because the system does what they want. The project team is happy because there are no confrontations about process change. The timeline is on track because nobody is fighting. And then, two years after go-live, the organization discovers that it cannot apply a platform update without breaking three ISV extensions and seventeen custom workflows, and the total cost of maintaining the customizations exceeds the cost of the original implementation.

Oracle takes a different approach. The vendor discourages customization of its cloud products, which creates less risk but also less flexibility. Oracle's "true cloud" model limits what customers can modify, which reduces the technical debt problem but creates a different risk: the organization may find that the standard product does not support critical business processes, and the options for addressing the gap are limited. Oracle customers tend to face the customization paradox not as a choice but as a constraint: the system will not let you customize, so you must either adapt or find a workaround, and the workarounds, which often involve manual processes, spreadsheets, or bolt-on tools, create their own form of technical debt even if they do not involve custom code.

The Customization Crisis in the Cloud

Customers will face a customization crisis with their ERP systems. Faced with the deficiencies of cloud products, customers will be forced to decide between accepting half-baked software or customizing to better fit their needs. Neither is ideal, so it will be a matter of choosing the lesser of two evils.

We predicted this crisis several years ago, and it has arrived. The cloud ERP products that vendors are pushing, and in some cases forcing, their customers to adopt are, in many areas, less functionally mature than the on-premise products they replace. S/4HANA does not yet have full parity with ECC. Oracle Cloud ERP does not yet match JD Edwards in manufacturing. Dynamics 365 is still consolidating functionality from the legacy AX, NAV, and GP products it subsumed.

This functional gap creates a customization dilemma that did not exist in the on-premise world. On-premise, the products were mature. The standard functionality was comprehensive. The customization decision was about whether to deviate from a complete product. In the cloud, the customization decision is about whether to compensate for an incomplete product. The dynamics are fundamentally different.

When the standard product lacks a capability that your business needs, you have three options. First, you can wait for the vendor to deliver the capability in a future release, which means going live without it and running a manual workaround in the interim. Second, you can build the capability as a customization or extension, which introduces technical debt and upgrade risk. Third, you can change your process to work without the capability, which may mean degrading the efficiency or effectiveness of that process.

None of these options is good. All of them have costs. And all of them are the customer's problem, not the vendor's. The vendor sold you the product as it exists today, with the roadmap as a non-binding suggestion of what might exist tomorrow. The gap between the product and your needs is yours to bridge, at your expense, on your timeline.

This is the customization crisis: the cloud model promises simplicity but delivers a less mature product, and the customer is left to choose between accepting the limitations, customizing around them, or changing their business. The machine presents this as a feature: "adopt the standard." The reality is that the standard is not yet finished, and the customer is paying to be a beta tester for a product that the vendor is still building.

A Decision Framework for Customization

The customization paradox cannot be resolved with a simple rule. It requires judgment, and that judgment must be grounded in a clear understanding of the organization's strategy, its competitive advantages, and its capacity for change. Here is a framework that I have used with hundreds of organizations to navigate this decision.

Step 1: Classify the process. For every process that surfaces a gap between the software's standard capability and the organization's current operation, ask a simple question: is this process a competitive differentiator? Does the way we do this create value that our competitors cannot easily replicate? If the answer is yes, the process deserves protection. If the answer is no, the process is a candidate for standardization.

Step 2: Assess the gap. How large is the difference between what the software does and what the process requires? A small gap may be addressable through configuration, which is different from customization. Configuration uses the vendor's built-in options to adjust behavior without modifying code. Customization involves writing new code, building extensions, or overriding standard functionality. Configuration carries minimal technical debt. Customization carries significant technical debt. The size of the gap determines which approach is appropriate.

Step 3: Calculate the true cost. The cost of a customization is not the cost of building it. It is the cost of building it, plus the cost of testing it against every future update, plus the cost of maintaining it for the life of the system, plus the cost of the specialized talent required to support it, plus the risk of it breaking at the worst possible moment. Most organizations calculate only the first cost. The other four are where the real money goes.

Step 4: Challenge the requirement. Before approving any customization, ask whether the requirement is a genuine business need or change resistance in disguise. Bring the business user, the process owner, and an independent advisor into the same room. Present the standard process. Explain the trade-offs. Ask: if you had never done it the old way, would you design it this way today? If the answer is no, the "requirement" is a habit, not a need, and the organization should adopt the standard.

Step 5: Document the decision. Whether you choose to customize or to standardize, document the rationale. Record what was decided, why, what the expected cost and risk are, and who is accountable for the outcome. This documentation is invaluable during post-implementation reviews, during future upgrade cycles, and during the inevitable conversation three years from now when someone asks why the system works the way it does.

Organizations that spent more time defining clear business processes prior to or early in their transformations were less likely to experience disruption. The customization decision is not a technology decision. It is a business process decision that happens to have technology implications. Organizations that invest in business process design before they start configuring software make better customization decisions, because they understand their processes well enough to distinguish between what is essential and what is habitual.

The organizations that skip this step, that move directly from vendor selection to system configuration without a rigorous process design phase, make the worst customization decisions. They customize reactively, responding to each gap as it surfaces during implementation, without a strategic framework for evaluating whether the customization is worth the cost. The result is a system that is customized haphazardly, where some processes are standardized that should not have been, and others are customized that should not have been, and nobody can explain the logic behind the decisions because there was no logic. There were just a series of individual negotiations between the implementation team and the business users, each resolved in isolation, each rational on its own, and collectively creating a system that is neither truly standard nor coherently customized.

The customization paradox does not have a universal solution. It has a decision-making process. Organizations that follow that process, that invest in understanding their own operations before they start modifying software, that distinguish rigorously between competitive differentiators and habits, and that calculate the true lifetime cost of every customization decision, will navigate the paradox far better than those that do not. The machine will not help you with this. The vendor wants you to adopt the standard because it is cheaper for them. The system integrator will accept whatever you decide because they get paid either way. The judgment must be yours, informed by independent advice and grounded in an honest assessment of what makes your business work.

In the next chapter, we will examine the latest entrant in the technology hype cycle: artificial intelligence. AI promises to solve problems that previous technology waves could not. It is also, as we will see, poised to repeat every mistake those waves produced -- with higher stakes and less organizational readiness than ever before.

Chapter 14

The AI Mirage

Every generation of enterprise technology arrives with the same promise: this is the one that changes everything. Client-server architecture was going to change everything. The internet was going to change everything. Cloud computing was going to change everything. Mobile was going to change everything. Blockchain was going to change everything. In each case, the technology was real, the potential was genuine, and the industry's ability to deploy it responsibly was approximately zero.

Now it is artificial intelligence's turn.

AI is the most powerful technology to enter the enterprise software landscape in decades. Its potential to transform business operations is not hype. Machine learning can detect patterns in data that human analysts cannot see. Natural language processing can automate interactions that previously required human judgment. Predictive algorithms can anticipate demand, identify risk, and optimize decisions at a speed and scale that was impossible five years ago. Agentic AI, the latest frontier, promises autonomous systems that can execute complex business processes with minimal human intervention.

None of this is fiction. The technology works. The question, as always, is not whether the technology works. The question is whether the organizations adopting it are ready for what it demands, whether the vendors selling it are being honest about what it can deliver, and whether the industry has learned anything from the previous waves of technology that promised to change everything and instead produced the same failure rates, the same cost overruns, and the same organizational wreckage.

The evidence so far suggests it has not.

The Failure Rate Nobody Talks About

More than 80 percent of AI projects fail to deliver on their intended objectives, according to research from RAND Corporation -- roughly twice the failure rate of traditional IT projects.

Let that number sit alongside the numbers from Chapter 1. Enterprise software implementations fail at a rate of 55 to 75 percent. AI projects fail at a rate of 80 percent or higher. The technology that is supposed to make enterprise systems smarter, more efficient, and more valuable is failing at an even higher rate than the enterprise systems themselves.

The reasons are familiar. They are the same reasons that ERP implementations fail, the same reasons that CRM implementations fail, the same reasons that every previous generation of enterprise technology failed. The technology is not the problem. The organizational readiness, the data quality, the change management, the governance, the leadership commitment -- these are the problems. And they are the problems that AI does not solve. AI amplifies them.

An ERP system running on bad data produces bad transactions. An AI system running on bad data produces bad decisions. The difference is that the AI system produces bad decisions faster, at greater scale, with more confidence, and with less visibility into how the decision was made. The failure mode of an ERP system is a processing error that someone catches in a reconciliation report. The failure mode of an AI system is a pattern of decisions that looks rational on the surface but is systematically wrong underneath, and nobody discovers the error until the damage has propagated through the business for weeks or months.

We have already seen this play out.

Watson, Amazon, and the Automation of Dysfunction

IBM's Watson for Oncology was intended to revolutionize cancer treatment by analyzing vast amounts of medical literature and patient data to recommend treatment options. Despite significant investment and high-profile partnerships with major cancer centers, Watson for Oncology failed to deliver meaningful improvements in patient outcomes. The system struggled with incomplete data, biased training sets, and the complexity of oncological decision-making that could not be easily reduced to algorithmic rules.

Watson was criticized for providing biased and sometimes unsafe treatment recommendations. The system was trained primarily on data from a single cancer center, limiting its generalizability to other patient populations and treatment protocols.

IBM spent years and hundreds of millions of dollars on Watson. The technology was sophisticated. The data science was real. The partnerships were prestigious. And the system produced recommendations that oncologists did not trust, because the AI had been trained on a narrow dataset that did not represent the diversity of cancer patients it was being asked to serve. The technology worked. The organizational and data infrastructure required to make it work responsibly did not exist. Watson for Oncology was eventually abandoned, not because AI cannot help with cancer treatment, but because IBM deployed it before the prerequisites were in place.

Amazon's AI-powered recruiting tool had to be abandoned when it was discovered that the system exhibited bias against women. The AI had been trained on historical hiring data that reflected existing gender biases in the tech industry, causing it to systematically downgrade resumes that included words associated with women.

Amazon's recruiting AI is the case study that should be required reading for every organization considering enterprise AI. The AI did exactly what it was designed to do: it learned from the data. The problem was that the data reflected a decade of biased hiring decisions. The AI did not introduce bias. It automated bias. It took the dysfunction that already existed in Amazon's hiring process and scaled it, accelerated it, and made it invisible by embedding it in an algorithm that appeared objective.

This is the fundamental danger of enterprise AI: it does not create dysfunction. It automates dysfunction. If your data is biased, your AI will be biased. If your processes are broken, your AI will optimize broken processes. If your organizational culture resists change, your AI will learn to work around the change, just as your employees do, but faster and at scale. AI is an amplifier. Point it at excellence and it amplifies excellence. Point it at dysfunction and it amplifies dysfunction. And in most organizations, the dysfunction is deeper, more pervasive, and more deeply embedded in the data than anyone wants to admit.

JPMorgan Chase's LOXM algorithm, designed for automated equity trading, had to be discontinued after it began making trading decisions that human traders could not understand or explain. This is the explainability problem: when an AI system produces a decision, can you trace the logic? Can you explain to a regulator, a board member, or a customer why the system made the choice it made? In many cases, the answer is no. The algorithm operates in a space of such mathematical complexity that the relationship between input and output is opaque even to the engineers who built it. This is not a theoretical concern. It is a governance crisis waiting to happen in every organization that deploys AI without establishing the oversight mechanisms to monitor, audit, and explain what the AI is doing.

The AI Arms Race

Investors are rewarding heavily software vendors that move to the cloud quickly or move their customers to the cloud quickly. And they are also rewarding heavily software providers that invest in AI and roll out AI capabilities quickly. So this is a clear cloud and AI arms race that the technology vendors are on, which is not a bad thing on the surface, but when you look under the hood, you find that the technology vendors now have a conflicting self-interest that conflicts with the interests of customers. Not every customer needs to go to the cloud right now. Not every customer needs to be using AI right now. A lot of customers do not even have their ducks in a row or their house in order to be able to leverage AI even if they wanted to.

The AI arms race is the cloud transition on steroids. The same investor pressure that forced every vendor to convert customers to the cloud is now forcing every vendor to embed AI into every product, whether the product needs it or the customer is ready for it. SAP is embedding Joule, its AI assistant, across the entire S/4HANA suite. Oracle is positioning AI-powered automation as a core differentiator. Microsoft is layering Copilot across Dynamics 365 and every other product in its ecosystem. Salesforce has Einstein. Workday has its AI agents. Every vendor, without exception, is racing to claim AI leadership, because AI is what investors are rewarding in 2025 and 2026 the way they rewarded cloud in 2020 and 2021.

The pressure to ship AI capabilities is producing the same dynamics we saw with cloud: features that are announced before they are ready, capabilities that are demonstrated in scripted demos but have not been deployed at scale in production, and claims about transformation that dramatically outpace the reality of what the technology can deliver today. As I discussed in Chapter 11, vendors are claiming thousands of AI agents built into their platforms. But how many of those agents are running in production at actual customer sites? How many have been validated against real-world data in real-world business processes? The honest answer, for most vendors, is very few.

These products are on one hand introducing artificial intelligence to customers, but on the other hand struggling to stabilize basic functionality such as manufacturing and warehouse management. The vendors are layering AI on top of products that are not yet functionally complete. They are selling intelligence before they have delivered competence. And the market is rewarding them for it, because the market values the promise of AI more than it values the reality of a working ERP system.

AI Washing

There is a term gaining traction in the industry that deserves wider recognition: AI washing. It is the practice of rebranding existing capabilities as "AI-powered" to capitalize on the hype without delivering genuinely new functionality.

A rules-based workflow that has existed in the software for a decade is relabeled as an "AI-driven process automation." A reporting dashboard that runs standard queries against a database is repositioned as "AI-powered analytics." A chatbot that follows a decision tree is marketed as a "conversational AI agent." In each case, the underlying technology has not changed. The marketing has.

AI washing is pervasive because it is profitable. Vendors that position themselves as AI leaders command higher stock prices, higher customer interest, and higher pricing premiums. The cost of relabeling existing features as "AI" is approximately zero. The revenue benefit is substantial. The incentive to AI wash is overwhelming, and the buyer's ability to distinguish genuine AI from rebranded automation is limited.

This matters because it erodes trust and distorts investment decisions. When everything is labeled AI, nothing is AI. The buyer cannot distinguish between a vendor that has made genuine, substantial investments in machine learning and a vendor that has slapped an "AI" badge on a feature set that has not changed since 2018. The result is that purchasing decisions are based on marketing rather than capability, and organizations invest in "AI" that is nothing more than the same software with a new label and a higher price tag.

The antidote to AI washing is specificity. When a vendor claims an AI capability, ask: what model is it using? What data was it trained on? How many customers are using it in production? What measurable outcomes has it delivered? What happens when the AI makes a wrong decision -- who is accountable? A vendor with genuine AI capabilities will have specific answers to these questions. A vendor that is AI washing will deflect, generalize, or refer you to a roadmap.

The Organizational Readiness Chasm

Even when the AI is real, even when the vendor has made genuine investments in machine learning and the capabilities are legitimate, the question of organizational readiness remains the dominant risk factor.

Seventy percent of all change initiatives fall short of their intended goals. That statistic applies to traditional change: process changes, system changes, organizational restructuring. AI-driven change is more disruptive, more ambiguous, and more threatening to the workforce than any of those. If organizations cannot manage traditional change successfully 70 percent of the time, what is their probability of managing AI-driven change?

You can spend big bucks on a new system with the greatest in AI, BI, IoT, and every other wonderful acronym of new technology, but if your employees continue working the same way they always have been, your investments will go to waste.

AI requires capabilities that most organizations do not have. It requires clean, governed data, as we discussed at length in Chapter 12. It requires people who can interpret AI outputs and exercise judgment about when to trust the algorithm and when to override it.

It requires governance frameworks that define who is accountable when the AI makes a decision that turns out to be wrong.

It requires a culture that is comfortable with ambiguity, because AI outputs are probabilistic, not deterministic -- the system gives you a best guess, not a guarantee. And it requires leadership that understands the technology well enough to ask the right questions and set the right boundaries.

Most organizations lack all of these capabilities. Their data is dirty, as we discussed. Their employees are already struggling to adopt the ERP system, let alone an AI layer on top of it. Their governance structures are weak. Their culture is change-averse. And their leadership is excited about AI because they read about it in a board report but cannot articulate what specific business problem AI will solve or how they will measure whether it is working.

The readiness chasm is the gap between what AI requires and what the organization can provide. In most cases, this gap is enormous. And it is growing.

This is the dynamic I described in Chapter 2: technology is changing exponentially faster than any single organization can absorb. That observation, which applies to cloud ERP and digital transformation broadly, becomes dramatically more acute with AI. The pace of AI development is unlike anything the enterprise technology industry has experienced. Large language models that did not exist three years ago are now being embedded into every vendor's product suite. Agentic AI, which was a research concept eighteen months ago, is being marketed as production-ready by vendors competing for investor attention. New capabilities are being announced monthly, each one requiring new skills, new governance frameworks, new data infrastructure, and new organizational muscles that take years, not months, to develop.

The result is that the gap between where organizations are and where the technology could take them is widening at an accelerating rate. Five years ago, an organization considering ERP modernization faced a gap between their current processes and what a cloud ERP could enable. That gap was manageable. It required change, but the change was comprehensible: new screens, new workflows, new reports. Today, an organization considering the same modernization faces that same gap plus an AI gap on top of it -- a gap that requires not just new processes but new capabilities that most organizations have never built: data science, model governance, AI ethics, human-AI workflow design, continuous model monitoring, and a workforce that can exercise judgment alongside algorithmic recommendations.

Each new wave of technology capability that the vendors release widens the chasm further. The organization has not yet absorbed the cloud migration, and the vendor is already selling AI. The organization has not yet cleaned its data, and the vendor is already marketing agentic AI that depends on clean data to function. The organization has not yet built basic change management competency, and the vendor is asking it to manage the most disruptive form of change the workforce has ever encountered. The technology is sprinting. The organizations are walking. And the industry's response to this widening gap is not to slow down and help organizations catch up. It is to sell faster, because the investors reward speed, not readiness.

And the industry's response to the gap is the same as its response to every other gap: sell the technology anyway and let the customer figure out the readiness part on their own.

I see this readiness chasm firsthand in the organizations we work with. At one food and beverage company with a mature Oracle environment, we conducted a three-day AI workshop that began by interviewing fifty employees across the organization about their understanding of and readiness for AI. The results were sobering but representative: most employees had only nascent knowledge of AI. Current processes were heavily Excel-driven. The organization's data -- inventory records, transaction histories, planning inputs -- was inconsistent and loosely governed. When we built a proof-of-concept AI agent using Oracle's own AI tools to detect inventory synchronization anomalies, the results were mixed. The agent could locate discrepancies, but it had no machine learning capability -- it did not learn unless explicitly programmed. Nothing revolutionary. The CIO observed that every Oracle integrator now seemed to claim they were an AI company, with solutions that were insanely expensive and biased toward doing everything within the Oracle ecosystem. The organization ultimately identified eight potential AI workstreams, but each one depended on the same prerequisite: clean master data, disciplined transactions, and reliable planning processes. Without those foundations, the AI recommendations could not be trusted. The technology was available. The organizational infrastructure to support it was not.

AI and the Data Problem, Revisited

In Chapter 12, I made the argument that data is the last remaining competitive advantage in a world of commoditized cloud ERP. That argument becomes even more consequential in the context of AI.

Every AI model is only as good as the data it is trained on. If your customer data contains duplicates, your AI will learn to treat duplicates as normal. If your inventory data contains inaccuracies, your AI will optimize around inaccurate inventory levels. If your pricing data reflects years of inconsistent entry and undocumented exceptions, your AI will learn the exceptions as rules and the errors as patterns. The AI does not know the data is wrong. It cannot distinguish between a signal and an artifact. It treats everything in the dataset as truth and builds its models accordingly.

The organizations that have invested in data governance -- that have clean master data, enforced quality standards, designated data owners, and documented data lineage -- will extract genuine value from AI. Their models will produce accurate predictions, reliable recommendations, and actionable insights, because the foundation is solid. These organizations are rare.

The organizations that have not invested in data governance -- which is the vast majority -- will deploy AI on top of dirty data and wonder why the results are unreliable. They will blame the AI. They will blame the vendor. They will hire more data scientists to tune the models. But the problem is not the model. The problem is the data. And fixing the data is not a technology project. It is an organizational transformation that takes years, requires executive commitment, and delivers no short-term gratification. The machine does not sell data governance. It sells AI. And the gap between the two is where most AI investments go to die.

There is also the strategic dimension I raised in Chapter 12 that bears repeating here: tens of thousands of organizations have opted in to allow their ERP vendors to use their proprietary data to train shared AI models. In a world where data is the last competitive differentiator, sharing that data with a model that benefits your competitors on the same platform is a strategic decision of extraordinary consequence. Organizations that recognize this are beginning to deploy independent AI toolsets outside their core ERP, preserving the proprietary value of their data.

We helped one global manufacturing client do exactly this. The company, a division of a Japanese industrial conglomerate, had identified over a dozen AI use cases across manufacturing scheduling, supply chain optimization, demand forecasting, and margin risk analysis. Rather than activating their ERP vendor's embedded AI -- which would have fed their operational data into a shared model -- they chose to build a custom AI platform on Microsoft Azure, housed within their own tenant, under their own data governance.

We evaluated Palantir, Snowflake, Databricks, and the custom build option, and the recommendation was clear: the custom build preserved data sovereignty, avoided vendor lock-in, and delivered a conservative five-year return of $1.5 to $3 million from partial automation alone, at an upfront investment of roughly $600,000. The economics and the strategy both pointed away from the vendor's bundled AI and toward independence.

This is not an approach that every organization can execute -- it requires technical sophistication and internal capability that many companies lack. But it illustrates the strategic calculus that more organizations will face as AI matures: do you feed your proprietary data into a shared model that benefits your competitors, or do you invest in an independent capability that preserves your competitive advantage?

The organizations that do not recognize this choice are clicking "accept" on terms of service updates and surrendering their last competitive advantage to a shared model that levels the playing field for everyone except the vendor, who benefits from all of it.

The Fear Factor

There is a dimension of AI adoption that distinguishes it from every previous technology wave, and it is the dimension that most implementations are least prepared to address: fear.

When an organization implements a new ERP system, employees worry about learning a new interface, mastering new processes, and adapting to new workflows. These are legitimate concerns, but they are concerns about competence, not survival. The employee may struggle with the new system, but they do not fear that the new system will eliminate their job.

AI is different. AI raises the specter of replacement, not just disruption. When an organization announces that it is deploying AI agents to automate procurement, or customer service, or financial analysis, the employees who perform those functions hear a message that no change management program can fully counteract: you may not be needed anymore.

Whether this fear is justified depends on the specific implementation. In many cases, AI augments rather than replaces human work. The procurement analyst still reviews the purchase orders; the AI just surfaces the anomalies. The customer service representative still handles the complex cases; the AI handles the routine ones. The financial analyst still interprets the numbers; the AI generates the first draft of the report. These are genuine productivity improvements that make jobs better, not obsolete.

But the nuance of "augmentation versus replacement" is difficult to communicate to a workforce that has watched automation eliminate jobs in other industries, other companies, and other departments. The fear is not irrational. It is experiential. Employees have seen what automation did to manufacturing floors, call centers, and retail checkout lanes. They are not comforted by the promise that "this time is different" because they have heard that promise before, and they have seen it broken.

The change management implications are profound. An ERP implementation requires people to change how they work. An AI implementation requires people to trust a system that they fear may replace them. These are fundamentally different challenges, and the standard change management playbook -- communications plans, training sessions, town halls -- is inadequate for the second one. Addressing the fear requires transparency about which roles will be affected and how, genuine investment in reskilling and redeployment, and leadership that is honest about the trade-offs rather than hiding behind platitudes about "empowering the workforce."

Organizations that ignore the fear factor will face resistance that is deeper, more emotional, and more difficult to overcome than anything they experienced during their ERP implementation. And because AI adoption depends on people trusting the system enough to use it, the resistance will not just slow the implementation. It will prevent the AI from delivering value, because a system that nobody trusts is a system that nobody uses.

The Ethics Nobody Wants to Discuss

Enterprise AI raises ethical questions that the industry has barely begun to address. When an AI system denies a customer credit, who is accountable for the decision? When an AI-powered supply chain algorithm routes inventory away from unprofitable markets, what is the impact on the communities that depend on those markets? When an AI recruiting tool screens out candidates based on patterns learned from biased historical data, is the organization legally liable for discrimination even if no human made the discriminatory decision?

These are not hypothetical questions. They are questions that organizations deploying enterprise AI are already facing, and in most cases, they do not have answers. The governance frameworks that should guide AI decision-making -- policies on bias detection, explainability standards, accountability chains, audit mechanisms -- do not exist in most organizations. The vendor does not provide them. The system integrator does not build them. The organization is left to figure it out on its own, usually after the AI has been deployed and the first problematic decision has already been made.

The ethical dimension of AI is not a compliance checkbox. It is a strategic risk. Organizations that deploy AI without governance frameworks are exposing themselves to regulatory action, litigation, reputational damage, and the loss of trust from employees, customers, and partners. The European Union's AI Act is already establishing regulatory requirements for high-risk AI applications. Other jurisdictions will follow. Organizations that get ahead of these requirements will be better positioned than those that are forced to retrofit governance after the fact.

Responsible AI adoption requires, at minimum: transparency about how AI decisions are made; explainability standards that allow decisions to be audited and understood; bias detection and mitigation processes that are continuous, not one-time;

accountability frameworks that define who is responsible when the AI makes a wrong or harmful decision; and ongoing monitoring that detects model drift, performance degradation, and emerging biases over time.

These are not optional features. They are the cost of deploying AI responsibly. And they are costs that the machine -- which is racing to embed AI into everything as fast as possible because investors are rewarding the speed -- has very little incentive to acknowledge.

AI Will Not Save You from the Machine

I want to close this chapter by connecting AI back to the central thesis of this book, because the temptation to view AI as the solution to the problems described in previous chapters is strong and must be resisted.

AI will not fix your organizational dysfunction. It will automate it. AI will not resolve your leadership vacuum. It will operate in it, making decisions without the governance that leadership should have provided. AI will not close your accountability gap. It will widen it, because when the AI makes a bad decision, everyone will point at the algorithm and nobody will accept responsibility. AI will not solve your change management problems. It will compound them, because the fear of replacement will make every other form of resistance seem mild by comparison.

AI is a tool. Like every tool, its value depends entirely on the hands that hold it and the foundation it rests on. In the hands of an organization with strong leadership, clean data, healthy culture, and robust governance, AI can be genuinely transformative. It can surface insights that drive competitive advantage. It can automate the mundane and free people for the meaningful. It can make decisions faster and better than humans alone.

In the hands of an organization that has not done this work -- that has dirty data, weak governance, change-averse culture, and leadership that views AI as a magic wand rather than a capability that must be built -- AI will produce the same results that every previous technology wave produced: expensive disappointment, delivered faster.

Google's DeepMind has achieved remarkable success in medical AI applications, particularly in ophthalmology and protein folding prediction. The key difference lies in the focus on specific, well-defined problems with high-quality training data and clear success metrics. The lesson is not that AI cannot work. It is that AI works when the prerequisites are in place: specific problems, quality data, clear metrics, human oversight, and organizational commitment. Without those prerequisites, AI is a mirage: a shimmering vision of transformation that recedes the closer you get to it.

The machine is already selling the mirage. Every vendor keynote, every analyst report, every conference session is telling you that AI will change everything. Some of that is true. Much of it is premature. And almost none of it comes with an honest assessment of what your organization must become before AI can deliver on its promise.

Do not be the organization that spends millions on AI before it has spent thousands on data governance. Do not be the organization that deploys AI agents before it has trained its people to work alongside them. Do not be the organization that buys the mirage because the demo was impressive and the vendor was convincing and the board asked why you were falling behind your competitors.

Be the organization that sees AI clearly: a powerful technology, a genuine opportunity, and a capability that must be built deliberately, governed rigorously, and deployed only when the foundation is ready to support it. The machine will tell you to move fast. The evidence says move thoughtfully. The organizations that listen to the evidence will be the ones that actually capture the value. The rest will be adding AI to the long list of technologies that promised to change everything and changed nothing, at extraordinary expense.

In the next chapter, we will examine the broader graveyard of emerging technologies -- blockchain, IoT, metaverse, and others -- that followed the same pattern of hype without readiness. The lesson is always the same, and it is the lesson that the machine is constitutionally incapable of learning: people, process, then technology. Always in that order. Never the reverse.

Chapter 15

The Emerging Tech Graveyard

In the previous chapter, I described AI as a mirage: a technology with genuine potential that the industry is deploying before the prerequisites are in place. But AI is not the first technology to follow this pattern. It is merely the latest. The enterprise technology industry has a long and well-documented history of seizing on emerging technologies, inflating their potential, selling them to organizations that are not ready, and moving on to the next innovation before the wreckage of the last one has been cleared.

This chapter is about the graveyard. Not a literal one, but a graveyard of initiatives, investments, and organizational ambitions that were buried by the gap between what emerging technology promised and what organizations were equipped to deliver. Blockchain. The Internet of Things. The metaverse. Robotic process automation. Each one arrived with breathless hype, attracted billions of dollars in investment, generated a gold rush of consulting engagements, and left behind a trail of failed pilots, abandoned platforms, and executives who quietly stopped mentioning the initiative in their quarterly updates.

The technologies themselves were not the problem. In each case, there were legitimate use cases, real capabilities, and organizations that deployed the technology successfully. The problem was the pattern: the industry's reflexive tendency to sell emerging technology to the broadest possible market before the technology is mature, before the use cases are proven, and before the organizations buying it have any realistic chance of making it work.

The pattern is always the same. And the lesson is always the same. And the industry never learns it.

The Pattern: Promise, Pilot, Plateau, Abandonment

Every emerging technology follows a lifecycle that is as predictable as it is wasteful.

Phase one is the promise. A new technology appears on the horizon. The early research is impressive. The potential applications are vast. The vendor community, always alert to the next revenue opportunity, begins incorporating the technology into its messaging. Conference keynotes are delivered. Analyst reports are published. The technology is positioned as the next great transformation, the innovation that will separate the leaders from the laggards.

Phase two is the pilot. Organizations, motivated by the fear of falling behind and the pressure from boards who have read the same analyst reports, launch pilot programs. These pilots are typically small, well-funded, and staffed with the organization's most capable people. They are designed to succeed, because the point of the pilot is to validate the investment, not to test whether the technology is appropriate for the business. The pilots produce results that are positive enough to justify expansion but not transformative enough to change anyone's mind about how the business operates.

Phase three is the plateau. The pilot is declared a success, but scaling it to the enterprise proves far more difficult than anyone anticipated. The pilot ran in a controlled environment with clean data, dedicated resources, and executive attention. The enterprise environment has none of those things. The integration complexity is higher than expected. The data quality is worse than assumed. The organizational change required to adopt the technology at scale exceeds the organization's capacity.

The initiative stalls. The budget is quietly redirected. The executive sponsor moves on to a new role. The pilot sits in the corner of the IT landscape, running but unloved, producing outputs that nobody uses.

Phase four is abandonment. The technology does not disappear. It finds its niche, serving the specific, well-defined use cases where it genuinely adds value. But the grand vision of enterprise-wide transformation evaporates. The consulting firms that built practices around the technology quietly retrain their staff on the next emerging trend. The vendor removes the technology from the keynote and replaces it with whatever is generating investor excitement this quarter. And the organizations that invested in the initiative write off the cost, absorb the lesson, and prepare to repeat the cycle with the next technology that promises to change everything.

This pattern has played out with remarkable consistency across every major emerging technology of the past two decades. Let me walk you through the graveyard.

Blockchain: The Solution Looking for a Problem

Many organizations rushed to implement blockchain technologies during the cryptocurrency boom of 2017-2018. Companies across various industries announced blockchain initiatives and made significant investments in distributed ledger technologies, often without clear use cases or understanding of the technology's limitations. Many of these initiatives failed to deliver tangible business value, resulting in wasted resources and damaged credibility for both the organizations and the blockchain technology itself.

Blockchain was supposed to revolutionize everything from supply chain management to financial transactions to identity verification. The technology was real: distributed ledgers that created immutable, transparent records without requiring a central authority. The concept was compelling: eliminate intermediaries, reduce fraud, increase trust. The conference circuit was on fire. Every major consulting firm stood up a blockchain practice. Every major vendor announced a blockchain strategy. Organizations that did not have a blockchain initiative were made to feel like they were falling behind.

The reality was less inspiring. Many organizations that invested heavily in blockchain technologies found that the technology's limitations -- including scalability issues, energy consumption concerns, and integration complexity -- made it unsuitable for their specific use cases. The vast majority of enterprise blockchain pilots never made it beyond the proof-of-concept stage. The technology worked in the lab. It could not work at scale, in real business environments, with the messy data, fragmented systems, and organizational complexity that define the enterprise landscape.

Walmart's use of blockchain for food traceability demonstrates what successful blockchain implementation looks like. The system enables the company to trace the source of food products within seconds rather than days, improving food safety and reducing the impact of contamination incidents. The success of this implementation stems from its focus on solving a specific business problem with clear value.

Walmart succeeded because they started with a specific problem -- food traceability -- that blockchain was uniquely suited to solve. They did not start with blockchain and go looking for a problem. The organizations that failed did exactly the opposite: they started with the technology because the hype told them to and then searched for a business justification after the investment was already committed. The technology was not the failure. The approach was.

The honest assessment from our own research was blunt: no one has a good handle on blockchain. The number of enterprise use cases is still small. That was true during the peak of the hype. It remains true today. Blockchain has found its niche -- supply chain provenance, certain financial transactions, digital identity -- but the grand vision of blockchain as the foundation of a new enterprise architecture is buried in the graveyard alongside the consulting decks that sold it.

The Internet of Things: Sensors Without Strategy

The Internet of Things -- the vision of connecting physical devices, sensors, and machines to enterprise systems through networked data flows -- promised to bridge the gap between the physical world and the digital one. Manufacturing floors would be instrumented with sensors that fed real-time data into AI-powered analytics. Supply chains would be tracked end to end through connected devices. Predictive maintenance would eliminate unplanned downtime by monitoring equipment health in real time.

The technology existed. Sensors were cheap. Connectivity was ubiquitous. Cloud platforms could ingest and process massive volumes of device data. The vision was sound. The execution was not.

General Electric's Predix platform was intended to create an industrial internet that would optimize manufacturing processes using AI and IoT sensors. Despite significant investment, the platform failed to gain widespread adoption and was eventually scaled back significantly. The failure was attributed to unclear value propositions, complex implementation requirements, and insufficient customer development.

GE is the defining IoT cautionary tale. Under CEO Jeff Immelt, GE invested billions of dollars in creating GE Digital and developing the Predix platform. The initiative showed initial promise, with GE Digital generating significant revenue and market excitement. However, when leadership changed and new priorities emerged, the organization failed to sustain its commitment. The lack of sustained leadership support, combined with cultural resistance and changing strategic priorities, ultimately led to the dismantling of GE Digital and massive write-downs.

Billions of dollars. Dismantled. The technology was not the problem. GE could build sensors and connect machines. What GE could not do was transform its organizational culture from an industrial conglomerate into a technology company. The Predix platform required customers to change how they operated their manufacturing facilities, and GE could not even change how it operated itself.

In contrast, Siemens successfully implemented AI-driven automation in its manufacturing processes using a focused, incremental approach that solved specific problems rather than attempting to transform entire industries simultaneously. The pattern is identical to the blockchain story: success comes from specific problems with clear value, not from grand visions that outrun organizational capability.

The frontier technology assessment was clear: few good business use cases exist for IoT in most enterprises. Adoption is based on trust, and trust comes from other people's successes. When nobody in your industry has successfully deployed IoT at scale, and when the most prominent company that tried spent billions and failed, the rational response is not to rush in. It is to wait for the technology to mature, the use cases to crystallize, and the implementation ecosystem to develop the expertise to deliver. That is not what the machine recommends, because waiting does not generate consulting revenue. But it is what the evidence supports.

The Metaverse: The Emperor's Virtual Clothes

If blockchain was a solution looking for a problem and IoT was a vision that outran its execution, the metaverse was something even more fundamental: a concept that the enterprise did not need.

Meta's significant investment in metaverse technologies has yet to generate substantial revenue, and user adoption of VR platforms remains limited. The company's experience highlights the challenges of investing in emerging technologies before markets are ready for widespread adoption.

Between 2021 and 2023, a remarkable number of organizations announced metaverse strategies. Virtual offices. Digital twins of retail stores. Immersive training environments. Corporate events held in virtual reality. The consulting firms built metaverse practices overnight. The vendor community issued press releases. And then, almost as quickly as it appeared, the enthusiasm evaporated. The user adoption was not there. The technology was clunky. The use cases were solutions in search of problems that nobody had.

The early adoption of virtual and augmented reality technologies by retailers and training organizations produced mixed results. While some found valuable applications in product visualization and employee training, many struggled to justify the significant investments required. The technology's limitations -- user adoption challenges, technical complexity, and high implementation costs -- led to numerous failed initiatives.

The metaverse is the clearest example in recent memory of the industry's capacity to create urgency around a technology that has no urgency. No customer was demanding a virtual office. No supply chain was going to collapse without a digital twin in VR. No competitive advantage hinged on whether your sales conference was held in a physical ballroom or a virtual one. The metaverse was pushed by vendors and consultants because it was novel, because it generated media attention, and because it created a new category of spending. The organizations that invested in it are now quietly decommissioning their metaverse pilots and hoping nobody asks about the ROI.

Robotic Process Automation: Automating the Wrong Things

RPA deserves its own mention in the graveyard because it represents a particularly instructive variant of the pattern: a technology that works as advertised but is deployed against the wrong problems.

RPA automates repetitive, rules-based tasks by mimicking human interactions with software interfaces. It can log into systems, copy data between fields, process forms, and execute simple workflows. For specific, well-defined tasks, RPA is genuinely useful. It can save time, reduce errors, and free people from tedious work.

The problem is what happened when the industry got hold of it. RPA was sold not as a tool for automating specific tasks but as a platform for "digital transformation." Organizations were told they could automate their way to efficiency without changing their underlying processes. Just point the robots at the manual work and watch the costs drop.

RPA implementations frequently fail when organizations underestimate the complexity of their existing processes or lack adequate governance frameworks. A major insurance company's attempt to automate claims processing resulted in significant customer service problems when the RPA system began processing claims that should have required human review.

RPA applied to a broken process automates a broken process. This is the same lesson from the AI chapter, and it is the same lesson from the ERP chapter, and it is the same lesson that the industry refuses to learn: technology cannot compensate for organizational dysfunction. If your claims processing requires human judgment to handle exceptions, automating it without building the exception-handling logic will produce exactly the disaster that the insurance company experienced. The technology did what it was told. It was told to do the wrong thing.

The RPA graveyard is littered with bots that were built to automate workarounds rather than eliminate them. Organizations that used RPA to copy data between systems that should have been integrated. Organizations that used RPA to reformat reports that should have been redesigned. Organizations that used RPA to fill gaps in their ERP system that should have been addressed through configuration. In each case, the RPA was technically successful and strategically pointless, because it preserved the dysfunction rather than resolving it.

The $5 Billion Tombstone: US Air Force ECSS

No discussion of the emerging tech graveyard would be complete without the single largest technology failure in the history of the United States government, and arguably the most expensive ERP failure ever documented.

The US Air Force began its Oracle ERP implementation in 2005 with the goal of replacing hundreds of legacy systems with a single, unified platform. What started as a straightforward implementation gradually expanded into a multi-system, multi-vendor effort that consumed eight years and over $5 billion before being canceled in 2012.

Five billion dollars. Eight years. Canceled. The system never delivered meaningful capability.

A US Senate subcommittee led by the late Senator John McCain performed a postmortem analysis of the root causes of failure. The outcome was a 44-page report. Two of the most powerful words in the Senate's report were its reference to the "organizational disaster" that resulted in the failure.

The Senate report is devastating not because it reveals technical flaws but because it reveals the same organizational failures that this book has described across every chapter. The project management and leadership team failed to properly identify and mitigate risks. They did not accurately estimate the amount of time, money, and resources required. Although the intent was to implement a single ERP system, the team ultimately veered off track to pursue multiple systems.

Another of the biggest flaws was that the team pursued a high degree of customization of the Oracle software, which escalated costs and risks. The willingness to customize -- even where the team perhaps did not need to -- was likely a symptom of the fact that there was so much resistance to change. The customization paradox from Chapter 13, playing out at billion-dollar scale.

Many within the Air Force viewed the organization as "too big to change." Key stakeholders and employees strongly resisted changes to future business processes and the capabilities of the Oracle technology. The organization's cultural problems and resistance to change culminated in an overall refusal to change and improve its business processes.

Even after eight years, the team still did not have an understanding of the complete inventory of systems and processes that they were trying to replace. This is comparable to planning a car trip to another city without knowing what city you are in.

There was no clear executive sponsor, and the organization's leaders delegated most major project decisions to the project team without providing adequate strategic direction. The leadership vacuum from Chapter 3.

The military's hierarchical structure and "can-do" attitude created an environment where project managers were reluctant to report problems or request assistance. Project status reporting was systematically biased toward positive outcomes, preventing senior leadership from making informed decisions about project continuation or cancellation.

The Air Force ECSS failure is not an emerging technology story in the narrow sense. Oracle's ERP was not emerging technology in 2005. But it is the ultimate illustration of the lesson that connects every entry in the graveyard: technology sophistication cannot compensate for organizational dysfunction. The most powerful software in the world, backed by billions in funding and the resources of the United States military, could not overcome a culture that refused to change, leadership that refused to lead, and an organization that could not honestly assess its own readiness.

The technology was not too complex. The organization was not ready. And nobody with the authority to stop the program was willing to say so. Five billion dollars later, a Senate subcommittee said it for them.

The Consultant Gold Rush

Every entry in the graveyard has one thing in common beyond the technology itself: a consulting gold rush that preceded the failure.

When blockchain emerged, every major consulting firm built a blockchain practice. When IoT peaked, every system integrator added IoT capabilities to its service offering. When the metaverse was briefly fashionable, consulting firms hired VR specialists and launched "metaverse strategy" engagements. When RPA took off, boutique firms popped up overnight, and the large SIs added RPA to their proposals alongside the ERP implementations they were already selling.

Not since Y2K has the industry faced such a synchronized spike in demand for implementations within the same timeframe. This will strain qualified resource availability. Of the ones that are available, many consultants will not have the appropriate experience with these newer products.

The gold rush dynamic is simple and damaging. A new technology creates demand. Demand creates revenue opportunity. Consulting firms, whose business model depends on staffing consultants on billable engagements, rush to build capability in the new technology. But building genuine expertise takes years. The demand is now. So the firms rebrand existing consultants, provide a week of training, and deploy them to client sites as "blockchain experts" or "IoT specialists" or "AI strategists." The client is paying premium rates for expertise that does not yet exist.

This is how the machine processes emerging technology. The same dynamics that produce the bait-and-switch in ERP implementations -- selling the A-team and delivering the B-team -- apply with even greater force to emerging technology, because the pool of genuine experts is even smaller and the gap between marketing and capability is even wider. The client is buying confidence and receiving improvisation. And because the technology is new and the client lacks the knowledge to evaluate quality, the improvisation is difficult to detect until the pilot fails and the consultant moves on to the next engagement.

Frontier technologies are seen as the wild west. Not nearly as ubiquitous in companies as the media might have you believe. Even where you might think advanced frontier technologies are in use, the likelihood is... not yet. The gap between the media narrative and the enterprise reality is the space where the gold rush operates. The consultants are selling the media narrative. The client is living the enterprise reality. And the two rarely meet.

The Lesson the Industry Cannot Learn

Every entry in the graveyard teaches the same lesson, and it is the same lesson that has appeared in every chapter of this book:

People, process, then technology. Always in that order. Never the reverse.

With new technologies such as artificial intelligence, robotics, machine learning, predictive analytics, blockchain, cloud computing, and other buzzwords filling the conversation, the focus often falls too much on technology and too little on people and processes. The difference between an ERP implementation and digital transformation is the holistic, full-scope essence that comes with evolving as an organization. Everything from effective organizational change management plans, business process management, and other people and process aspects of a project are much more important than the technology. Your project can succeed with subpar technology, but it cannot succeed without strong business processes and people enablement.

Read that last sentence one more time. Your project can succeed with subpar technology. It cannot succeed without strong business processes and people enablement. This is not an opinion. It is a finding from the data across more than a thousand implementations. The technology is the least important variable. The people and the processes are the most important variables. And yet the industry -- the vendors, the consultants, the analysts, the conference keynotes, the media -- spends 90 percent of its energy on the technology and 10 percent on the people and processes.

The graveyard is full of organizations that got the sequence backwards. They bought the technology before they understood their processes. They deployed the platform before they prepared their people. They launched the pilot before they assessed their readiness. They did these things because the machine told them to, because the vendor had a quota to meet, because the consultant had a practice to staff, because the analyst said they were falling behind, because the board read an article and demanded action.

These products are on one hand introducing artificial intelligence and blockchain to customers, but on the other hand struggling to stabilize basic functionality such as manufacturing and warehouse management. The vendors are selling the future before the present works. The consultants are staffing the future before they can deliver the present. And the organizations are buying the future because the present is boring, and boring does not get funded by a board that just read about AI in the Wall Street Journal.

The lesson is not that emerging technology is bad. Blockchain has legitimate use cases. IoT has legitimate use cases. AI has extraordinary potential. Even the metaverse may eventually find its place. The lesson is that technology deployed without organizational readiness -- without clean data, clear processes, capable people, committed leadership, and robust governance -- will fail regardless of how sophisticated it is. The sophistication of the technology is irrelevant if the organization cannot absorb it.

This is the lesson the industry cannot learn, because learning it would require the machine to slow down. The machine does not slow down. The machine sells the next technology, hires the next wave of consultants, publishes the next analyst report, and processes the next wave of organizations through the same cycle of promise, pilot, plateau, and abandonment. The graveyard grows. The machine moves on.

In Part III, we will turn to the operators of the machine: the system integrators and consulting firms that are hired to guide your transformation and whose business model, as we will see, is fundamentally misaligned with your success. If Part I was about the fuel, and Part II has been about the engine, Part III is about the people at the controls. And what they are doing at those controls should concern you deeply.

Chapter 16

The Buyer's Revolt

The first five chapters of Part II have described the engine of the machine: how the cloud business model reshaped the industry's economics, how the vendor playbook exploits information asymmetry, how integration and data migration are chronically underestimated, how the customization paradox has no clean resolution, how AI is being sold before the prerequisites exist, and how the graveyard of emerging technology keeps growing because the industry cannot learn its own lessons.

This chapter is about the counter-movement. It is about the growing number of organizations that are refusing to be processed by the machine on the machine's terms. They are pushing back on forced migrations. They are demanding data portability and exit rights. They are rejecting monolithic platform bundles in favor of composable architectures. They are deploying third-party tools on top of legacy systems instead of migrating to cloud products that offer less functionality at higher cost. They are, in ways large and small, beginning to revolt.

Whether this revolt will change the market is an open question. The machine is powerful, well-funded, and deeply entrenched. But the signals of buyer resistance are real, and they are growing louder. Understanding them is important, because they point toward a different way of navigating the technology landscape -- one that puts the buyer's interests, not the vendor's, at the center of every decision.

The Refusal

The most visible signal of the buyer's revolt is the growing number of organizations that are simply refusing to migrate.

Forty percent of SAP customers have not yet started their journey to S/4HANA. Despite years of strong-arm tactics and incentives -- the RISE program, the discontinuation of maintenance and support in 2030 -- despite all these tactics, 40 percent of customers still have not even started the migration.

That is not a statistic about laziness or ignorance. That is a statistic about rational economic behavior. These organizations have done the math. They have looked at the cost of migration, the risk of disruption, the functional gaps in the cloud product, and the dubious business case, and they have concluded that the migration does not make sense. Not yet. Maybe not ever.

If S/4HANA public cloud was such a great product, you would see a lot more companies moving to it en masse. If it had such a strong business case, you would see people moving to it en masse. The fact that they are not tells you everything you need to know about the gap between the vendor's marketing and the customer's reality.

Kingfisher, the global retailer with thousands of locations, is the most public example. As I discussed in Chapter 10, Kingfisher refused to migrate to S/4HANA because the cost was estimated at twenty times what they were currently spending. Instead, they deployed third-party AI tools on top of their existing ECC system, using the data they already had and the technology they had already paid for. They presented their strategy at a Gartner conference, openly and unapologetically. They rejected the premise that innovation requires a platform migration. They chose to innovate on their terms, not the vendor's.

Kingfisher is not alone. Across our client base and across the market, I am seeing a pattern: organizations that have been told they must migrate are asking why. They are asking for the business case. They are discovering that the business case does not exist. And they are choosing a different path.

This whole forced migration is causing SAP to lose a lot of goodwill in the industry. So much so that a lot of legacy customers are actually questioning their decision to be on SAP and are secondguessing that decision and evaluating other options.

When your best customers start evaluating your competitors, the forced migration strategy is not working. It is backfiring. And the backfire is the first phase of the revolt.

The Demand for Rights

The second signal of the revolt is the changing language in procurement. Buyers are no longer accepting vendor contracts at face value. They are demanding specific protections that did not appear in enterprise software contracts five years ago.

Buyers are pushing back on forced migrations, proprietary extension models, and take-it-all platform bundles. RFPs increasingly demand data portability, exit rights, transparent pricing, open standards, and proof of interoperability with competitors.

Let me unpack what each of these demands means, because they represent a fundamental shift in the power dynamic between buyer and vendor.

Data portability means the right to extract your data from the vendor's platform in a usable format, at any time, without penalty. In the on-premise world, your data was in your data center. You owned it. You controlled it. In the cloud world, your data lives on the vendor's infrastructure, in the vendor's format, behind the vendor's APIs. Getting your data out -- in a format that another system can consume -- is often difficult, slow, and sometimes impossible without the vendor's cooperation. Data portability clauses require the vendor to make your data accessible and extractable, on your timeline, in standard formats.

Exit rights mean the contractual ability to leave the platform without prohibitive financial penalties. Cloud subscription agreements often include multi-year terms, auto-renewal clauses, and steep early termination fees that make leaving economically irrational even when the product is not delivering value. Exit rights give the buyer a contractual off-ramp: defined terms under which the agreement can be terminated, with reasonable notice periods and without punitive financial consequences.

Transparent pricing means visibility into how the subscription fee is calculated, what it includes, what it excludes, how it will change at renewal, and what consumption-based charges will apply for AI, analytics, and other variable-cost services. The opacity of enterprise software pricing has been a source of buyer frustration for decades. Cloud pricing, with its layers of subscription fees, consumption charges, and bundled modules, has made the problem worse, not better. Transparent pricing demands that the vendor disclose the full cost structure, including renewal escalation formulas, before the contract is signed.

Open standards mean the use of non-proprietary data formats, APIs, and integration protocols that allow the buyer's systems to communicate with any vendor's platform, not just the incumbent's. Proprietary extension models -- like SAP's BTP or Salesforce's Force.com -- create additional lock-in by requiring customers to build on the vendor's proprietary tools. Open standards demand that the vendor support interoperability with competitor products, reducing the switching cost and preserving the buyer's architectural flexibility.

Proof of interoperability means requiring the vendor to demonstrate, during the sales cycle, that their product can connect to and exchange data with the buyer's existing landscape of systems, including systems from competing vendors. This is the practical test of open standards: not whether the vendor claims to support them, but whether they can prove it.

When you are entering into a subscription-based contract with a cloud vendor, try to incorporate clauses that outline termination and what it would look like if your organization chose to go a different direction. How can you get out of the contract? This is basic procurement discipline, but it is discipline that many organizations failed to exercise during the initial wave of cloud migrations, when the urgency to move and the vendor's sales pressure created an environment where contract terms were accepted rather than negotiated.

The buyers who are demanding these rights are the vanguard of the revolt. They are saying, in contractual language: we are willing to be your customer, but we are not willing to be your hostage.

There is a specific contractual mechanism in cloud agreements that deserves particular attention: the upgrade control clause. In many cloud contracts, the vendor dictates when upgrades happen and which software versions the customer is required to run. The customer has no choice. The upgrade is pushed to their environment on the vendor's schedule, whether the customer is ready or not. This is a form of control that did not exist in the on-premise world, where the customer decided when to apply patches and when to upgrade. In the cloud, that decision has been transferred to the vendor -- and with it, the customer's ability to manage the pace of change within their own organization. Buyers should insist on contractual provisions that give them advance notice of mandatory upgrades, the ability to defer upgrades within a defined window, and testing environments that allow them to validate compatibility before the upgrade is applied to production.

The Composable Alternative

The most architecturally significant expression of the buyer's revolt is the emergence of composable ERP as a genuine alternative to the monolithic suite.

For nearly forty years, organizations relied on monolithic ERP platforms -- massive, tightly integrated systems designed to centralize every business function under one roof. While these systems delivered consistency and control, they also created rigidity. Implementations often spanned years, upgrades disrupted operations, and customization meant heavy dependence on vendors. Now, that model is being replaced by composable ERP.

Instead of multi-year, big-bang migrations to a monolithic suite, organizations assemble capabilities module by module, connected by clean APIs and shared data products. Finance might modernize first, followed by supply chain planning, then manufacturing execution -- each on the best-fit platform, each governed by a common integration and identity model. This approach lowers switching costs, reduces program risk, and allows innovation to move at the speed of the business rather than the pace of a single vendor's roadmap.

The composable model is not a rejection of ERP. It is a redefinition of it. ERP remains essential, but it is no longer the singular gravitational center of the enterprise stack. Rather than forcing every process into one suite, organizations are decomposing the stack: ERP handles standardized records and controls, while surrounding platforms deliver agility, analytics, and differentiated experience.

This shift reflects a fundamental change in mindset. Where once ERP dictated process design, now process design dictates ERP configuration. The technology serves the business, not the other way around. That is a sentence I have written in some form in every chapter of this book, and it is a sentence that the composable model, for the first time, makes architecturally possible at enterprise scale.

In Chapter 12, I described the composable paradox: more components mean more integration points. That remains true. Composable architecture is not simpler than monolithic architecture. In many ways it is more complex. But it is a different kind of complexity -- one that the buyer controls rather than the vendor. In a monolithic model, the vendor controls the upgrade cycle, the extension model, the integration framework, and the data architecture. In a composable model, the buyer controls all of those things. The complexity is real, but the agency is the buyer's.

That agency is what the revolt is about.

LeasePlan's story is a real-world proof point for the composable alternative. After investing €92 million in an SAP implementation that was ultimately declared unfit for purpose, the company did not attempt another monolithic deployment. It moved to a best-of-breed approach, assembling capabilities from multiple vendors rather than betting everything on a single platform. The decision was born from pain, not theory. But it illustrates that the composable path is not just an architectural aspiration -- it is a survival strategy for organizations that have been burned by the monolithic model.

The Dual-Track Strategy

Not every organization can abandon its existing ERP vendor tomorrow. The switching costs are high, the organizational disruption would be significant, and the available alternatives may not yet be mature enough to replace every capability the monolithic system provides. The revolt is not, for most organizations, a sudden departure. It is a gradual repositioning.

Many organizations are adopting dual-track strategies: extracting value from current suites while introducing independent data, AI, and workflow layers to preserve optionality.

The dual-track strategy works like this. On one track, the organization continues to run its existing ERP system -- whether that is SAP ECC, Oracle EBS, or an older version of any other platform -- and invests in maintaining and optimizing it. Third-party support providers like Rimini Street offer maintenance at a fraction of the vendor's price, extending the useful life of the legacy system without paying the vendor's premium for support on a product the vendor would prefer you to abandon.

On the second track, the organization begins building independent capabilities outside the ERP. A modern data platform -- Snowflake, Databricks, or a custom Azure or AWS environment -- that aggregates data from across the enterprise and serves as the foundation for AI, analytics, and decision intelligence. Independent workflow tools that handle the processes where the ERP falls short. Best-of-breed applications for CRM, planning, HCM, or other functions where the monolithic suite's offering is not competitive.

The dual-track strategy preserves optionality. The organization is not locked into the vendor's migration timeline. It is not forced to adopt a cloud product that is less mature than the on-premise product it replaces. It is not paying twice -- maintenance on the old system and subscription on the new system -- for the privilege of being a beta tester.

Instead, it is making incremental investments in capabilities that deliver value today while reducing dependency on the monolithic vendor over time.

Kingfisher's approach is a version of the dual-track strategy. They kept ECC running, deployed third-party AI on top of it, and refused the migration. The Japanese manufacturer I described in Chapter 14 is another version: they kept their existing ERP and built a custom AI platform on Azure rather than activating the vendor's embedded AI. In both cases, the organization chose to invest in independence rather than deepen dependency.

The reflex to put everything into multi-tenant SaaS is replaced by a pragmatic hybrid model. Commodity processes move to SaaS to gain speed and evergreen upgrades; differentiating capabilities may remain on-prem or private cloud for latency, control, or sovereignty.

This is the cloud-smart approach, and it is the opposite of the vendor's message. The vendor says: move everything to our cloud, on our timeline, using our tools. The cloud-smart buyer says: I will move what makes sense, when it makes sense, on my timeline, using the tools that serve my interests. The difference between those two approaches is the difference between being a customer and being a captive.

The Consulting Model Shift

The buyer's revolt extends beyond technology decisions to the consulting relationships that support them.

Organizations favor independent consultancies and flexible talent networks that blend process, data, AI, cybersecurity, architecture, and change skills across multiple technologies. Delivery models become modular and outcome-based: short, cross-functional sprints with shared KPIs rather than long, monolithic SI engagements.

For decades, the default consulting model was the large system integrator: Deloitte, Accenture, Capgemini, Infosys, or one of their peers. These firms brought scale, brand credibility, and deep vendor partnerships. They also brought the conflicts of interest described in Part III of this book: incentives misaligned with client success, vendor dependencies that biased their recommendations, and a business model that profited from duration and complexity.

The revolt is changing this. Buyers are increasingly seeking independence over scale. They want advisors who do not partner with the vendor, who do not earn commissions on software deals, and whose only incentive is the client's success. They want delivery models that are outcome-based rather than time-and-materials, where the consultant shares the risk rather than passing it entirely to the client. They want flexible teams assembled for specific needs, not hundreds of consultants deployed on a multi-year engagement whose primary purpose is to generate billable hours.

This market shift gives buyers more leverage, more objectivity, and better knowledge transfer. It also gives them something the monolithic SI model never provided: a relationship where the consultant's success is measured by the client's outcomes, not by the consultant's revenue.

This shift is not complete. The large SIs still dominate the market by revenue. But the trend line is clear. The organizations that are leading the revolt are choosing advisory models that reflect the same principles they are applying to their technology decisions: independence, flexibility, and alignment of incentives.

The Regulatory Tailwind

The buyer's revolt is receiving an unexpected ally: regulators.

As I described in Chapter 10, the European Union is investigating SAP for potential and alleged antitrust behavior. SAP has made it extremely difficult for customers to use third-party options for maintenance. The investigation is focused on whether SAP's practices -- including punitive terms for customers who switch to third-party maintenance providers and barriers that prevent competitor software from integrating with SAP systems -- constitute an abuse of market dominance.

Whether the EU investigation results in meaningful enforcement remains to be seen. But the investigation itself has created a new dynamic: the vendor's lock-in tactics are now on the public record, subject to regulatory scrutiny, and available as leverage in contract negotiations. A buyer who can point to an active antitrust investigation when negotiating data portability clauses or exit rights has a different kind of leverage than a buyer who is negotiating in a vacuum.

The European Union's AI Act, the Digital Markets Act, and emerging data sovereignty regulations are all creating a regulatory environment that favors the buyer. Data portability is moving from a nice-to-have in contract negotiations to a legal requirement in some jurisdictions. Interoperability is being mandated for dominant platforms. The vendor lock-in strategies that the market has tolerated for decades are beginning to encounter legal constraints that the market alone did not provide.

The regulatory tailwind does not solve the buyer's problem. Regulations are slow, enforcement is uncertain, and the vendors have armies of lawyers who specialize in navigating regulatory frameworks without changing fundamental business practices. But the direction is clear: the era of unconstrained vendor lock-in is ending. The question is how quickly, and the answer depends in part on how aggressively buyers exercise the rights that regulators are beginning to protect.

Will the Revolt Succeed?

The honest answer is: partially.

The buyer's revolt will not dismantle the machine. The economic forces that drive the machine -- investor demand for recurring revenue, executive compensation tied to cloud conversion, sales incentives that prioritize subscription deals, ecosystem alignment between vendors, consultants, and analysts -- are too powerful and too deeply entrenched to be overturned by buyer resistance alone.

But the revolt will change the terms. It already has. Five years ago, no buyer demanded data portability in an ERP contract. Today, sophisticated buyers demand it as standard. Five years ago, composable ERP was a theoretical concept. Today, organizations are building composable architectures in production. Five years ago, refusing a forced migration was considered reckless. Today, Kingfisher presents its refusal at Gartner conferences to applause.

There is one dimension of the cloud transition whose full consequences have not yet been felt, and it should add urgency to the revolt: cloud-to-cloud switching costs. The current wave of cloud migrations has been going on for roughly ten years. In another ten years, the organizations that migrated first will begin to outgrow their systems, discover that the vendor's roadmap has diverged from their needs, or face the same obsolescence pressures that drove them from on-premise to cloud in the first place. When that happens, they will discover that switching from one cloud platform to another is more painful, more risky, and more costly than the on-premise-to-cloud migration they just completed. The data is deeper. The AI models are trained. The integrations are more tightly coupled. The contractual barriers are higher. We have not even begun to see this pain yet, but it is on the horizon. The organizations that are making architectural decisions today -- choosing composable over monolithic, building independent data layers, preserving optionality through dual-track strategies -- are the ones that will be best positioned when the cloud-to-cloud switching wave arrives. The organizations that went all-in on a single vendor's cloud, with maximum lock-in and minimum independence, will discover that the marriage they entered has no exit clause they can afford to exercise.

The market will not correct itself through the revolt alone. But informed buyers, armed with contractual protections, architectural alternatives, independent advisory support, and a clear-eyed understanding of how the machine works, can navigate the market on their own terms. They can choose which parts of the cloud to adopt and which to defer. They can build independent data and AI capabilities that preserve competitive advantage. They can negotiate contracts that protect their rights and their data. They can select consulting partners whose incentives align with their outcomes.

I have never seen this level of distrust, frustration, and anger towards enterprise technology providers as I am seeing right now. That distrust is the fuel of the revolt. Whether it translates into sustained market change depends on whether buyers maintain their resolve when the vendor offers a discount, when the SI promises it will be different this time, and when the board asks why the company has not migrated yet.

I think about companies like Commodore 64, Blackberry, Blockbuster Video, and someday I just have this feeling that SAP is going to be on that list. That may be too bold a prediction for this book. Or it may be exactly right. What is certain is that the vendors that treat their customers as revenue streams to be optimized rather than partners to be served are building a debt of their own -- not technical debt, but trust debt. And trust debt, once accumulated, compounds just as relentlessly as the technical kind.

The buyer's revolt is not a revolution. It is an evolution. It is the slow, difficult process of informed buyers reclaiming agency over their own technology decisions. The machine will resist. The vendors will adapt their tactics. The consultants will rebrand their services. But the underlying shift -- from vendor-dictated architecture to customer-owned architecture, from monolithic lock-in to composable flexibility, from information asymmetry to informed decision-making -- is underway. And for the organizations that lead it, the rewards are significant: lower costs, less dependency, more flexibility, and a technology landscape that serves the business rather than the machine.

This concludes Part II: The Technology. We have examined the engine of the machine from every angle -- the economics that power it, the playbook it uses, the technical challenges it underestimates, the customization paradox it ignores, the AI mirage it sells, the graveyard of technologies it leaves behind, and the revolt that is beginning to push back.

In Part III, we turn to the operators of the machine: the system integrators and consulting firms whose role is to guide your transformation and whose business model, as we will see, is designed to profit from your struggle. If the technology is the engine, the consultants are the people at the controls. Understanding how they operate -- and how their incentives diverge from yours -- is essential to surviving the machine.

Part III: THE CONSULTANT

Operators of the Machine

"The people you hire to guide you through the machine are often the ones feeding you into it."

Chapter 17

The Fox Guarding the Henhouse

We have now reached the third and final gear of the machine.

Part I examined the client: the organization that feeds itself into the machine through leadership vacuums, cultural dysfunction, process rigidity, and the failure to prepare for the magnitude of change that digital transformation demands. Part II examined the technology: the cloud economics that drive the machine's behavior, the vendor playbook that exploits information asymmetry, the integration and customization challenges that are chronically underestimated, and the AI mirage that the industry is selling before the prerequisites exist.

Part III is about the operators of the machine. The system integrators and consulting firms that are hired to guide your transformation. The people who are supposed to be on your side.

They are not.

That is a provocative statement, and I want to be clear about what I mean by it. I am not saying that every consultant is dishonest, that every system integrator is incompetent, or that every advisory relationship is exploitative. There are excellent consultants and capable firms doing genuinely valuable work. I have had the privilege of working alongside some of them. But the business model within which the vast majority of system integrators operate is structurally, fundamentally, and irreparably misaligned with the interests of the client. The individuals may be well-intentioned. The system they operate within is not.

This chapter is about that system. It is about the conflict of interest that sits at the heart of the system integrator model -- a conflict so pervasive that the industry has normalized it, so deeply embedded that most clients do not even recognize it, and so profitable that no one inside the machine has any incentive to change it.

The systems integrator should not be the one to self-assess how things are going and where the risks lie. This is akin to the fox guarding the henhouse.

The Business Model

Start with how system integrators make money, because everything else flows from this.

The big system integrators have hundreds of thousands of consultants that they need to keep staffed. Deloitte has over 400,000 employees. Accenture has over 700,000. These are not boutique firms that deploy small, specialized teams. They are staffing machines. Their revenue is a function of how many consultants are billing hours, at what rate, on how many projects. The economics are simple: more bodies, more hours, more revenue.

This creates the first conflict. They probably "need" to staff 100 or 200 on your project to make it worth their while. Not because your project requires 100 or 200 consultants. Because their business model requires 100 or 200 consultants to generate the revenue that justifies the engagement for their practice leadership. The staffing level is determined not by your project's needs but by the firm's financial requirements.

The time-and-materials contract structure compounds the conflict. Under T&M, the SI bills for every hour worked. If the project takes longer, the SI bills more. If the project encounters problems that require additional resources, the SI bills more. If the timeline slips, the budget expands, and the scope creeps -- all of which happen in the vast majority of implementations -- the SI's revenue increases.

Read that again. When your project struggles, the SI profits.

The longer the program continues, the more money the supplier makes. This is the perverse incentive at the core of the T&M model. The SI has no financial incentive to deliver your project on time or under budget. In fact, they have a financial disincentive. An on-time, on-budget delivery means the engagement ends sooner, revenue stops earlier, and consultants need to be redeployed to the next project. A project that runs over, that encounters "unforeseen" complexity, that requires additional phases, additional resources, additional change orders -- that project is a gift that keeps giving.

ERP system integrators do not have an incentive to be realistic about their estimated implementation duration and cost. This could explain why most implementations take more time and money than expected.

The Vendor Partnership

The second layer of conflict is the SI's relationship with the software vendor.

Your ERP systems integrator should not be involved in your ERP software selection. They are aligned with one or more of the ERP vendors, and their recommendation will be biased depending on which arm of the firm you are working with.

The large system integrators are not independent technology advisors. They are vendor partners. Deloitte has an SAP practice and an Oracle practice and a Microsoft practice and a Workday practice. Each practice generates revenue by implementing that vendor's products. Each practice has revenue targets that depend on a pipeline of implementations. When you ask Deloitte to help you select software, the answer you receive is shaped not by what is best for your business but by which practice within Deloitte has the capacity to staff the implementation.

I know this because I lived it. As I described in Chapter 1, one of the first projects I worked on at PricewaterhouseCoopers was an ERP evaluation where a client paid nearly $1.5 million for what they believed was an independent assessment. The answer was SAP from day one. The Denver office had a large SAP practice, and the job was to feed it business. Every software selection I participated in at that firm ended the same way.

The vendor partnership creates a specific economic incentive that goes beyond software selection. Many system integrators earn commissions on the software deals they help close. They receive referral fees from the vendor for steering clients toward the vendor's products. They earn a cut of subscription revenue over time. The concept of being "Accentured" or "Deloitted" stems from these firms embedding themselves in multiple channels across your company and aligning assessments and budgets in their favor.

In some cases, the consulting firm makes more money from the vendor than from the client. When a system integrator earns recurring commissions on cloud subscriptions over the life of the customer's contract, their economic relationship with the vendor can be more lucrative than their relationship with the client they are supposed to be advising. The client thinks they hired a consultant. They actually hired a sales channel.

Billing the Client to Bill the Client More

There is a behavior pattern within the large consulting firms that I witnessed firsthand early in my career and that has been confirmed by every subsequent engagement I have had with organizations that employ them. It is the practice of billing clients for time spent on internal firm activities that serve the firm's interests, not the client's.

At PricewaterhouseCoopers, I spent significant time in client conference rooms with only consultants present, strategizing about how to increase the firm's footprint at the client. How to get five or ten more people on the project. How to neutralize the one person who was calling us out on our performance. How to keep competing firms out of the picture. The client was billed for all of it.

The consulting firm was literally charging the client for the time spent figuring out how to charge the client more.

This is not an isolated practice confined to one firm or one era. It is a structural feature of the business model. The large consulting firms deploy account management resources -- account executives, partner-level relationship managers -- whose explicit purpose is to protect and expand the firm's revenue at each client. This individual's only focus is to keep the client happy, wine and dine, keep them from talking to any other consultants and, most importantly, to distract them from any issues or risks on the project.

The distraction function is particularly corrosive.

As a large system integrator takes over more and more aspects of a project, they are better able to push, delay, or simply hide potential project risks. This is with the intention of preventing disruption to their "cash cow," which can be countless consultants working a project. Any risk of slowing or reducing the run-rate hits the Partners directly.

The project is not just a consulting engagement. It is a revenue stream. And the people managing the relationship are managing the revenue stream, not the project. The client experiences this as attentive account management. The firm experiences it as revenue protection. The two are not the same thing, and the gap between them is where client value is lost.

There is another dimension of this dynamic that I witnessed firsthand: the positive-spin machine. At the large consulting firms, significant time is spent not on solving the client's problems but on figuring out how to present bad news in a way that preserves the engagement. I sat in meetings -- hours-long meetings -- where the sole agenda was crafting a narrative that would make a struggling project look acceptable to the steering committee. The focus was not on fixing what was broken. It was on messaging what was broken in a way that the client would accept without reducing the headcount or questioning the SI's performance. The client was billed for this time. They paid for the hours the SI spent managing the client's perception of the project rather than managing the project itself.

Locking Out the Independent Voice

Of all the tactics in the SI playbook, the most damaging to the client's interests is the systematic effort to eliminate independent oversight.

An independent quality assurance advisor, a third-party project manager, or a client-side consultant whose job is to hold the SI accountable is a direct threat to the SI's revenue model. The independent advisor sees things the SI does not want the client to see. They ask questions the SI does not want answered. They provide the client with the context and the expertise to challenge the SI's decisions, timelines, staffing levels, and change orders.

The SI knows this. And they act accordingly.

They will offer "free" services to keep other consultants out. I have experienced this personally. Early in my independent consulting career, I spent a full day meeting with a services company that had engaged a major SI for an SAP implementation. We discussed the scope of independent advisory work, the value of third-party oversight, and how our engagement would protect the client's interests throughout the implementation. The meeting went well. Two days later, I received a call letting me know that the SI had offered the "same" work as part of their implementation at no additional charge.

Does anyone not see the conflict of interest here? The SI is offering to provide quality assurance oversight on its own implementation. The party being evaluated is offering to evaluate itself. And the "free" price tag makes it impossible for the client to justify hiring an independent advisor, because how do you explain to your CFO that you are paying for something that another firm will do for free?

The "free" is not free. It is a subsidy from the SI's implementation revenue, invested specifically to prevent independent scrutiny of that implementation. The SI is spending money to avoid accountability. And the client, attracted by the apparent savings, loses the one resource that would have been genuinely on their side.

At least one of these firms has shared directly with me that they have specialized training as part of their management program on how to deflect advisory firms that attempt to offer additional services to their clients. This is not incidental. It is institutional. The effort to lock out independent voices is trained, practiced, and integrated into the firm's management development curriculum. Protecting the account is protecting the revenue. And nothing threatens the revenue like an independent advisor who can see the project clearly.

The territorial behavior is striking in its parallels. The large SIs protect client accounts the way crime families protect territory. They do not "play nice with others" -- those are the industry's own words, not mine. They offer services below cost to lock out the competition. They train their people to neutralize outsiders who threaten the revenue stream. They station dedicated account managers whose explicit purpose is to keep the client from talking to anyone else. The language of the industry itself -- "Accentured," "Deloitted," the concept of being captured by a firm -- carries the connotation of something less than voluntary. This is not collaboration. This is territorial control. And the client who does not recognize it is the client who ends up owned.

Accenture or Deloitte cannot provide quality assurance on their own activities. They will tell you they can, but make absolute certain this is being managed internally or by an independent consulting firm. Otherwise, the fox will be guarding the henhouse.

When the Fox Raids the Henhouse: Queensland Health

If you want to understand how far the conflict of interest can go, study the Queensland Health payroll disaster. It is one of the most thoroughly documented cases of SI misconduct in the history of the industry, and the details are as damning as they are instructive.

What began as a $6.19 million payroll system replacement project with IBM ultimately cost taxpayers AU$1.25 billion. A billion and a quarter Australian dollars. For a payroll system. Serving healthcare workers -- doctors and nurses who, in many cases, were either incorrectly paid or not paid at all.

The system went live with over 2,000 known defects, including 14 showstoppers. Over 35,000 payroll errors affecting healthcare workers. Over 80,000 workers across 24,000 different combinations of wage payments and withholdings. The complexity was significant, but it was known complexity. The payroll requirements of the Queensland Health system were not a mystery. They were documented. The problem was not that the requirements were unknown. The problem was how IBM obtained the engagement in the first place.

The official inquiry found that IBM had acted improperly and corruptly in forming and submitting its tender to the government. Key IBM staff had been provided confidential information by government executives relating to the available budget, and the company used its pre-existing system access from other projects to retrieve internal government documents related to the tender.

Additionally, IBM staff improperly accessed the proposals of its competitors. The inquiry concluded that had the government been aware of these failures, IBM would have been automatically excluded from the procurement process.

Let me make sure the severity of this registers. IBM, one of the most storied names in technology, obtained a government contract by accessing confidential budget information and reading its competitors' proposals. The tender process -- the mechanism designed to ensure fair competition and protect taxpayer interests -- was corrupted from the inside. The SI did not just fail to deliver. It cheated to win the right to fail.

And then, having won the contract through corrupt means, IBM delivered a system that was catastrophically defective. Healthcare workers went unpaid. Strikes followed. Staff departed. The operational disruption to a public health system -- the system responsible for caring for the sick and injured -- was immense and prolonged. The remediation cost taxpayers over a billion dollars, more than two hundred times the original budget.

Queensland Health is an extreme case. But the dynamic it illustrates -- an SI that prioritizes winning the deal over delivering value, that uses information asymmetry to its advantage, and that faces minimal consequences when the project fails -- is not extreme. It is the business model, operating at maximum dysfunction.

The Accountability Void

One of the most striking features of the SI model is the near-total absence of financial consequences for failure.

When a project runs over budget, the SI does not absorb the overrun. The client does, through change orders, extended timelines, and additional staffing. When a project fails to deliver the promised benefits, the SI does not refund its fees. The statement of work was for services rendered, not outcomes delivered. When a project is so catastrophically dysfunctional that it ends in litigation, the SI's exposure is typically limited to a fraction of the fees paid, because the contract's liability cap -- negotiated by the SI's lawyers, who do this for a living -- protects the firm from the full consequences of its failure.

The result is an accountability void: the SI profits from successful projects and suffers minimal consequences from unsuccessful ones. The economic asymmetry is remarkable. The client bears essentially all of the downside risk. The SI captures a disproportionate share of the upside revenue. This is not an accident of contract negotiation. It is the intended design of the standard SI engagement model.

In my work as an expert witness analyzing over fifty implementations embroiled in litigation, I have seen this pattern repeatedly. The SI's contract includes limitations of liability that cap the firm's financial exposure at a fraction of the total engagement value. The consequential damages -- the operational disruption, the lost revenue, the organizational damage, the cost of remediation -- are excluded from the SI's liability. The client sues to recover damages. The SI's lawyers point to the contract. The settlement, if there is one, represents a fraction of the actual cost of the failure.

The SI walks away. The client absorbs the loss. And the firm's next proposal to its next prospect says nothing about the failure, because there is no mechanism in the market to force that disclosure.

The OCM Conflict

There is one specific manifestation of the SI conflict that deserves separate attention, because it affects the single most important workstream in any digital transformation: organizational change management.

It is simply a bad idea to hire your SI to perform change management. Even if you are working with a large system integrator such as Deloitte, Accenture, or Capgemini, and even if they allege to have a "change team," you do not want to give this level of control to one organization. Getting the system up and running quickly and getting users acclimated can be a conflict of interest.

The conflict is specific and measurable. The SI's primary incentive is to get the system configured and go-live achieved. Change management, when done properly, slows the project down. It requires time for organizational readiness assessments. It requires workshops that pull key resources away from configuration activities. It requires honest communication about the impact of the change, which may raise concerns that create resistance, which may delay timelines. Every element of effective change management conflicts with the SI's desire to maintain velocity toward go-live.

When the SI owns both the implementation and the change management, the implementation always wins. Testing gets compressed, but so does training. Communication plans are created but not executed with rigor. Organizational readiness assessments are conducted but their findings are downplayed to avoid delaying the timeline. The change management workstream becomes a checkbox rather than a genuine effort to prepare the organization.

The organizations that separate implementation from change management -- that hire an independent firm to manage the human side of the transformation while the SI manages the technical side -- consistently outperform those that consolidate everything under one provider. The independent change management team has no incentive to protect the SI's timeline. Their incentive is to ensure the organization is ready, even if readiness requires slowing down. That tension between the SI's desire for speed and the change team's insistence on readiness is productive. It is the check and balance that the foxes-and-henhouse model eliminates.

What the Industry Thinks About Its Own

When we published our analysis of system integrator conflicts, we received more than a hundred responses from industry professionals. Not a single person came to the defense of the large system integrators. Not one. From a pool of current and former consultants, client executives, project managers, and industry analysts, the response was unanimous: the model is broken, and everyone inside it knows it.

The quotes were devastating in their consistency:

"When a vendor 'owns' everything, you gain nothing but risk and the costs associated with that risk."

"The problem is not just confined to the really big firms. There is a constant information disparity. The client never quite knows who to trust."

"At firms like Deloitte, you really cannot even get a straight answer internally -- ask 10 managers the same question, get 10 different answers."

"Most Big ones in the IT/Business consulting field come from an Accounting/Audit background, even Accenture -- Arthur Andersen. Remember Enron?"

The Enron reference is telling, and it deserves more than a passing mention, because the history it invokes is directly relevant to the consulting industry's present.

In 2001, the collapse of Enron exposed one of the most destructive conflicts of interest in modern business history. Arthur Andersen, one of the Big Five accounting firms, had been simultaneously auditing Enron's financial statements and providing lucrative consulting services to the same company. The consulting revenue created an economic incentive to preserve the audit relationship, which created an incentive to overlook the accounting irregularities that would have ended it. The result was catastrophic: investors lost billions, employees lost their retirement savings, and Arthur Andersen -- a firm that had existed for nearly ninety years -- was destroyed.

The regulatory response was swift and unambiguous. The Sarbanes-Oxley Act of 2002 imposed strict separation between audit and consulting services. The message was clear: the conflict of interest between auditing a company and consulting for the same company was too dangerous to tolerate. The same firm could not objectively evaluate an organization's financial health while simultaneously profiting from advisory engagements that depended on the relationship continuing. Independence was not optional. It was mandated by law.

Two decades later, the technology consulting industry operates with conflicts of interest that are structurally identical to the ones that destroyed Arthur Andersen -- and it operates without any equivalent regulation. The same firm that implements your ERP system evaluates its own work. The same firm that partners with a software vendor recommends that vendor's product. The same firm that profits from project duration estimates how long your project will take. The same firm that benefits from your dependency promises to transfer knowledge. Every one of these conflicts mirrors the audit-consulting conflict that Sarbanes-Oxley was designed to eliminate -- and every one of them is perfectly legal in the technology consulting industry.

The industry has not learned from the Enron era. It has drifted back toward the same conflicts that created the crisis in the first place. The Big Four firms -- the direct descendants and successors of the firms that were forced to separate audit and consulting -- have rebuilt massive consulting practices that now generate more revenue than their audit practices. The separation that Sarbanes-Oxley imposed was structural but narrow: it applied to audit-consulting conflicts, not to technology-consulting conflicts. The result is that the same firms that cannot audit and consult for the same client can implement and evaluate their own technology work for that client. The ethical principle that demanded separation in one context is ignored in another, because the technology consulting industry has never faced its own Enron moment -- at least not yet.

The foxes are not just guarding the henhouse. They designed it. And because no regulator has told them they cannot, they continue to operate the henhouse exactly as they please.

Why Clients Do Not See It

The natural question is: if the conflict is this obvious, why do clients tolerate it?

The answer is information asymmetry. The client does not know what they do not know. Most organizations undertake a major digital transformation once every ten to fifteen years. The executives making the decisions have never done this before. They do not understand how the SI's business model works. They do not know that the staffing level is determined by the firm's revenue targets rather than the project's needs. They do not know that the "free" OCM offering is a tactic to eliminate oversight. They do not know that the vendor recommendation was predetermined by the firm's partnership structure. They do not know that the timeline was compressed to win the deal, not because it was realistic.

The SI knows all of this. The SI has done this hundreds of times. The SI has entire departments dedicated to business development, proposal strategy, and account management. The client has a project sponsor who is trying to do their day job while simultaneously overseeing the most complex initiative their organization has ever undertaken.

The asymmetry is overwhelming. And the machine exploits it at every turn.

This is why independent advisory exists. Not because clients are incapable of managing their own transformations. But because the information gap between the client and the SI is so vast that without someone in the room who understands the SI's playbook, the client is negotiating blindfolded against a counterparty that can see everything.

The fox guarding the henhouse is not a metaphor. It is the operating model of a trillion-dollar industry. And the first step to protecting yourself is understanding that the animal in the room is not a sheepdog.

In the next chapter, we will examine one of the most damaging tactics in the SI's arsenal: the bait-and-switch between the team that wins your business and the team that delivers your implementation. The A-team that sold you is not the team you will get. Understanding why -- and what to do about it -- is essential to surviving Part III of the machine.

Chapter 18

The Bait and Switch

In the previous chapter, I described the structural conflicts of interest that define the system integrator business model: the T&M incentives that reward duration over delivery, the vendor partnerships that predetermine recommendations, the revenue protection tactics that lock out independent oversight. Those are the systemic issues. This chapter is about how those issues manifest in the most immediate, most visible, and most personally frustrating way: the people who show up to do the work.

The bait and switch is the oldest trick in the consulting playbook, and it is so pervasive that it has become an industry punchline. The team that wins your business is not the team that delivers your implementation. The brilliant partner who presented in the boardroom will appear at your steering committee once a quarter, if that. The seasoned project manager who answered every question during the proposal will be replaced by someone who has never managed a project of this complexity. The functional experts who impressed your team during discovery will be rotated off within months, replaced by consultants who are learning your system on your dime.

Many times, you will be promised the A-team and left with the D-team when it comes time for implementation.

This is not an exception. It is the standard operating procedure. And understanding why it happens, and what you can do about it, is essential to surviving the machine.

Two Organizations Wearing the Same Logo

The first thing you need to understand about a large system integrator is that the sales organization and the delivery organization are, for all practical purposes, two different companies. They share a brand name, a website, and a business card template. They do not share people, incentives, or, in many cases, knowledge.

The sales team's job is to win the deal. They are compensated on deal size, win rate, and revenue booked. They deploy the firm's most polished, most experienced, most impressive professionals for the proposal, the orals presentation, and the executive workshops that precede the contract. These people are skilled presenters who know the right things to say, the right concerns to address, and the right level of confidence to project. They have done this hundreds of times. They are very, very good at winning business.

The delivery team's job is to implement what the sales team promised. They are compensated on utilization -- the percentage of their available hours that are billed to a client. They are staffed from a resource pool that is managed by practice leadership, whose primary concern is ensuring that every consultant is deployed and generating revenue. The delivery team did not write the proposal. They may not have seen the proposal. They are handed a statement of work, a timeline, and a budget that were crafted to win the deal, and they are told to make it work.

The gap between what was sold and what can be delivered is the space where the bait and switch operates. The sales team made commitments about timeline, scope, staffing, and capability that the delivery team must now honor with different people, different skill levels, and frequently different assumptions about what is actually possible.

The Staffing Pyramid

The economics of SI staffing follow a pyramid structure that is as old as the consulting industry itself. At the top are the partners, who sell the work and maintain the client relationship. Below them are the managers, who oversee workstreams and manage the day-today engagement. Below the managers are the senior consultants, who bring functional or technical expertise. And at the bottom, forming the widest layer of the pyramid, are the junior consultants -- the analysts, the associates, the people who were hired out of school six months ago and have never configured an ERP system in a production environment.

The pyramid exists because it is profitable. A partner bills at $500 to $700 per hour. A junior consultant bills at $150 to $250 per hour. The firm's cost for the junior consultant is far less than the billing rate. The margin on junior resources is higher than the margin on senior resources. The more junior bodies the firm can deploy on your project, the more profitable the engagement becomes.

This is why the staffing plan that accompanies the proposal always looks different from the staffing that actually shows up. The proposal features named senior resources with impressive resumes. The delivery features a rotating cast of junior consultants whose resumes you never reviewed and whose names you did not see in the proposal. The senior resources appear for the first few weeks -- long enough to establish credibility and create a perception of quality -- and then quietly transition to other engagements where they are needed to win the next deal. The junior resources remain.

The big system integrators are notorious for employing kids right out of school and charging their clients to train them. They are also notorious for outsourcing a majority of work to people with limited skillsets.

I know this because I was one of those kids. As I described in Chapter 1, my first consulting engagement at PricewaterhouseCoopers put me on a Fortune 500 project at twenty-four years old with no practical experience. The team scaled from twenty or thirty consultants to forty or fifty. I was adding maybe five to ten hours of real value per week, yet I was expected to bill fifty to sixty. I remember the creeping dread of impostor syndrome, the feeling that at some point the client was going to find me out.

They never did. The client had no idea what each of us was doing. The team had grown like an amoeba, absorbing more bodies at every opportunity, and the client simply did not have the visibility or the expertise to question it.

I was not a bad consultant. I was a junior consultant on a learning curve, being billed at a fully loaded rate to a client who believed they were getting experienced professionals. The firm knew I was not experienced. The client did not. And nobody told them, because telling them would have reduced the headcount, reduced the revenue, and violated the fundamental logic of the staffing pyramid.

The Bench Pressure

The bait and switch is not always deliberate. In many cases, it is a structural consequence of how large consulting firms manage their workforce.

Consulting firms carry a "bench" -- consultants who are between engagements and not generating revenue. The bench is expensive. Every consultant on the bench is a cost without a corresponding revenue stream. Practice leaders are measured, in part, on the size of their bench: a large bench means poor resource management and wasted capacity. The pressure to minimize the bench is intense and constant.

When a new project is sold, practice leadership looks at two things: what the project needs and who is available. In a perfect world, these align. In reality, they rarely do. The project needs a senior supply chain consultant with ten years of SAP experience. The bench has a mid-level consultant with three years of Oracle experience and a junior consultant who just finished training. The senior supply chain consultant is available but is being held for a larger deal that might close next month.

Guess who gets staffed on your project?

The bench pressure means that the team you receive is often determined not by your project's requirements but by who happens to be available at the time your project starts. The SI will never tell you this. They will present the staffing plan as though it was carefully designed for your specific needs. In reality, it was assembled from whoever was on the bench, supplemented by whoever could be pulled from other engagements, and backfilled with junior resources whose primary qualification is that they are not yet assigned to anything else.

I have seen this play out in ways that would be comical if they were not so expensive. At one mid-market manufacturer, the SI proposed over one hundred consultants for an implementation that, based on our independent assessment, required twenty to thirty. The proposal was not designed for the client's project. It was designed for the SI's bench. Every available body in the practice area was assigned to the project, regardless of whether the project needed them, because the alternative was leaving them unbilled.

The "Up or Out" Culture

The internal culture of the large consulting firms compounds the staffing problem in ways that the client never sees.

Success at Big Four firms is measured by deal size, utilization rates, and vendor commissions -- never by whether the client's implementation actually succeeded. There was no discussion of client outcomes. The metrics were purely internal: how much did we bill, how big was the project, how much commission did we earn from SAP.

The "up or out" model that defines career progression at these firms creates a specific dynamic: consultants advance by selling and staffing, not by delivering. A consultant who closes a $30 million deal is promoted. A consultant who delivers a $10 million project on time, under budget, with measurable client satisfaction is... adequate. The incentive structure rewards revenue generation over delivery excellence, which means the firm's best people are pulled toward sales and away from the work.

The people who remain on delivery are either genuinely passionate about the work -- and there are many such people, and they are valuable -- or they are the ones who could not advance on the sales track and have settled into a delivery role by default. The client does not know which type they are getting. The firm does not distinguish between the two in its staffing plan. And the client's assumption that the people on the project are the firm's best delivery professionals is, in many cases, an assumption that the firm's internal incentive structure has made unlikely.

The Offshore Illusion

The bait and switch has a global dimension that has become more pronounced over the past decade: offshoring.

"Their primary value proposition is cheap offshore staff and replacing people with automation." This quote, from one of the hundred-plus industry professionals who responded to our SI analysis, captures a dynamic that has reshaped the consulting industry's economics.

The large SIs have built massive offshore delivery centers -- in India, the Philippines, Eastern Europe, Latin America -- where consultants work at a fraction of the cost of their onshore counterparts. The economics are compelling for the firm: bill the client at onshore rates, deliver the work through offshore resources at offshore costs, and pocket the margin differential. Some of this savings is passed to the client through blended rates that are lower than fully onshore staffing. Much of it is retained by the firm as profit.

The quality implications are significant and varied. Offshore teams can be highly capable, particularly for technical work like coding, data migration, and integration development.

The challenge arises when offshore resources are deployed for work that requires deep understanding of the client's business context, industry-specific expertise, and the ability to facilitate real-time decision-making with business users who are in a different time zone and a different cultural context.

The bait and switch in the offshore model works like this. The proposal features a blended team with senior onshore resources handling the client-facing work and offshore resources handling the technical execution. In practice, the senior onshore resources are thinner than promised, the offshore team takes on more client-facing work than was planned, and the communication challenges -- time zone differences, language barriers, and the difficulty of building trust through a video screen -- create friction that slows the project and frustrates the client.

The client signed up for a team that would work alongside them in their conference rooms, understanding their business, building relationships with their people. What they got is a resource plan where half the work happens twelve time zones away, managed by an onshore coordinator who may or may not have the authority or the context to ensure the offshore team's output meets the client's needs.

But the quality concern, while real, is not the primary reason the offshore model persists. The primary reason is economics. Offshore resources are, for the large system integrator, the equivalent of junior consultants on a global scale: low cost, high margin. A consultant in Bangalore or Manila costs the firm a fraction of what a consultant in Chicago or London costs. The billing rate to the client, while discounted from onshore rates, still carries a margin that is often higher in percentage terms than the margin on senior onshore resources. Offshore delivery is not a staffing strategy. It is a profit strategy. The SI is not offshoring to save you money. They are offshoring to make more money. Whatever discount you receive on the blended rate is a fraction of the margin the firm captures on the cost differential.

This is the same pyramid economics operating at global scale. Just as the domestic staffing pyramid puts junior consultants at the base because their margin is highest, the global staffing model puts offshore resources at the base for the same reason. The client sees a blended rate that looks competitive. The firm sees a margin structure that is more profitable than a fully onshore team. And the quality trade-off -- the communication friction, the context gaps, the time zone challenges -- is the client's problem, not the firm's.

The Competency Gap

Beyond the staffing mechanics, there is a deeper problem with the quality of what large SIs deliver, and it goes to the nature of the skills that digital transformation requires.

One of the most common themes we heard from people is that the big system integrators have significant knowledge gaps that harm their clients' chances of ERP success.

The large SIs excel at technical configuration. They can configure SAP modules, build Oracle integrations, and customize Dynamics 365 workflows. These are the tangible, billable activities that form the core of their delivery model. What they consistently struggle with -- and what the staffing pyramid is not designed to provide -- are the intangible skills that determine whether the transformation succeeds or fails: organizational change management, strategic program governance, business process redesign, data governance, stakeholder alignment, and the ability to navigate the political dynamics of a large organization undergoing significant change.

They are often described as "hiring functional 'experts' with no program management abilities, and that is why they are weak in business needs like readiness, data migration, and similar areas."

The competency gap is structural. The skills that the SI's staffing model produces -- technical configuration, system testing, report building -- are necessary but insufficient. The skills that determine success -- navigating resistance, building organizational readiness, designing governance structures, facilitating difficult conversations between executives who disagree -- are not taught in the SI's training programs, not measured in the SI's performance reviews, and not valued in the SI's career progression model. The SI is a machine for producing technical consultants. Digital transformation requires something far broader.

This is why so many implementations are technically sound but organizationally disastrous. The system is configured correctly. The integrations work. The data is migrated. But the people are not ready, the processes have not been redesigned, the governance is weak, and the leadership has not been engaged. The SI delivered what the SI knows how to deliver: technology. What the organization needed was transformation. Those are different things, and the gap between them is the competency gap.

The methodology gap is as important as the skill gap. Technology vendors and system integrators typically have well-documented, branded methodologies for deploying software -- Activate for SAP, Oracle Unified Method, Microsoft Sure Step, and their successors. These methodologies cover the technical workstream competently. What they consistently lack are methodologies for the workstreams that determine success: business process improvement, organizational change management, organizational redesign, solution architecture, and enterprise integration strategy. The SI arrives with a playbook for configuring software. They do not arrive with a playbook for transforming the organization. And because their methodology does not include these workstreams, their staffing model does not include the talent to deliver them. The competency gap is not an accident. It is the predictable consequence of a methodology that was designed to deploy technology, not to transform businesses.

The AI Irony

There is one final dimension of the staffing and billing model that deserves attention, because it exposes the most glaring hypocrisy in the consulting industry today.

Artificial intelligence should be dramatically reducing the number of billable hours required for an enterprise implementation. AI-powered code generation can accelerate development. AI-assisted testing can compress testing cycles. AI-driven data migration tools can automate the most tedious and error-prone aspects of data cleansing and transformation. AI-enabled project management can surface risks earlier and optimize resource allocation. The technology exists today to reduce the labor intensity of an ERP implementation by 20, 30, perhaps 40 percent or more.

It is not happening.

The reason is simple: reducing billable hours runs directly counter to the economic interests of the system integrators. The SI's revenue is a function of hours billed. Any technology that reduces the number of hours required to deliver an implementation reduces the SI's revenue proportionally. AI applied to the SI's own delivery model is not an innovation. It is a threat. It threatens the staffing pyramid. It threatens the offshore profit margins. It threatens the bench utilization metrics. It threatens the entire economic architecture that makes large system integrators the most profitable services firms in the world.

And so the large SIs have adopted a remarkable posture: they sell AI to their clients while resisting AI in their own operations. They stand on conference stages and tell you that AI will transform your supply chain, your finance function, your manufacturing operations, your customer service. They build AI practices, hire AI specialists, and embed AI into their proposals. And then they staff your project with the same number of consultants they would have staffed five years ago, billing the same number of hours, at the same rates, as though AI did not exist.

The irony is breathtaking. The same firms that are allegedly helping the world's largest corporations streamline their businesses with AI are the same firms resisting AI's ability to streamline their own businesses. They are selling efficiency to you while protecting inefficiency in themselves. They are telling you to embrace automation while ensuring that their own labor-intensive delivery model remains untouched.

Some firms are beginning to use AI internally for code generation and testing automation. But the productivity gains are not being passed to the client in the form of lower fees or shorter timelines. They are being captured by the firm in the form of higher margins. The consultant who used to take forty hours to write a module now takes twenty, but the client is still billed for forty. The AI has made the consultant more productive. The client has not benefited. The firm has.

This dynamic will eventually change, because the market will eventually force it to. Independent firms and smaller consultancies that embrace AI-driven delivery will be able to offer comparable quality at lower cost and shorter timelines, creating competitive pressure that the large SIs cannot ignore indefinitely. But for now, the large firms have the market power, the client relationships, and the brand credibility to maintain the status quo. And the status quo is: AI for thee, but not for me.

I say this not as a theoretical observation but as someone who is building the alternative. At Third Stage Consulting, we developed an AI platform called Mission Control that does exactly what the large SIs refuse to do: it uses AI to reduce the cost and improve the quality of implementation delivery. Mission Control draws on the collective knowledge of over a thousand implementation project teams we have worked with over the past eight years. It automates documentation, risk identification, and quality assurance activities that would otherwise require hundreds of hours of senior consultant time. The result is not just lower cost for the client. It is higher quality -- more detailed documentation, more consistent methodology, more thorough risk coverage than any individual consultant, no matter how experienced, could produce manually.

Mission Control has changed how I operate as a CEO and as an advisor. I lead a firm with over one hundred active client engagements each year. Two years ago, maintaining meaningful visibility into each of those projects was impossible. I could review status reports, attend steering committees, and rely on my team's judgment. But the depth of insight I could bring to any single engagement was constrained by the same limitation that constrains every human: time. Mission Control gives me insights into each of our projects -- patterns, risks, anomalies, cross-project trends -- in ways that I never could have imagined just two years ago. It allows me to scale my knowledge and my approach across every engagement, so that every client benefits from the cumulative experience of every project we have ever done. That is what AI is supposed to do: amplify expertise, not replace it. The large SIs could do this too. They choose not to, because doing so would undermine the billable hour model that funds their existence.

Taking Back Control: The Internal Staffing Imperative

AI-driven delivery is one antidote to the SI overstaffing and overbilling problem. But the more fundamental one is shifting the balance of power on the project itself by building internal capability.

One of the most effective countermeasures to SI overreach is deceptively simple: hire more of your own people to run the project. Not to replace the SI entirely -- there is legitimate value in specialized implementation expertise -- but to ensure that the client's organization has enough internal resources, managed by internal leadership, to oversee the SI rather than be overrun by it. When the PMO is staffed by the SI, the SI is managing itself. When the PMO is staffed internally, the client has a team whose sole purpose is to represent the client's interests: challenging timelines, questioning staffing levels, validating deliverables, and holding the SI accountable for what they promised.

This is why Third Stage created a staffing arm alongside our advisory practice. We help clients recruit and deploy internal project resources -- program managers, change management leads, business analysts, data migration specialists -- who report to the client, not to the SI. These resources are embedded within the client's organization, managed by the client's leadership, and aligned with the client's outcomes. They are the client's eyes and ears on the project. They provide the institutional knowledge that persists after the SI leaves. And they fundamentally change the power dynamic on the project, because the client is no longer dependent on the SI to tell them how things are going.

By ensuring the PMO is established internally and managed by someone who represents the client's best interests -- not the SI's revenue targets, not the vendor's migration timeline -- the client has effectively reprogrammed the machine. The playing field tilts in favor of the organization that is paying for the transformation and living with the consequences. This is not a radical idea. It is how every other major business initiative is managed: by the people who own the outcome. The fact that digital transformation has been an exception to this principle, with the SI running the project on behalf of the client, is one of the most consequential structural failures in the industry. Fixing it starts with putting the client's people in charge of the client's project.

The Workday Warning

The bait-and-switch dynamic is not limited to the Big Four. It extends to every tier of the consulting ecosystem, and in some cases, smaller firms are more dangerous because they have fewer resources to cover the gaps.

In one Workday implementation I analyzed as an expert witness, the system integrator stopped work with the project only 56 percent complete. The client had paid over $800,000 in consulting fees. The SI's team was under-resourced in critical functional areas -- grants, projects, general ledger, and engagement management were all understaffed. Configuration changes were made on the fly with no documentation. The financial lead billed 160 hours in a single month with no recorded activity. Four different engagement managers were cycled through the project, each inheriting the dysfunction of their predecessor without the context to address it. End-to-end testing was zero percent complete when the relationship collapsed.

Four engagement managers. Each rotation represents a loss of institutional knowledge, a reset in the client relationship, and a period of ramp-up where the new manager is learning the project rather than leading it. By the fourth rotation, the client had lost all confidence in the SI's ability to deliver. The project was abandoned at the halfway mark, and the client estimated it would cost an additional $300,000 to hire a new partner and rebuild what had been done incorrectly.

This case illustrates a variant of the bait and switch that is particularly common among mid-tier firms: the SI wins the deal by committing to a team they cannot sustain. The named resources leave -- poached by other projects, promoted out of delivery, or simply burned out -- and the SI backfills with whoever is available. The client signed a contract for specific expertise. They received a revolving door.

What the Client Can Do

The bait and switch is difficult to prevent entirely, but it is not impossible to mitigate. Here is what informed buyers do.

Contractualize the team. Name the key resources in the contract. Specify the roles, the individuals, and the minimum tenure. Include a clause that requires the SI to notify you and obtain your approval before any named resource is removed from the project. If the SI will not agree to this, they are telling you something important about their intentions.

Conduct independent resume reviews. Do not accept the SI's assertion that their team is qualified. Review the resumes yourself. Better yet, have an independent advisor review them. Look for specific experience with your industry, your vendor platform, and the functional areas that are most critical to your implementation. A resume that lists "ERP experience" without specifying which platform, which modules, and which client environments is a resume that is hiding something.

Establish a governance model for resource acceptance. Make sure you have leverage on the resources that are brought in, that you have a governance model on resource qualification and acceptance. This means the right to interview consultants before they are deployed to your project, the right to request replacements for consultants who are not performing, and a defined process for escalating resource quality concerns to the SI's practice leadership.

Separate evaluation from delivery. Ask the vendor to include a solution architect and professional services or delivery team resource in the demonstration if possible. This will keep the sales team honest. If the delivery team is in the room during the sales cycle, the promises become more modest and the expectations become more realistic. If the sales team refuses to include delivery resources, the gap between what is being sold and what will be delivered is wider than they want you to see.

Insist on knowledge transfer from day one. Do not wait until the SI is leaving to discover that all the institutional knowledge walks out the door with them. Require documentation standards, knowledge transfer milestones, and the active involvement of your internal team throughout the implementation. If the SI resists knowledge transfer -- and many will, because your dependency is their future revenue -- treat that resistance as a red flag.

Engage independent oversight. The single most effective countermeasure to the bait and switch is having someone in the room who understands the SI's playbook, who can evaluate the quality of the resources being deployed, and who has the authority to challenge staffing decisions that serve the SI's interests rather than yours. This is not a luxury. It is a prerequisite for any organization engaging a large system integrator.

Be cognizant that promises are empty until confirmed in a contract. Whatever the SI commits to in the sales process is what they will be obligated to fulfill. If they will not put it in writing, it is not a commitment. It is a sales pitch. And the distance between a sales pitch and a delivery plan is the distance between the A-team and the D-team.

An Honest Staffing Model

I want to close this chapter by describing what an honest staffing model looks like, because the contrast with the standard SI approach is instructive.

An honest staffing model starts with the project's needs, not the firm's bench. It identifies the specific roles, skills, and experience levels required for each phase of the implementation, and it staffs to those requirements. If the project needs twelve consultants, it proposes twelve, not fifty. If the project needs a senior supply chain architect, it commits that person by name and guarantees their availability for the duration of the engagement.

An honest staffing model is transparent about who is junior and who is senior. It does not hide junior resources behind ambiguous titles or blended rates that obscure the actual experience level. It tells the client: this person is a year out of school, they are learning, and their billing rate reflects that. The client can make an informed decision about whether to accept that resource rather than discovering three months in that the "functional consultant" who has been configuring their financials module has never done a month-end close.

An honest staffing model includes knowledge transfer as a core deliverable, not an afterthought. It plans for the client's internal team to shadow the consultants, to participate in configuration decisions, and to build the capability to operate the system independently after the SI leaves. The goal is to make the SI unnecessary, not indispensable.

An honest staffing model measures success by client outcomes, not by utilization rates. It tracks whether the implementation is delivering value, whether the timeline is realistic, whether the team is right-sized, and whether the client is building the internal capability to sustain the transformation. These are the metrics that matter. They are also the metrics that the standard SI model does not track, because tracking them would reveal truths that the model would prefer to hide.

The honest staffing model is rare in the industry. It is rare because it is less profitable for the firm. Fewer bodies, lower revenue. Transparent pricing, lower margins. Knowledge transfer, reduced future dependency. Every element of an honest model runs counter to the economic incentives of the standard SI model. Which is precisely why the standard model persists and the honest model remains the exception.

In the next chapter, we will examine the timeline lie: why every system integrator proposes an eighteen-month implementation regardless of the actual complexity of the project, and what happens when reality collides with the fiction that was sold.

Chapter 19

The 18-Month Lie

There is a number that appears in nearly every system integrator proposal I have ever reviewed, regardless of the client's size, complexity, industry, or readiness. It appears in proposals for $500 million global manufacturers and $50 million regional distributors. It appears in proposals for organizations with a single ERP instance and organizations with seventeen. It appears for greenfield implementations and for migrations from legacy systems that have been running for thirty years.

The number is eighteen months.

More often than not, SIs provide an overly optimistic plan -- it looks like eighteen months regardless of how big or how complex the implementation is.

Eighteen months has become the universal timeline for enterprise software implementation proposals. It is a fiction so pervasive that it has achieved the status of convention. Nobody inside the industry believes it. The SI's delivery team does not believe it. The experienced project managers do not believe it. The vendor's own implementation methodology does not support it. And yet it appears, again and again, in the proposals that land on the desks of executives who have never done this before and who have no basis for questioning whether the number is real.

This chapter is about why eighteen months is a lie, why the lie persists, and what happens when reality catches up.

The Lowball Strategy

The eighteen-month timeline is not an estimate. It is a sales tactic.

The logic is straightforward. In a competitive bid, the SI that proposes the shortest timeline and the lowest cost has a significant advantage. The client's executive team, which is under pressure from the board to transform quickly and affordably, gravitates toward the proposal that promises the least disruption and the smallest investment. The SI that says "eighteen months and $15 million" wins over the SI that says "thirty months and $30 million," even if the second estimate is far more realistic.

ERP system integrators do not have an incentive to be realistic about their estimated implementation duration and cost. This could explain why most implementations take more time and money than expected.

The lowball strategy works because of confirmation bias. The executives evaluating the proposals want the shorter timeline to be true. They want to believe that their transformation can be completed in eighteen months because they have already told the board it will be. The budget has been approved for a certain amount. The organizational patience for disruption has a shelf life. The eighteen-month proposal tells them what they want to hear, and the human tendency to accept information that confirms existing beliefs does the rest.

The SI knows the timeline is unrealistic. Not every individual at the firm knows, but the partners and the senior delivery leads who have done this hundreds of times know. They know that an eighteen-month timeline for a complex, multi-module, multi-site ERP implementation is not achievable without compressing activities that should not be compressed: business process design, organizational change management, testing, data migration, training. They know that the compression will produce defects, delays, and change orders. And they know that the change orders are where the real money is.

This is the lowball strategy in its purest form: win the deal with an unrealistically low number, then manage the inevitable cost increases through change orders once the client is committed and cannot easily switch providers. The initial contract is the foot in the door. The change orders are the revenue model.

The pressure is even more intense in private equity-backed organizations. PE firms operate on hold periods -- typically three to seven years -- during which they must improve the portfolio company's operations and exit at a profit. Every month of implementation is a month without the efficiency gains that the PE firm's investment thesis depends on. The PE partner sitting on the board does not want to hear that the transformation will take thirty months. They want to hear eighteen, because eighteen fits within the financial model. The SI, sensing the pressure, delivers the number the PE partner wants. The organization, caught between an SI that is lowballing and a board that is demanding speed, accepts a timeline that nobody in the room believes -- because the alternative is a confrontation with the people who own the company.

There is a variant of the eighteen-month lie that deserves specific attention because it takes the optimism to an extreme that borders on irresponsible: the accelerated methodology.

Vendors like NetSuite market implementation programs -- such as SuiteSuccess -- that promise go-live in as little as 90 days. Ninety days. Three months from contract signing to a live production system. The pitch is compelling, particularly for mid-market and smaller organizations that want speed, simplicity, and a quick return on investment. And to be fair, it is technically possible to deploy software in 90 days. You can configure modules, load data, flip the switch, and declare go-live within that timeframe.

But deploying software is not the same as implementing a transformation. A system that is live is not the same as a system that is used. A system that is used is not the same as a system that delivers value. The 90-day methodology gets you to go-live. It does not get you to adoption. It does not get you to process improvement.

It does not get you to organizational readiness. It does not get you to the business outcomes that justified the investment in the first place.

In 90 days, you cannot conduct a meaningful organizational readiness assessment. You cannot redesign business processes. You cannot build a change management program that prepares the workforce for a new way of working. You cannot cleanse decades of accumulated data quality problems. You cannot test integrations at production volume. You cannot train users deeply enough that they can operate the system without reverting to spreadsheets and workarounds on day two. You can do all of these things superficially. You can check the boxes. But checking the boxes and doing the work are different things, and the difference shows up the moment real transactions start flowing through the system and real employees start trying to do their jobs.

The accelerated methodology is the eighteen-month lie compressed to its logical extreme. It optimizes for the vendor's metric -- time to go-live -- at the expense of the client's metric -- time to value. The vendor can claim a successful deployment. The client is left with a system that is technically live but operationally hollow: configured but not adopted, deployed but not delivering, live but not working. Even for the smallest and simplest organizations, implementing technology that is actually used by employees and is delivering actual business value is nearly impossible to do in anywhere close to 90 days. The organizations that believe otherwise discover the gap between deployment and value the hard way -- in the weeks and months after go-live, when the stabilization effort consumes the budget that the 90-day timeline was supposed to save.

A Project Is Not a Program

There is a more fundamental reason why the eighteen-month timeline is always wrong, and it has nothing to do with the SI's honesty or lack thereof. It has to do with a structural mismatch between what the SI proposes and what the client actually needs.

When you hire a system integrator and a software vendor, they are really the project lead for a technical workstream. The project management is typically focused on deploying technology. But your transformation typically entails a lot of other work that is just as if not more important than the technical implementation.

The SI's proposal is a software project plan. It covers technical configuration, system design, unit testing, data migration, and go-live. These are the activities the SI knows how to do, the activities the SI can staff, and the activities the SI can estimate with some degree of confidence. The proposal reflects a technical project because the SI is a technical firm. The eighteen-month timeline is, in many cases, a defensible estimate for the technical work alone.

The best analogy I have found for this is building a house. When you build a house, you do not start by hiring the plumber and telling them to begin installing pipes. You start with an architect who creates a blueprint -- the vision of what the finished house will look like. You lay a foundation before you frame the walls. You hire a general contractor who manages the plumber, the electrician, the roofer, the flooring installer, and every other subcontractor, ensuring that their work is coordinated, sequenced, and aligned with the blueprint. The plumber is essential. But the plumber is not the general contractor. The plumber does not create the blueprint. The plumber does not manage the electrician. The plumber does one thing, and does it well, within a structure that someone else is responsible for governing.

Hiring a system integrator to run your digital transformation is like hiring the plumber to be your general contractor. They will do excellent plumbing. But they will not create the architectural blueprint for your business. They will not manage the change management team or the data migration team or the process redesign team. They will not ensure that the foundation is solid before they start building on top of it. They will do their piece -- the technical configuration -- and they will do it according to their timeline and their plan, without visibility into or accountability for all the other pieces that must come together for the house to stand.

And here is the part that should give every executive pause: when you build a house, there are building codes, inspections, and a general contractor who answers to you. When you build a digital transformation, there are none of these things. No building codes. No mandatory inspections. No general contractor who is contractually accountable for the whole structure. The SI is accountable for their workstream. Nobody is accountable for the house. Unless you create that accountability yourself.

But a digital transformation is not a technical project. It is a program -- a collection of interdependent workstreams that must be planned, staffed, funded, and governed as a coordinated whole. The technical implementation is one workstream. The others include:

Architecture, data, and integration. The overarching technical thread that ties together multiple technologies, defines how systems connect to one another, manages data migration and cleansing, and establishes the analytics and reporting foundation. This workstream touches the SI's technical project but is typically out of scope in their proposal.

Organizational change management. Everything related to the people side of the transformation: change readiness assessments, change impact analysis, organizational design, roles and responsibilities definition, stakeholder engagement, and sustained communication and reinforcement. The SI will tell you they do change management. What they mean is technical training -- teaching people which buttons to click. That is one subset of a comprehensive change management program, and it is the least important subset. The change impact work, the readiness assessment, the organizational design -- these are the activities that determine whether the organization can absorb the transformation, and they are almost never adequately scoped in the SI's proposal.

Business process re-engineering. The definition of current-state processes, the design of future-state processes, the gap analysis between the two, and the quantification of business value. Without clarity on what you want your processes to be, the technical configuration becomes aimless. Every decision about how to configure the system requires a business process decision, and if those decisions have not been made in advance, they get made reactively during configuration workshops -- slowly, contentiously, and expensively. This is one of the primary reasons technical projects run over: the business process work that should have preceded the configuration was never done, and now the configuration team is waiting for decisions that nobody anticipated needing to make.

Program management. The overarching governance function that ties all of these workstreams together: integrated project plans across all workstreams, project governance and controls, the business case as a decision-making framework, resourcing across workstreams, risk management, and the escalation mechanisms that ensure problems are surfaced and resolved before they become crises.

The things that are most likely to slow down a project and create disruption and cause a project to take longer than expected are organizational change management and business process re-engineering -- not the technical implementation. The SI's timeline does not account for these workstreams because the SI did not scope them. The client assumes the SI's proposal represents the full effort. It does not. It represents one workstream out of four or five, and it is typically not even the workstream that determines whether the transformation succeeds or fails.

This is the structural mismatch that makes the eighteen-month lie almost inevitable. Even if the SI were being perfectly honest about the technical timeline, the proposal would still be wrong, because the proposal describes a project and the client needs a program. The difference between eighteen months and thirty months is not padding. It is the work that the SI did not include because it is not work they do -- or not work they want to highlight, because highlighting it would make the proposal larger, more expensive, and harder to sell.

Perhaps most importantly, by having program management in place, you the implementing organization -- not the system integrator, not the software vendor -- now have control and ownership of the overall program. The program management office should be yours. It should be staffed by your people, managed by your leadership, and accountable for your outcomes. The SI reports to the PMO, not the other way around. When the client owns the program and the SI owns a workstream within it, the power dynamic shifts fundamentally. The SI is no longer running the show. They are delivering a defined scope of technical work within a program that the client controls. That is a very different engagement than the one the SI's proposal describes, and it is the engagement model that produces better outcomes.

The Change Order Cascade

Change orders are the mechanism through which the eighteen-month lie becomes a thirty-six-month reality. Understanding how they work is essential to understanding why every ERP implementation costs more than the proposal said it would.

A change order is a formal modification to the original statement of work. It can add scope, extend the timeline, increase the budget, or some combination of all three. Change orders are a legitimate part of project management -- requirements evolve, business conditions change, and some adjustments are genuinely necessary. But in the SI's business model, change orders serve a different function: they are the revenue recovery mechanism for the scope that was deliberately excluded from the original proposal to keep the price low.

Here is how the cascade works. The original proposal scopes the core ERP implementation: finance, supply chain, manufacturing, procurement. It includes configuration, unit testing, and basic data migration. It does not include, or includes only superficially, the activities that experience tells you will consume a substantial portion of the budget: comprehensive organizational change management, business process redesign, integration development for the forty systems that connect to the ERP, end-to-end testing with realistic data volumes, cutover planning and rehearsal, post-go-live stabilization support, and the hundreds of decisions that must be made during implementation but that nobody anticipated during the sales cycle.

Each of these excluded or underscoped activities surfaces during the implementation as a "discovery" -- a requirement that was not in the original scope but that is essential for the project to succeed. The SI presents each one as a change order.

The client, who is now six or twelve months into the project with millions already spent, has no practical alternative but to approve the change order, because stopping the project is more expensive than continuing, and the excluded activity is genuinely necessary.

One change order is manageable. Five are concerning. Fifteen are a pattern. And by the time the cascade is complete, the $15 million project is a $35 million project, the eighteen-month timeline is a thirty-month timeline, and the client is explaining to the board why the numbers have changed. The SI, meanwhile, has increased its revenue by 100 percent or more relative to the original proposal, and none of that increase comes with the competitive pressure that the original bid was subjected to. The change orders are negotiated bilaterally, without the benefit of alternative proposals, because by the time they surface, the switching cost of replacing the SI is prohibitive.

The average cost overrun for ERP implementations reaches 189 percent. One hundred and eighty-nine percent. If you budgeted $10 million, you spent $29 million. If you budgeted $50 million, you spent $145 million. This is not an anomaly. It is the average. And the primary mechanism that transforms a proposal into a bill that is nearly three times larger is the change order cascade, fueled by a lowball strategy that the industry has refined into an art form.

The Fixed-Price Illusion

Some organizations, having been burned by T&M overruns or having heard horror stories from peers, insist on fixed-price contracts. The logic seems sound: if the price is fixed, the SI bears the risk of overruns, and the client's budget is protected.

The logic is wrong.

A fixed-price contract in enterprise software implementation is not what it appears to be. The price is fixed, but the scope is not. Or more precisely, the price is fixed for the scope that is defined in the statement of work, and the statement of work is defined with sufficient ambiguity to give the SI an escape route for anything that was not explicitly included.

Here is the dynamic. The SI proposes a fixed price. To make the fixed price competitive, the scope must be narrowed. Activities that are expensive and unpredictable -- change management, data cleansing, integration testing, post-go-live support -- are either excluded from the fixed-price scope or included with limiting assumptions that are buried in the appendix. The client reads the headline number and feels protected. The SI's lawyers have drafted a contract that protects the firm.

When the excluded activities prove necessary -- as they always do -- the SI presents them as out-of-scope additions. The fixed-price contract does not cover them. They require a separate engagement, billed at T&M rates, with no competitive pressure. The client's "fixed-price" project now has two components: the fixed-price base, which covers the easy, predictable work, and a growing T&M extension that covers the hard, unpredictable work that the fixed price was supposed to protect against.

The total cost of the project is often higher than it would have been under a straightforward T&M arrangement, because the fixed-price structure incentivizes the SI to define the scope as narrowly as possible, which means more activities end up as out-of-scope additions. The client pays more, not less, for the illusion of cost certainty.

The truly honest contract structure -- one that aligns the SI's incentives with the client's outcomes -- would be an outcome-based engagement where the SI's compensation is tied to the successful delivery of defined business outcomes within an agreed timeline and budget. This model is almost nonexistent in the industry, because it requires the SI to share the risk rather than transfer it, and sharing risk is not the machine's preferred operating mode.

What the Data Actually Says

If eighteen months is the lie, what is the truth? The data from our research across more than a thousand implementations provides a clearer picture.

For mid-size companies with revenue between $50 million and $1 billion, most implementations require 14 to 16 months. For companies larger than $1 billion in revenue, this number increases to 31 to 34 months.

Let me unpack those numbers. The fourteen to sixteen-month range for mid-market companies is actually close to the eighteen-month proposal -- but only for the simplest implementations with the narrowest scope. A mid-market company implementing a single ERP module, in a single geography, with clean data, a strong internal team, and minimal integration complexity might achieve a fourteen-month timeline. That describes almost nobody. The moment you add a second module, a second site, a complex integration landscape, dirty data, or an organization that has never done this before, the timeline extends. Sixteen months becomes twenty. Twenty becomes twenty-four. And the eighteen-month proposal that assumed the simplest scenario encounters the complex reality of an actual enterprise.

For large companies, the gap between the proposal and reality is even wider. Thirty-one to thirty-four months is the average. The SI proposed eighteen. The actual duration is nearly double. And these are averages, which means that a significant number of implementations take even longer. I have worked with organizations where the implementation consumed four years, five years, and in extreme cases, was abandoned after seven years with nothing to show for the investment.

These figures are trending higher in the last two years, largely because the major vendors are concurrently releasing newer, less proven, and less mature flagship ERP products in the market. The cloud products that are replacing the on-premise systems are less functionally complete, which means more customization, more workarounds, and more time to achieve functional parity. The eighteen-month lie is getting further from the truth, not closer.

Why Nobody Says No

If the data is this clear, why do clients keep accepting eighteen-month proposals?

The answer involves three parties, all of whom have reasons to maintain the fiction.

The SI proposes eighteen months because that is what wins deals. A realistic proposal of thirty months at twice the budget would lose to every competitor who is willing to lowball. The SI that tells the truth finishes last in the selection process. Honesty is a competitive disadvantage in a market where the buyer rewards optimism.

The vendor supports the eighteen-month timeline because it accelerates the license or subscription revenue. The sooner the customer goes live, the sooner they begin paying the full subscription fee and the sooner the vendor can book the deal as a completed implementation in its metrics. The vendor's sales team reinforces the SI's timeline because a longer timeline might cause the client to delay the contract or reduce the scope, both of which reduce the vendor's revenue.

The client accepts the eighteen-month timeline because they need it to be true. The board approved a budget based on eighteen months. The CFO modeled the cash flow based on eighteen months. The CEO told the organization that the transformation would be complete by a specific date. Accepting a longer timeline means going back to the board, revising the budget, extending the disruption, and admitting that the transformation is bigger, harder, and more expensive than anyone said it would be. Nobody wants to deliver that message, especially before the project has even started.

The result is a conspiracy of optimism. Every party at the table knows the timeline is unrealistic, or should know, and every party has a reason to pretend it is not. The SI wins the deal. The vendor books the revenue. The client gets the approval. And twelve months later, when the timeline is already slipping and the change orders are accumulating, everyone acts surprised.

The Compression Tax

The damage from an unrealistic timeline is not merely financial. It is operational and organizational, and the costs compound in ways that the original budget never anticipated.

When the timeline is compressed, the activities that suffer first are always the same: business process design, organizational change management, testing, and training. These are the "soft" workstreams -- the ones that do not produce tangible technical deliverables, the ones that are hardest to measure and easiest to cut. They are also the workstreams that determine whether the transformation succeeds or fails.

Business process design gets compressed into a series of rushed workshops where the SI presents the system's standard processes and asks the business users to accept them, without adequate time to evaluate the implications, identify the gaps, or design the future state workflows that will actually work in the client's environment. The result is a system configured to generic standards rather than the client's specific needs, which surfaces as defects and workarounds after go-live.

Change management gets compressed into a communications plan and a training schedule, without the organizational readiness assessment, the stakeholder engagement, or the sustained reinforcement that genuine change management requires. The result is an organization that is informed about the new system but not prepared for it, which surfaces as resistance, low adoption, and reversion to legacy processes.

Testing gets compressed because the configuration ran late, the integrations were delivered late, and the data migration was behind schedule. The testing that was supposed to take eight weeks gets four. The defects that should have been caught in testing are instead caught in production, which is the most expensive environment in which to discover and fix a defect.

Training gets compressed because the system was not stable enough to train on until two weeks before go-live. Users receive a crash course in a system they have never seen, are expected to operate it competently on Monday morning, and discover within hours that the training did not cover the scenarios they actually encounter in their jobs.

Each of these compressions has a cost. But the costs do not appear on the project budget during the implementation. They appear after go-live, in the form of operational disruption, extended stabilization, additional consulting fees, and the organizational damage of a workforce that has been put through a poorly managed transformation. Fifty-one to fifty-four percent of companies experienced a material operational disruption at the time of go-live. The costs of these disruptions increased the initial cost of the implementation by anywhere from 50 to 300 percent.

The compression tax is the price the organization pays for the eighteen-month lie. It is not on the invoice. It is not in the proposal. But it is real, it is substantial, and it is paid by the client long after the SI has moved on to the next engagement.

The Hall of Infamy

The history of enterprise software is littered with projects that started with ambitious timelines and ended in catastrophe. A few of the most instructive examples:

Waste Management partnered with SAP on an implementation that was supposed to deliver $106 million to $220 million in annual benefits within eighteen months. Eighteen months. For the largest waste services company in North America. The project failed entirely. No benefits were realized. The lawsuit reached $500 million before settling.

The US Air Force began its Oracle ERP implementation in 2005 with the goal of replacing hundreds of legacy systems with a single, unified platform. What started as a straightforward implementation gradually expanded into a multi-system, multi-vendor effort that consumed eight years and over $5 billion before being canceled in 2012. The system never delivered meaningful capability. Eight years. Five billion dollars. Not eighteen months. Not close.

Hershey's attempted to simultaneously implement SAP, Siebel CRM, and Manugistics supply chain software on an overly aggressive timeline. The go-live happened just before the Halloween candy season -- the single most important revenue period for a candy company -- resulting in $100 million in unfulfilled orders. The timeline was the weapon that inflicted the wound.

Lidl spent seven years and approximately €500 million on an SAP implementation before abandoning the project entirely and reverting to their legacy systems.

FoxMeyer Drug's SAP implementation was plagued by unrealistic timelines, inadequate testing, insufficient training, and a fundamental misunderstanding of how the new system would integrate with existing business processes. The failure contributed to the company's bankruptcy.

In every one of these cases, the original timeline was a fraction of what the implementation actually required. In every one of these cases, the compressed timeline contributed directly to the failure. And in every one of these cases, the people who proposed the timeline knew, or should have known, that it was not achievable.

A Framework for Realistic Timelines

If eighteen months is the lie, what is the truth? The honest answer is: it depends. But it depends on variables that are knowable, measurable, and estimable -- if anyone bothers to measure them.

Based on twenty-five years of data across more than a thousand implementations, here is a framework for realistic timeline estimation.

Start with the baseline. A single-module, single-site, cloud ERP implementation for a mid-market company with clean data and a capable internal team takes twelve to sixteen months. This is the minimum. Anything shorter is either a miracle or a disaster waiting to happen.

Add for scope. Each additional module -- manufacturing, warehouse management, advanced planning, HCM, CRM -- adds three to six months, depending on complexity. Multi-module implementations are not additive; they are multiplicative, because the integration between modules creates complexity that does not exist in a single-module deployment.

Add for geography. Each additional site, region, or legal entity adds complexity in the form of localization requirements, multi-currency accounting, regulatory compliance, and the logistical challenge of managing a project across time zones. A global rollout across five regions is not a twelve-month project. It is a three-to-five-year program with phased deployments.

Add for data. If your data is dirty -- and it almost certainly is -- add three to six months for data cleansing and migration. If you have no data governance framework, add more. If you are migrating from a legacy system that is twenty or thirty years old, with undocumented data structures and decades of accumulated quality issues, add significantly more.

Add for organizational readiness. If your organization has never done this before, if your leadership is not aligned, if your culture is change-averse, if your employees are exhausted from previous initiatives -- add time. The organizational work is not optional, and it cannot be compressed without consequence.

Add for integration complexity. Count your integrations. Then double the count, because the sales cycle always underestimates. Each bidirectional integration adds weeks of development and testing. EDI migrations for hundreds of trading partners can add months.

Build in contingency. A realistic plan includes contingency. Not 5 percent. Twenty to thirty percent. Because in a program of this complexity, something will go wrong that nobody anticipated, and the only question is whether you have the budget and the timeline to absorb it or whether you are forced to compress the activities that should not be compressed.

When you apply this framework honestly, the eighteen-month proposal for a complex, multi-module implementation at a large enterprise becomes a twenty-four to thirty-six-month program. That is the truth the SI will not tell you, because telling it would lose the deal. But it is the truth that the data supports, that experience confirms, and that every post-mortem eventually reveals.

The eighteen-month lie is the entry point of the machine. It is the number that gets the client to sign. It is the fiction that launches a thousand change orders. And it is the expectation that, once set, creates the timeline pressure that compresses the activities most critical to success, producing the operational disruptions that affect the majority of implementations and the cost overruns that nearly triple the original budget.

The antidote is simple in concept and difficult in practice: demand honesty. Demand that the SI present a timeline based on your actual complexity, not a generic number designed to win the bid. Demand that the timeline include the full scope of work -- change management, data migration, integration development, testing, training, stabilization -- not just the technical configuration. And demand that the SI explain, in detail, what happens to the timeline when reality diverges from the plan, because it will.

If the SI cannot present a realistic timeline without losing the deal, that tells you something important about the market you are buying from. It tells you that the machine is optimized for winning, not for delivering. And the first step to surviving the machine is refusing to accept a lie as the foundation of your program.

In the next chapter, we will examine what happens after the implementation is complete -- or rather, what happens when it is not complete, and the organization discovers that the SI has created a dependency that was never intended to end. The knowledge hostage. The consulting engagement that becomes permanent.

Chapter 20

The Knowledge Hostage

In the previous three chapters, I described how the system integrator's business model creates conflicts of interest, how the bait and switch replaces the team that sold you with the team that was available, and how the eighteen-month lie compresses timelines in ways that guarantee cost overruns and operational disruption. These are the problems of the implementation phase -- the period during which the SI is actively engaged, billing hours, and delivering (or failing to deliver) the system.

This chapter is about what happens after the implementation is supposed to be over. It is about the moment when the SI's contract winds down, the consultants begin to transition off the project, the organizational knowledge that accumulated over twelve or twenty-four or thirty-six months of implementation starts walking out the door, and the client discovers a truth that nobody mentioned during the sales cycle:

They cannot operate their own system.

This is the knowledge hostage. It is the state in which an organization has paid tens of millions of dollars for a system it does not understand, configured by consultants who have left, documented in specifications that the internal team cannot interpret, and maintained through a managed services contract that costs millions per year and has no natural end date. The organization did not plan for this. The SI did not warn them about it. And the vendor does not care, because the license fees are being paid regardless of whether the client can use the product.

The knowledge hostage is not a failure of the implementation. It is a feature of the business model.

The Broken Promise

Every system integrator contract includes a section on knowledge transfer. The language is reassuring. The SI commits to ensuring that the client's internal team is equipped to operate and maintain the system after the engagement concludes. There will be documentation. There will be training. There will be a transition plan. The client reads these provisions and feels confident that when the consultants leave, the organization will be self-sufficient.

In practice, knowledge transfer is one of the most consistently broken promises in the industry.

The reasons are both structural and economic. Structurally, the implementation team is building the system under time pressure for the entirety of the engagement. There is no natural pause in the work where the team can stop, document everything they know, and teach it to the client's internal resources. Knowledge transfer is supposed to happen alongside the build, but in reality, it is always the activity that gets deferred when the timeline is tight. And the timeline is always tight.

Knowledge transfer from your system integrator will not occur through osmosis, so you will need something more deliberate. This sounds obvious, but in most implementations, osmosis is exactly what the client is counting on. The theory is that by having internal team members work alongside the SI's consultants during the implementation, knowledge will transfer naturally through proximity and participation. The internal team member sits in the configuration workshops, observes the decisions being made, and absorbs the logic through exposure.

The theory does not survive contact with reality. The internal team members are participating in the implementation while simultaneously doing their day jobs. They attend the workshops, but they do not have the bandwidth to absorb the technical depth of every configuration decision. They see the what but not the why.

They observe the consultant selecting a setting but do not understand the downstream implications of that choice, the alternatives that were considered, or the specific business requirement that drove the decision. The knowledge that transfers through osmosis is surface knowledge. The deep knowledge -- the why behind every configuration choice, the workarounds that were built to address gaps, the integration logic that connects one module to another -- stays in the heads of the consultants.

And then the consultants leave.

The Economic Disincentive

The structural challenge of knowledge transfer is compounded by an economic disincentive that is rarely discussed openly but that every experienced professional in the industry understands.

The SI has no financial incentive to transfer knowledge effectively. In fact, the SI has a financial incentive not to.

If the client's internal team can operate the system independently, the client does not need the SI's managed services contract. If the internal team understands every configuration decision and every custom development, the client does not need to call the SI when something breaks. If the documentation is thorough enough that a new hire can learn the system from the documentation alone, the client does not need the SI's ongoing support.

Effective knowledge transfer reduces the SI's post-implementation revenue. The machine is not designed to make itself unnecessary. It is designed to create dependency. And the most effective way to create dependency is to ensure that the knowledge required to operate the system resides with the SI's consultants rather than with the client's employees.

I am not suggesting that every SI deliberately withholds knowledge. Most consultants, as individuals, want to do a good job and leave their clients well-prepared. But the system within which they operate provides neither the time, the incentive, nor the structure for thorough knowledge transfer. The consultants are under pressure to complete the build. Their utilization targets require them to be billing on the next project before the current one is finished. The firm's business development team is already selling managed services to the client, positioning post-go-live support as a natural extension of the implementation. The knowledge transfer that was promised in the contract becomes a box to check rather than a capability to build.

"The difference is whether they do it 'to' you as opposed to 'with' you. One leaves a legacy and a capability, while with the other approach, everything falls apart once they are gone." That distinction -- doing the implementation to the client versus with the client -- is the difference between a knowledge transfer and a knowledge hostage. In the vast majority of implementations I have observed, the SI does the work to the client, the client watches, and when the SI leaves, the client discovers that watching is not the same as understanding.

The Managed Services Trap

The knowledge hostage does not become apparent immediately after go-live. It reveals itself gradually, through a sequence that follows a predictable pattern.

Phase one is hypercare. For the first two to four weeks after go-live, the SI maintains a support team on site to address the immediate post-go-live defects and stabilization issues described in Chapter 8. This period is intense, firefighting-oriented, and essential. The SI's team is resolving the urgent problems that surface when the system goes into production with real data at real volume.

Phase two is the drawdown. After hypercare, the SI's contract calls for a rapid reduction in on-site resources. The SI's best consultants -- the ones who built the system, who understand the configuration decisions, who know the workarounds and the integration logic -- are transitioned to their next engagement. They are replaced by a smaller managed services team that may not have the same depth of knowledge. In some cases, the managed services team is staffed by different people than the implementation team, working from a different location, often offshore.

Phase three is the discovery. The deeper, more systemic problems that did not surface during hypercare begin to emerge. Month-end close processes that work differently than expected. Intercompany transactions that fail under specific conditions. Reporting discrepancies that only become visible when the first quarterly financials are prepared. The internal team encounters these issues and discovers that they do not understand the system well enough to diagnose or resolve them. They escalate to the managed services team. The managed services team, which did not build the system, reviews the issue, researches the configuration, and responds within the service level agreement -- which may be days, not hours.

Phase four is the dependency. The organization realizes that it cannot operate its own system without the SI's ongoing support. The managed services contract, which was supposed to be a transitional arrangement, becomes permanent. The annual cost is substantial -- typically ranging from several hundred thousand dollars to several million per year, depending on the complexity of the system and the breadth of the support required. And there is no natural end date, because the internal team has never built the capability to replace the external support.

I have worked with organizations that were still paying their system integrator millions of dollars per year, three, four, and five years after go-live, because they could not operate their own system. Not because the system was too complex for their internal team to learn. Because the knowledge transfer never happened, and the internal team was never given the opportunity, the documentation, or the training to become self-sufficient. The dependency was not inevitable. It was the predictable result of a business model that profits from it.

The Institutional Knowledge Drain

The knowledge hostage problem is compounded by a dynamic that is less visible but equally damaging: the loss of institutional knowledge that occurs when the consultants who built the system leave the project.

During a twelve-to-thirty-six-month implementation, the SI's team accumulates an enormous amount of knowledge about the client's system. They understand why the pricing logic was configured a particular way. They know the workaround that was built to handle the exception for the client's largest customer. They remember the integration decision that was made in month three and the downstream implications it had in month eighteen. They know which data mapping rules are critical and which were quick fixes that should be revisited. They carry the institutional history of every decision, every compromise, and every shortcut that was made during the build.

This knowledge is almost never adequately documented. The implementation methodology calls for documentation, but the documentation that is produced is typically technical specification documents that describe what was configured, not why. They describe the settings. They do not describe the business context, the alternatives that were evaluated, the trade-offs that were accepted, or the rationale for the decisions that were made.

A technical specification tells you that the revenue recognition rule is set to method A. It does not tell you that method A was chosen because the client's industry-specific requirements eliminated methods B and C, and that if the requirements change, the configuration must be revisited or the financial reporting will be incorrect.

When the consultants leave, they take this contextual knowledge with them. What remains is a system that works, a set of technical documents that describe how it is configured, and an internal team that was never taught the why behind the how. The internal team can operate the system -- they can process transactions, run reports, execute standard workflows. But they cannot troubleshoot non-standard scenarios, they cannot evaluate the impact of configuration changes, and they cannot adapt the system to evolving business requirements without calling the consultants who built it.

The institutional knowledge drain is particularly devastating when key consultants leave not just the project but the SI's firm entirely. Consulting has high turnover. The senior consultant who built your financial module may have moved to a competitor, started their own practice, or left the industry altogether. The knowledge they carried about your system is gone -- not just from your organization, but from the firm you are paying for managed services. The managed services team that answers your support tickets may have no more insight into your system's configuration history than your own internal team does.

The Documentation Deficit

If the knowledge hostage has a single root cause, it is documentation -- or more precisely, the systematic failure to document the decisions, rationale, and context that make a complex system comprehensible to people who did not build it.

There are three types of documentation that a well-run implementation should produce. The first is technical documentation: what was configured, how the integrations work, what the data model looks like. This is the documentation that most SIs produce, and it is the least valuable of the three, because it describes the system as it exists but provides no context for why it exists that way.

The second is decision documentation: what decisions were made, what alternatives were considered, what the rationale was, and what the implications are if conditions change. This documentation is almost never produced, because it requires the consultant to pause the build, reflect on the decision, and write it down in a format that a non-participant can understand. The timeline does not allow for this. The SI is not incentivized to produce it. And the client does not know to demand it until it is too late.

The third is operational documentation: how the system should be operated on a day-to-day basis, what the standard procedures are, what the exception-handling processes are, and what the escalation paths are when something goes wrong. This documentation should be produced by the client's internal team, with the SI's support, and it should be tested by having the internal team operate the system using only the documentation as a guide. If the internal team cannot operate the system from the documentation, the documentation is inadequate, and the knowledge transfer is incomplete.

In most implementations, only the first type of documentation is produced, and it is produced at the end of the project, under time pressure, by consultants who are already mentally transitioning to their next engagement. The result is documentation that is technically accurate but operationally useless -- a snapshot of the system's configuration that tells you what but not why, and that becomes outdated the moment the first post-go-live change is made.

Breaking Free

The knowledge hostage is not a permanent condition. It can be broken. But breaking it requires deliberate investment, sustained leadership commitment, and a willingness to prioritize internal capability building over the convenience of external dependency.

Overdependence on consultants is a problem that many encounter. Another common problem is deferring too much to your system integrator because you do not know enough about the software. Both challenges can be mitigated by better building your internal competencies to become self-sufficient sooner.

Here is what breaking free looks like in practice.

Start during the implementation, not after. The biggest mistake organizations make is treating knowledge transfer as a post-go-live activity. By the time the SI is leaving, it is too late to build the internal capability that should have been developing throughout the implementation. From day one, the client's internal team should be embedded in every workstream -- not as observers, but as participants who are doing the work alongside the consultants. The internal team member does not watch the consultant configure the module. The internal team member configures the module, with the consultant coaching. The difference is profound: one produces familiarity, the other produces competence.

Demand decision documentation. Make it a contractual requirement that every significant configuration decision is documented with its rationale, its alternatives, and its implications. This documentation should be reviewed and approved by the client's internal team before it is finalized. If the internal team cannot understand the documentation, it is not adequate.

Build a Center of Excellence. A Center of Excellence is an internal team dedicated to owning, maintaining, and evolving the enterprise system after the SI leaves. It should include functional experts who understand the business processes the system supports, technical experts who understand the configuration and integration architecture, and a governance function that manages change requests, evaluates enhancement opportunities, and maintains the documentation. The Center of Excellence should be established during the implementation, not after, so that its members accumulate knowledge alongside the consultants who are building the system.

But a Center of Excellence is only effective if its members are equipped with the right knowledge from the beginning -- not after the SI has left and the gaps have already opened. This means investing in training that goes far beyond the vendor's standard curriculum.

There are two dimensions of training that most organizations neglect, and both are critical. The first is software training for the internal core team and extended team members -- not the end-user training that happens two weeks before go-live, but deep, hands-on training in the software platform that begins early in the implementation. The core team members who will participate in design workshops, make configuration decisions, and eventually own the system need to understand the software before they are asked to make decisions about it. An untrained core team member sitting in a design workshop is not a participant. They are an audience member, watching the SI make decisions on their behalf and nodding along because they lack the knowledge to challenge or contribute. Training the core team on the software early in the implementation transforms them from passive observers into active decision-makers -- and that transformation is what prevents the knowledge hostage from forming.

The second dimension is implementation best practices. Most internal team members have never been through a digital transformation. They do not know what good governance looks like, what a realistic timeline should be, how to evaluate an SI's performance, how to manage change orders, or what questions to ask when something feels wrong. Training them on these practices -- the mechanics of how implementations work, the risks to watch for, the governance frameworks that protect the client -- gives them the confidence and the vocabulary to take ownership of the project from day one rather than deferring to the SI on every decision.

At Third Stage, we have built our entire model around this principle. Before our clients' implementations begin, we train their core teams and extended team members to equip them with the knowledge and tools to take ownership of the project from the start. This is not a one-day orientation. It is a structured program that covers the software platform, implementation methodology, change management fundamentals, governance and risk management, and the specific dynamics of working with a system integrator -- including the conflicts of interest described in this book. When the SI arrives, the client's team is not starting from zero. They have context. They have confidence. They have the ability to ask informed questions and challenge assertions that do not feel right. That preparation fundamentally changes the power dynamic of the engagement.

Our staffing arm extends this further. As I discussed in Chapter 18, we help clients recruit and deploy internal project resources -- program managers, change management leads, business analysts, data migration specialists -- who report to the client and are managed by the client's leadership. These are not temporary contractors who disappear after go-live. They are professionals who build institutional knowledge throughout the implementation and carry it forward into operations. They are the antidote to the knowledge hostage, because they ensure that the knowledge lives inside the organization, not inside the SI.

And for the documentation deficit -- the systematic failure to capture the decisions, rationale, and context that make the system comprehensible -- we built Mission Control. As I described in Chapter 18, Mission Control is our AI platform that draws on the collective knowledge of over a thousand implementation projects to automate the documentation, risk identification, and quality assurance activities that SIs typically do not do well and that clients typically cannot do at all. Mission Control produces the decision documentation, the risk logs, the governance artifacts, and the quality assurance records that should exist on every implementation but almost never do -- not because anyone decided they were unimportant, but because nobody had the bandwidth to produce them while simultaneously building the system. AI changes that equation. The documentation that would require hundreds of hours of senior consultant time is generated continuously, at higher quality and greater consistency than any manual process could achieve. The result is that when the SI leaves, the client has a comprehensive record of what was built, why it was built that way, what the risks are, and what needs attention going forward. That record is the difference between a knowledge hostage and an informed owner.

There is another category of tools that can accelerate capability building and reduce SI dependency: technology-agnostic employee adoption platforms. These tools train employees on business processes and workflows in an automated, on-demand way -- embedded tutorials that work across multiple web-based systems and guide employees while they are actually working. Unlike the SI's technical training, which happens in a classroom two weeks before go-live and is forgotten within days, adoption platforms provide continuous, contextual reinforcement that persists long after the SI has left. They are not tied to a single vendor's product. They work across any web-based application, which means the organization is not adding another vendor dependency. And they reduce the need for the SI's training resources, which is one of the most common mechanisms through which post-go-live dependency is sustained.

Test the knowledge transfer. Before the SI's contract ends, conduct a readiness assessment of your internal team's ability to operate and maintain the system independently. This is not a quiz or a certification exam. It is a practical test: give the internal team a set of realistic scenarios -- a configuration change request, a data quality issue, an integration failure, a user support ticket -- and evaluate whether they can diagnose and resolve them without SI assistance. If they cannot, the knowledge transfer is incomplete, and the SI's contract should not be allowed to conclude until it is.

Negotiate managed services with an exit strategy. If you need managed services in the short term, negotiate a contract that includes a defined exit ramp. The managed services agreement should include declining support hours over time, explicit knowledge transfer milestones tied to fee reductions, and a target date by which the internal team is expected to be self-sufficient. A managed services contract with no end date and no exit strategy is not a support agreement. It is a subscription to dependency.

One way to mitigate that risk is to bring more capabilities in-house and avoid becoming dependent on a consulting or implementation partner. This is not just post-implementation advice. It is a principle that should guide the entire engagement, from the first day of the implementation to the last day of managed services. The goal is not to eliminate the SI. There is legitimate value in specialized expertise. The goal is to ensure that when the SI leaves, the organization can stand on its own.

The Capability Maturity Model

Based on our work with hundreds of organizations navigating post-implementation dependency, we have developed a framework for assessing and building organizational capability. It is a maturity model with five levels:

Level 1: Dependent. The organization cannot operate or maintain the system without external support. The SI or managed services provider handles all non-routine activities. The internal team processes transactions but cannot troubleshoot, configure, or adapt the system. This is the knowledge hostage.

Level 2: Assisted. The internal team can handle routine operations and basic support tickets. Non-routine issues, configuration changes, and system enhancements still require external support. The dependency is reduced but not eliminated.

Level 3: Capable. The internal team can operate, troubleshoot, and make configuration changes to the system. External support is used selectively for complex issues or specialized expertise. The team has documented processes, trained backups, and a governance model for change management.

Level 4: Proficient. The internal team can not only operate the system but optimize it. They identify opportunities for process improvement, evaluate vendor updates and new features, and implement enhancements without external assistance. The organization is self-sufficient and uses external consultants only for strategic initiatives.

Level 5: Leading. The internal team operates the system at a level that exceeds the capability of the original implementation team. They have built institutional knowledge, developed proprietary best practices, and are continuously evolving the system to drive competitive advantage. External dependency is zero for operational activities.

Most organizations emerge from implementation at Level 1. With deliberate investment, they can reach Level 3 within twelve to eighteen months post-go-live. Reaching Level 4 typically takes two to three years. Level 5 is rare but achievable for organizations that treat their internal capability as a strategic asset rather than a cost center.

The progression from Level 1 to Level 3 is where the knowledge hostage is broken. It requires dedicated resources, sustained leadership attention, and an investment that the original project budget almost certainly did not include. This investment is not optional. It is the cost of ownership that the sales cycle never mentioned, that the SI's proposal never scoped, and that the vendor never warned you about. It is the price of freedom from the machine's most insidious form of dependency.

The Machine's Final Lock

The knowledge hostage is the machine's last lock. The vendor locked you in with a subscription model and high switching costs. The SI locked you in with a business model that profits from duration and complexity. The knowledge hostage locks you in by ensuring that even after the vendor is paid and the SI has left, you cannot operate independently. You are dependent on people who no longer work for you, for knowledge that should have been yours, paying for support that should have been unnecessary.

Breaking this lock requires the same thing that breaking every other lock in this book requires: understanding how the machine works, refusing to accept its defaults, and investing in the organizational capability that the machine is designed to prevent you from building.

The organizations that break free are the ones that plan for independence from day one. They embed their people in the implementation. They demand documentation that transfers knowledge, not just records configuration. They build Centers of Excellence before go-live, not after. They negotiate managed services contracts with exit strategies. And they treat the development of internal capability not as a post-implementation afterthought but as a core deliverable of the transformation itself.

The organizations that do not break free are the ones that wake up three years after go-live, still writing checks to their system integrator, still unable to make a configuration change without calling for help, and still wondering why the transformation that was supposed to make them more efficient has made them more dependent than ever.

The knowledge hostage is not inevitable. But it is the default. And breaking the default requires intention, investment, and the courage to insist on independence in an industry that profits from your dependence.

In the next chapter, we will examine the process by which organizations select their system integrators -- a process that is, in many cases, as rigged as the software selection it follows. The SI selection is the moment when the machine's final gear engages, and understanding how it works is your last opportunity to choose a partner whose interests align with yours rather than one whose interests align with the machine's.

Chapter 21

The Elephant in the Room

In the previous four chapters, I have described the system integrator's structural conflicts of interest, the bait and switch between sales and delivery teams, the eighteen-month lie that launches every engagement, and the knowledge hostage that persists long after the implementation is supposed to be complete. Each of these is a problem that the client must manage once the SI has been selected.

This chapter is about the selection itself. Because the uncomfortable truth is that the SI selection process is, in the majority of cases, neither independent nor competitive. It is a curated exercise in which the vendor recommends its preferred partners, the client selects from a pre-approved list, and the outcome is shaped by economic relationships that the client does not see and that nobody discloses.

The SI selection is the last decision the client makes before the machine fully engages. It is also the decision with the highest leverage, because the SI you select will determine the quality of your implementation team, the realism of your timeline and budget, the degree of organizational change support you receive, and the nature of the dependency you will carry for years after go-live. You are, in a very real sense, choosing your captor -- the firm that will create the dependency described in the previous four chapters. Getting it right is essential. Getting it wrong is expensive. And the process by which most organizations make this decision is designed to produce the wrong answer.

The Curated List

Most SI selection processes begin the same way: the organization asks the software vendor to recommend implementation partners.

This seems reasonable. The vendor knows the product better than anyone. They know which firms have the most experience implementing it. They know which partners have the certifications, the trained resources, and the track record. Who better to recommend an implementation partner than the company that built the software?

The answer is: almost anyone. Because the vendor's recommendation is not based on which partner will deliver the best outcome for your specific organization. It is based on which partner has the strongest commercial relationship with the vendor.

The major software vendors maintain tiered partner ecosystems. SAP has its Diamond, Platinum, and Gold partners. Oracle has its Cloud Elite and Cloud Premier partners. Microsoft has its Inner Circle and Solutions Partner designations. These tiers are determined primarily by the volume of business the partner generates for the vendor -- how many licenses they sell, how many implementations they deliver, how much revenue they drive into the vendor's pipeline. The partners at the top of the tier system are the ones who generate the most revenue for the vendor. They are not necessarily the ones who deliver the best outcomes for the client.

When the vendor recommends three or four partners from its ecosystem, the client receives a curated list of firms that have been pre-selected for their commercial alignment with the vendor, not for their fit with the client's specific needs. The "competition" between the recommended partners is real in the sense that they are competing against each other, but it is constrained in the sense that every firm on the list represents the same vendor's product and operates under the same vendor partnership model. The client is choosing between variations of the same conflict of interest.

Choosing your SI from the vendor's recommended partner list is like asking the Don to recommend a good accountant. You will get a name. It will be someone in the family. The tiered partner ecosystem — Diamond, Platinum, Gold — is a made-man system.

The more business you generate for the family, the higher your rank, the more territory you control, the more protected you are. The firms at the top of the tier structure are "made" — they operate with the vendor's blessing and in return are expected to deliver clients to the family's implementation pipeline. The firms outside the family do not get the recommendations, the co-selling support, or the access. It is not a meritocracy. It is a loyalty structure.

The conflict is even more insidious when the SI and the software evaluator are the same firm. The large consultancies -- Deloitte, Accenture, PwC, KPMG, EY -- maintain multiple product practices under one roof. They have an SAP practice, an Oracle practice, a Microsoft practice, and in some cases a Workday or Salesforce practice. They will tell you they are independent. They will tell you that their software evaluation is objective, that their recommendation is based purely on what is best for your business. They are not independent. They cannot be, because every recommendation they make feeds one of their own practices at the expense of the others.

Here is how it actually works. Before the evaluation begins, the firm's leadership conducts an internal assessment of which solution has the best chance of winning the client's business. This assessment is shaped by which practice has available capacity, which practice has the strongest relationship with the client's executives, and which vendor is offering the most attractive partner incentives at that moment. The firm then aligns politically behind that solution. They do not want to compete with themselves. The SAP practice and the Oracle practice within the same firm are not going to present the client with an honest, balanced comparison and let the chips fall where they may. One practice will be positioned as the recommended path. The other practices will be quietly sidelined. The client receives what appears to be an independent recommendation from a prestigious firm. What they actually receive is the output of an internal political negotiation that the client was never invited to observe.

I know this because I was part of that machine. At PricewaterhouseCoopers, I sat in the rooms where these political alignments were made. I watched the partners negotiate internally about which practice would get the engagement before the client had any idea the decision had already been shaped. I participated in software evaluations where the answer was predetermined, where the analysis was reverse-engineered to justify a conclusion that the firm's economics had already dictated. I was a junior consultant at the time, and I did not have the power to change it. But I had the clarity to see it. And that clarity is what eventually led me to leave the Big Four and build a practice that operates on the other side of the table. When I tell you the process is not independent, I am not speculating. I am remembering.

Your ERP systems integrator should not be involved in your ERP software selection. They are aligned with one or more of the ERP vendors, and their recommendation will be biased depending on which arm of the firm you are working with. The same logic applies in reverse: the vendor should not be involved in your SI selection, because the vendor's recommendation will be biased toward partners who generate the most revenue for the vendor.

The curated list creates an illusion of competition. The client conducts a "selection process" -- they review proposals, attend presentations, check references -- but the pool of candidates has been pre-filtered by the party with the least alignment to the client's interests. The outcome feels rigorous because the process followed a structured methodology. But the inputs to the process were controlled by someone whose interests diverge from the client's.

RFP Theater, Act Two

In Chapter 11, I described the vendor RFP as theater. The SI selection RFP is the second act of the same performance, with the same structural flaws.

The SI's proposal is written by the sales team. It is crafted to check boxes, make commitments that are ambitious enough to impress the evaluation committee but vague enough to provide escape routes if the delivery team cannot honor them. The named resources have impressive resumes. The timeline is competitive. The pricing is aggressive. The methodology is branded and proprietary and represented as proven across hundreds of engagements.

What the proposal does not tell you is which of the named resources will actually be on your project and for how long. It does not tell you that the timeline was compressed to win the bid. It does not tell you that the pricing excludes workstreams that will surface as change orders. It does not tell you that the methodology, while branded, will be adapted on the fly by a delivery team that may or may not have the experience to adapt it effectively.

If you are using a system integrator, there are often salespeople that minimize the problems and exaggerate the functionalities. Many times, you will be promised the A-team and left with the D-team when it comes time for implementation.

The evaluation committee reviews the proposals and scores them on a matrix. The matrix includes criteria like experience, methodology, team qualifications, timeline, and price. Each criterion is weighted. The scores are tabulated. The winner is announced. The process feels objective because it used a matrix and assigned numbers.

But the matrix is only as good as the information it is scoring, and the information in the proposal is marketing material produced by a sales team whose compensation depends on winning. The experience cited in the proposal may be the firm's experience, not the team's experience. The methodology may be a slide deck, not a delivery approach. The team qualifications may describe the people who will appear for the first two weeks and then rotate off.

The price may exclude the workstreams that will drive 40 percent of the actual cost.

Scoring marketing material with a matrix does not produce objectivity. It produces the appearance of objectivity, which is more dangerous than no process at all, because it gives the organization confidence in a decision that was made on incomplete and misleading information.

The Reference Check Charade

Every SI selection process includes reference checks, and every reference check follows the same pattern: the SI provides a list of references, the client calls them, the references say positive things, and the evaluation committee records the feedback as confirming evidence.

This is almost completely useless. The SI curates their reference list the same way the vendor curates its partner list: they select clients who had good experiences, who are willing to speak positively, and who will not mention the problems that every implementation encounters. No firm provides a reference who will say "we went 200 percent over budget and the team was underqualified." The references are marketing assets, deployed strategically, and the information they provide is filtered through the same incentive structure that produced the proposal.

It is essential to take up references and much better to find your own than to take the ones offered by the SI, especially if you can find clients who are willing to discuss why things have not gone so well.

The valuable references are the ones the SI does not provide. They are the clients who had difficult experiences. The projects that ran over. The implementations where the team was swapped out, the timeline doubled, and the change orders accumulated. These references exist -- every SI of any size has them -- but finding them requires effort that most evaluation committees do not invest. It requires networking. It requires asking industry peers. It requires engaging independent advisors who have visibility across the market and can identify organizations with relevant experience, positive or negative, that the SI would prefer you not discover.

Independent review platforms like Raven Intel have emerged to address this gap, providing unfiltered reviews of system integrators from actual clients. These platforms are imperfect -- the sample sizes are small, the reviews are self-selected, and the incentive to post is often strongest for clients with extreme experiences, either very positive or very negative. But they provide a data point that the curated reference list does not: the unscripted voice of the client.

When the Process Is Corrupted

The dynamics I have described so far -- curated lists, proposal theater, reference charades -- are the standard dysfunction of SI selection. They are the baseline. In some cases, the dysfunction is far worse.

In one SI selection that I analyzed as an expert witness, an insider within the client organization shared confidential bid information with a preferred vendor during the selection process. The insider provided the preferred vendor with access to competitor proposals, allowing them to see exactly what their competitors were bidding and to adjust their own proposal accordingly. The insider also provided confidential budget information, enabling the preferred vendor to price their proposal at precisely the level the client had available.

The insider received approximately $50,000 in undisclosed payments from the preferred vendor. The payments were not disclosed to the client organization. The selection process, which appeared competitive and rigorous from the outside, was corrupted from the inside. The preferred vendor won. The implementation failed. The litigation that followed revealed the corruption, but only after millions had been spent and the damage had been done.

This case is extreme. But the dynamic it illustrates -- the use of insider information and undisclosed financial relationships to influence the selection outcome -- operates on a spectrum. At the extreme end is outright corruption. In the middle is the vendor's recommendation of preferred partners based on commercial relationships that are not disclosed to the client. At the other end is the analyst firm's research report that recommends vendors and partners whose sponsorship fees fund the analyst's business. Each point on the spectrum represents a selection process that is shaped by economic relationships the client does not fully understand.

The Analyst Problem

Analyst firms -- Gartner, Forrester, IDC, and their peers -- play a significant role in the SI selection process, and their influence deserves scrutiny.

These firms publish research reports, rankings, and recommendations that heavily influence which vendors and which implementation partners organizations consider. A Gartner Magic Quadrant placement or a Forrester Wave ranking can make or break a vendor's pipeline. Organizations rely on these reports as independent, expert assessments of the market.

But the analyst firms are not independent in the way most buyers assume. They operate a business model in which the vendors and implementation partners being evaluated are also paying customers. Vendors pay for access programs that allow them to brief analysts, influence research agendas, and ensure their products receive attention. Partners pay for inclusion in directories, for speaking slots at analyst-sponsored events, and for co-branded research that positions them favorably. The financial relationship between the analyst and the firms being evaluated is substantial, ongoing, and not always visible to the buyer reading the report.

I am not saying that analyst research is worthless. The best analysts produce genuinely insightful work that reflects deep market knowledge and rigorous methodology. But the financial relationships create a structural bias that the buyer should understand. A vendor or partner that invests heavily in analyst relations is more likely to receive favorable coverage than one that does not, not because the analyst is corrupt, but because the vendor that invests in the relationship has more opportunities to shape the analyst's understanding of its product, its strategy, and its competitive position.

The buyer should treat analyst research as one input among many, not as the definitive assessment. Cross-reference analyst rankings with independent client reviews, peer references, and your own evaluation. Be aware that the firms at the top of the analyst's ranking may be there in part because they invest more heavily in the analyst relationship than their competitors do. And ask yourself a simple question: if the analyst's revenue depends on the vendors and partners it evaluates, can its recommendations truly be independent?

What a Genuine SI Selection Looks Like

If the standard SI selection process is theater, what does a genuine process look like? Based on our experience facilitating hundreds of SI selections, here is a framework that produces better outcomes.

Step 1: Inception. Before you issue an RFP, define your scope, your approach, and your commercial principles. What are you implementing? What is the timeline? What is the budget range? What delivery model do you prefer -- time and materials, fixed price, capped T&M, or outcome-based? These decisions should be made by the client, informed by independent advice, before any SI has been invited to the table. The inception phase sets the terms of the engagement. If you let the SI define these terms through their proposal, you have already lost control of the process.

Step 2: Down-select. Conduct a paper-based evaluation against weighted criteria to narrow the field to three or four candidates. Three is the sweet spot -- enough competitive tension to keep the bidders honest, not so many that the process becomes unwieldy. The criteria should span functional capability, technical expertise, commercial terms, delivery credentials, and cultural fit. And the candidates should not be limited to the vendor's recommended partners. Cast a wider net. Include mid-tier firms. Include independents. Include firms the vendor did not suggest, because those firms may have capabilities and perspectives that the vendor's preferred partners do not.

Step 3: Collate and issue the RFP. The RFP should evaluate two dimensions: software fit, which is relatively objective, and implementor capability, which is subjective. Credentials, experience, trust, cultural fit, and confidence matter equally as much as objective considerations such as price. These softer criteria are correspondingly much harder to measure but are usually the most important factors. The RFP should require the SI to provide not just a methodology and a timeline but named resources with detailed resumes, a governance model, a knowledge transfer plan, and draft terms and conditions. Getting the commercial terms on the table early prevents the discovery, after selection, that the SI's contract contains provisions that are unacceptable.

Step 4: Scripted demonstrations. Do not let the SI control the demo. Provide a script based on your actual business scenarios, your actual data, and your actual processes. Require the delivery team -- not the sales team -- to conduct the demonstration. It was discovered at one vendor demo session that the client was not seeing a live demo but a pre-recorded video of the system in use, with the long gaps for performance problems edited out. Scripted demonstrations that use your scenarios, conducted by the people who will actually do the work, are the most revealing activity in the entire selection process.

Step 5: Independent reference checks. Do not rely on the SI's curated reference list. Find your own references. Ask industry peers. Engage an independent advisor who has visibility across the market. Ask the references what went wrong, not just what went right. Ask them what they wish they had known. Ask them whether the team that was proposed was the team that showed up. The references that the SI does not provide are more valuable than the ones they do.

Step 6: Meet the actual team. Cultural fit is important. Meet the individual team members -- from the engagement manager down to front-line technical consultants. Do not accept the assertion that the team will be finalized after the contract is signed. If the SI cannot commit to specific individuals during the selection process, they are telling you that the team in the proposal is not the team you will get.

Step 7: Negotiate before you commit. "Too often, the vendor is selected before any commercial dialogue has been held, and this weakens the client position." Negotiate the commercial terms, the liability provisions, the knowledge transfer requirements, the resource commitment clauses, and the exit terms before you sign. There are all too frequent instances where contracts are simply signed without any discussion of terms with the vendor at all. Some of these contracts have onerous terms for clients, and it is only when things are going wrong that the client finds out they have no rights to terminate for cause or for liquidated damages.

Step 8: Due diligence before final commitment. After selecting a preferred vendor, conduct discovery or blueprinting workshops as a "decision in principle" -- not a final commitment. If anything material surfaces during due diligence that contradicts what was represented during the selection, reopen the tender. This is your last opportunity to validate the SI's claims before the contract is signed and the leverage shifts permanently in the SI's favor.

The Question Nobody Asks

There is one question that I encourage every client to ask during the SI selection process, and it is a question that almost nobody asks because it feels impolite:

What is the worst implementation your firm has delivered in the past three years, and what did you learn from it?

Every SI of any size has failed implementations. Every one. The honest firms will acknowledge this, describe what went wrong, and explain what they changed as a result. The dishonest firms will claim that they have never had a failed implementation, or they will redefine failure so narrowly that their failures do not qualify.

The answer to this question tells you more about the firm's culture, its self-awareness, and its commitment to improvement than every other element of the selection process combined. A firm that cannot honestly discuss its failures is a firm that has not learned from them. And a firm that has not learned from its failures will repeat them -- on your project.

Would you prefer to be a big fish in a small pond or a small fish in a big pond? This is the other question that deserves more attention than it receives. If your organization has $500 million in revenue and you hire a system integrator with $50 billion in revenue, you are a rounding error in their portfolio. Your project will be staffed from the bench, managed by whoever is available, and prioritized behind larger, more lucrative engagements. If you hire a firm where your project is one of the largest in their portfolio, you get their best people, their senior attention, and a partnership where your success matters to their business. Size is not a virtue in SI selection. Fit is.

The Captor You Chose

Here is the uncomfortable truth: the SI selection process, as practiced by the majority of organizations, is designed to produce an outcome that serves the vendor's ecosystem, the SI's revenue targets, and the analyst's business model. It is not designed to produce an outcome that serves the client.

But there is a deeper truth behind this one, and it is the insight that the entire industry would prefer you not reach: the SI selection may be the most overrated decision in your entire transformation.

I do not say this to be dismissive. The implementation partner matters. Technical competence matters. Cultural fit matters. The quality of the people who configure your system, build your integrations, and migrate your data matters. But the SI is one workstream in a program that has four or five workstreams, and it is not the workstream that determines whether your transformation succeeds or fails. As I discussed in Chapter 19, the things that are most likely to slow down a project and cause it to fail are organizational change management and business process re-engineering -- neither of which is the SI's core competency. The leadership commitment described in Chapter 3, the cultural readiness described in Chapter 4, the accountability structures described throughout Part I -- these are the variables that determine outcomes. The SI selection does not appear on that list.

The industry wants you to believe that choosing the right SI is the most critical decision you will make, because the industry profits from the selection process, from the implementation engagement, and from the managed services that follow. The more weight you assign to the SI decision, the more power the SI has in the relationship. But the data tells a different story. The data tells you that vendor choice has minimal statistical impact on outcomes, and the same is true of the SI. The organizations that succeed are the ones that invest in the non-technical dimensions of transformation -- the people, the processes, the governance, the change management -- regardless of which SI they hired. The organizations that fail are the ones that hired a prestigious SI and assumed the prestige would compensate for the organizational work they did not do.

The SI selection is important. It is not the most important thing. And the sooner you internalize that distinction, the sooner you will stop outsourcing your transformation's success to a firm whose incentives are misaligned with yours and start investing in the capabilities that actually determine whether you succeed or fail.

The organizations that make better SI selection decisions are the ones that refuse to accept the standard process. They cast a wider net than the vendor's recommended list. They evaluate the delivery team, not the sales team. They find their own references. They negotiate the commercial terms before they commit. They ask the uncomfortable questions. And they engage independent advisory support from someone who has no economic relationship with any of the firms being evaluated.

The SI selection is the last decision you make before the machine fully engages. Make it with your eyes open. The best time to choose wisely is before the captivity begins. Because once the contract is signed, the leverage shifts, the consultants arrive, and the dynamics described in the previous four chapters begin to play out. The SI you selected becomes the SI you are stuck with. Choose accordingly.

Reducing Dependency Before It Starts

The best defense against the SI selection problems described in this chapter is not just a better selection process. It is reducing your dependency on the SI before the engagement begins.

As I discussed in Chapters 18, 19, and 20, the SI handles one workstream -- the technical implementation. They are not equipped to manage the overall program. Do not let them convince you otherwise. Change management, program governance, business process optimization, solution architecture, data migration strategy, integration to third-party systems -- these are workstreams that should be owned by the client or by independent advisors who represent the client's interests. When the SI controls all of these workstreams, they control the entire transformation. When you control them, the SI becomes what they should be: a technical delivery partner operating within a program that you own.

One of the most effective ways to reduce SI dependency is to hire software vendor specialists from outside the vendor and partner community. The conventional wisdom is that if you need SAP consultants, you hire them through the SAP partner ecosystem. If you need Oracle specialists, you go to Oracle's partner network. But every consultant sourced through the vendor's ecosystem carries the same conflicts of interest that the SI carries: vendor alignment, partnership incentives, and a career path that depends on maintaining the vendor relationship.

The alternative is to source technical talent independently. Experienced SAP, Oracle, Microsoft, and Workday specialists exist outside the partner ecosystem -- professionals who have deep platform knowledge but are not beholden to the vendor or the SI for their next engagement. These independent specialists can be deployed on the client's team, reporting to the client's PMO, working alongside the SI's consultants but accountable to the client. They provide the technical depth that the internal team may lack without the conflicts of interest that come with sourcing through the vendor's partner network.

This is another reason we built our staffing arm at Third Stage. We help clients source and deploy independent technical specialists -- SAP functional consultants, Oracle architects, D365 developers, data migration leads -- who work for the client, not for the SI. These resources sit on the client side of the table. They review the SI's work with informed eyes. They challenge configuration decisions that do not make sense. They ensure that knowledge transfer is happening in real time, because they are building the knowledge themselves rather than watching the SI build it. And when the SI's engagement ends, these specialists remain, carrying the institutional knowledge that would otherwise walk out the door.

The combination of an independent PMO, client-sourced technical specialists, and AI-powered documentation through tools like Mission Control creates an engagement model that is fundamentally different from the one the machine defaults to. The SI is still there. Their technical expertise is still valuable. But they are operating within a structure that the client controls, surrounded by resources that represent the client's interests, producing documentation that the client owns. The power dynamic has shifted. The client is no longer a passenger in their own transformation. They are driving it.

In the next chapter, we will examine what happens in the rare cases where the consulting relationship actually works -- where the SI delivers genuine value, where the advisory model is aligned with the client's interests, and where the transformation produces the outcomes that were promised. These cases exist. They are the exception, not the rule. But understanding what makes them work is essential to knowing what to demand from every consulting engagement you enter.

Chapter 22

What Good Looks Like

I have spent the last five chapters describing what bad looks like. The structural conflicts of the SI model. The bait and switch. The eighteen-month lie. The knowledge hostage. The rigged selection process. Reading these chapters back to back, you might conclude that every consulting engagement is doomed to fail and that the only rational response is to do everything yourself.

That is not what I am saying. What I am saying is that the default model is broken, and that if you accept the default, you will get the default outcome. But the default is not the only option. There are consulting relationships that work. There are implementations that deliver what they promise. There are organizations that emerge from digital transformation stronger, more efficient, and genuinely better at what they do.

These cases are the exception, not the rule. But they are real. And understanding what makes them work is essential, because it gives you a standard to hold every consulting engagement against and a set of principles to demand from every partner you hire.

This chapter is about what good looks like.

Independence Is Not Optional

The single most important characteristic of an effective advisory relationship is independence. Not independence as a marketing claim. Independence as a structural reality.

An independent advisor does not partner with the software vendor. They do not earn commissions on software deals. They do not receive referral fees for steering you toward a particular product.

They do not have an SAP practice that needs to be fed or an Oracle practice that needs to be staffed. When they walk into your conference room, there is exactly one set of interests they are there to serve: yours.

This sounds simple. It is extraordinarily rare.

The vast majority of consulting firms in the enterprise technology space operate under some form of vendor affiliation. They partner with SAP, Oracle, Microsoft, or Workday. They earn revenue from those partnerships. Their recommendations are shaped, consciously or unconsciously, by those economic relationships.

When they tell you they are independent, they mean something different from what you understand the word to mean. They mean they are independent within the constraints of their partnerships. They are not independent of them.

"It is not an either-or proposition: you can get the best of the system integrator and augment with the more strategic and specialized skill sets of others." The model that works is not one where you eliminate the SI. The SI brings technical expertise that you need. The model that works is one where the SI delivers the technical workstream within a program that is governed by the client, advised by an independent party, and structured so that no single firm controls both the delivery and the oversight.

There is a common assumption in the industry that the advisor and the implementer should always be separate firms. I want to challenge that assumption, because the nuance matters.

A biased advisor should never be your implementer. When a firm that partners with SAP advises you to select SAP and then implements SAP, the entire engagement -- from recommendation to delivery -- is shaped by a commercial relationship that has nothing to do with your best interests. That is the fox-guarding-the-henhouse model described in Chapter 17, and it should be rejected categorically.

But an independent, tech-agnostic advisor who also provides implementation support is a fundamentally different model. When the firm advising you has no vendor partnerships, earns no commissions, and arrived at the technology recommendation purely through an analysis of your business needs -- and that same firm then helps you implement the solution, manage the change, redesign the processes, govern the program, and build internal capability -- the alignment of interests is preserved throughout the engagement. There is no moment where the incentive structure shifts from your interests to the vendor's, because the vendor was never in the equation.

In fact, there is a strong argument that the independent advisor is better positioned to support implementation than a vendor-aligned SI, precisely because their scope extends beyond technology. The vendor-aligned SI delivers a technical workstream. The independent advisor delivers a program: organizational change management, business process improvement, data migration strategy, integration architecture, PMO governance, and the human dimensions of transformation that determine success or failure. The firms that can do both -- advise independently and deliver holistically -- offer a model that eliminates the gap between what was recommended and what gets built. The recommendation and the delivery are governed by the same set of interests: yours.

The bright line is not between advisory and implementation. The bright line is between independence and affiliation. An advisor who is affiliated with the vendor cannot provide objective guidance regardless of whether they also implement. An advisor who is independent of the vendor can provide objective guidance and, in many cases, deliver a more complete and more aligned implementation than the vendor's preferred partners, because their scope is not limited to the technology workstream and their incentives are not divided between your interests and the vendor's.

There is also a financial dimension to independence that is rarely discussed but that represents one of the most tangible returns on investing in an independent advisor: cost savings.

Large SI teams typically show up on day one of the project and begin billing immediately -- whether or not the client is ready to optimize that time. The SI's incentive is to deploy resources as early as possible and keep them deployed as long as possible, because that is how their revenue model works. If the client is not ready for design workshops because the business process work has not been completed, the SI's team is still on site, still billing, still consuming budget while waiting for the client to catch up. If the SI has staffed forty consultants but only twenty are productive in a given phase, the other twenty are still billing. The meter is running from the moment the contract is signed, and the client is paying for the SI's readiness, not their own.

An independent advisor focused on client success manages this dynamic actively. They help the client sequence the work so that SI resources are brought on only when the organization is ready to use them productively. They challenge staffing levels that reflect the SI's bench pressure rather than the project's actual needs. They review invoices and utilization reports to ensure that the hours being billed correspond to value being delivered. They negotiate phase gates that tie SI resource deployment to the client's readiness milestones rather than the SI's revenue targets. In some cases, we have helped clients reduce their SI run rate by 20 to 30 percent simply by managing the timing and staffing of the engagement more carefully -- not by cutting scope, but by eliminating the waste that the SI's default deployment model builds into every project.

This cost management function alone often pays for the independent advisor's fees several times over. The most expensive consulting engagement is not the one with the highest billing rate. It is the one where forty consultants are billing full-time and only half of them are doing productive work. An independent advisor with visibility into the SI's staffing plan, utilization data, and delivery timeline can identify that waste in real time and redirect the spending toward activities that actually move the program forward. The SI will not do this for you. They benefit from the waste. The independent advisor benefits when you eliminate it.

Meeting Clients Where They Are

One of the hardest lessons I have learned in twenty-five years of advisory work is that being right is not enough. You can have the correct diagnosis. You can see the risks clearly. You can know exactly what the organization should do. And the organization may not do it.

Clients do not always listen, and that has to be okay. They may lack the resources, budget, people, or organizational will to do things the "right" way. Effective advisors stay for the entire journey regardless -- the solution has to be the client's, not the consultant's.

I have worked with consultants who take an absolutist approach: if the client does not follow the recommendation, the consultant disengages. "If they are not going to listen, I do not want to be part of this project." I understand the frustration. But that position is dangerous, because it abandons the client at precisely the moment they need guidance most.

The best advisory relationships are not the ones where the client follows every recommendation perfectly. They are the ones where the advisor provides the best possible counsel, the client makes their own decision based on their own reality, and the advisor stays to help navigate the consequences -- whether the decision was the one the advisor would have made or not. The advisor's job is not to be right. It is to be useful. And being useful means adapting your recommendations to the client's actual capacity, actual budget, actual culture, and actual constraints, rather than insisting on an idealized approach that the organization cannot execute.

Being effective in this work often means being part consultant, part therapist. Listening to and understanding the client's problems is half the battle. The executives leading a transformation are under enormous pressure -- from their boards, from their employees, from the vendors, from the SIs, from the timeline, from the budget. They need someone who can hear what they are worried about, who can validate the concerns that are legitimate and challenge the ones that are not, and who can do so with the empathy and the patience that the situation requires. The consulting firms that approach every engagement as a technical exercise, deploying methodology and deliverables without first understanding the human dimension, miss the most important part of the work. The organizations going through transformation are not machines to be optimized. They are communities of people navigating uncertainty. Meeting them where they are starts with understanding who they are.

This does not mean accepting bad decisions silently. It means documenting the risks, presenting the alternatives, making the recommendation clearly, and then -- if the client chooses a different path -- helping them execute that path as effectively as possible while continuing to surface the risks that the decision creates. The client owns the outcome. The advisor's job is to ensure the client makes informed decisions, not to make the decisions for them.

My favorite client in twenty-five years of consulting is also one of the most difficult I have ever worked with, and the combination is not a contradiction -- it is the point. This is a company in the steel industry that completely disrupted its sector. They took an old-school, traditional industry and transformed it with an innovative operating model that reshaped how their market works. They are brilliant operators and fierce competitors. They are also deeply skeptical of consultants. They do not trust outsiders. They do not defer to external expertise. Their culture either accepts you or rejects you, and the rejection is swift and unambiguous.

For the first several months of our engagement, we were tested constantly. Every recommendation was challenged. Every deliverable was scrutinized. Every assumption was questioned -- not because the client was being difficult, but because that is who they are. They did not become the most innovative company in their industry by accepting advice at face value. They became that company by thinking for themselves, by demanding proof, and by holding everyone around them to the same standard they hold themselves.

We could have walked away. Many consultants would have. Instead, we adapted. We learned their culture. We earned their trust the only way it can be earned in an organization like that: by demonstrating, over time, that we were adding value on their terms, not ours. We met them where they were. We fit our approach to their reality, not the other way around.

That client has been with us for years. We have helped them through multiple major transformation initiatives -- enterprise-wide ERP deployments, business intelligence programs, and strategic technology decisions that have shaped their competitive position. It is the most rewarding advisory relationship of my career. And it only exists because we were willing to endure the difficulty of the early months rather than insisting that the client conform to our model. The advisory relationship that works is the one where the advisor adapts to the client's culture, not the one where the client adapts to the advisor's preferences.

Transparent Governance

In effective consulting relationships, the client has real-time visibility into what the consultants are doing, why they are doing it, and how it connects to the project's objectives. This sounds basic. In most engagements, it does not exist.

The standard SI engagement operates with a significant information asymmetry: the SI knows far more about the project's status, risks, and trajectory than the client does. Status reports are filtered. Risk registers are curated. Steering committee presentations highlight progress and minimize problems. The client receives a version of reality that has been shaped by the SI's interest in maintaining the engagement, protecting the timeline narrative, and avoiding difficult conversations that might slow the project or reduce the headcount.

Transparent governance eliminates this asymmetry. It means the client has access to the same project data the consultants have: unfiltered risk registers, real utilization numbers, actual versus planned progress at the task level, defect counts and severity distributions, change order histories, and resource deployment reports that show who is working on what and for how many hours. It means the program management office -- which, as I have argued throughout Part III, should be owned by the client -- has the authority and the tools to monitor the SI's performance in real time, not through quarterly reviews that are scripted by the SI's account management team.

This is another area where tools like Mission Control make a material difference. AI-powered project oversight can process the vast quantities of project data that a human PMO cannot -- across RAID logs, status reports, resource plans, configuration documents, testing results, and change order histories -- and surface the patterns, anomalies, and risks that manual governance processes miss. The technology to achieve transparent governance exists. The question is whether the client demands it and whether the SI tolerates it. The SIs that resist transparency are the ones with something to hide. The SIs that welcome it are the ones confident in their delivery. That distinction, all by itself, tells you a lot about which SI to hire.

Outcome-Based Relationships

The T&M model, as I described in Chapter 17, creates a perverse incentive: the SI profits when the project takes longer. The fixed-price model, as I described in Chapter 19, creates a different perversion: the SI profits by narrowing the scope and billing everything else as out-of-scope additions. Neither model aligns the SI's financial interests with the client's outcomes.

What would alignment look like? It would look like an engagement where at least a portion of the consultant's compensation is tied to the achievement of defined business outcomes. Not go-live -- go-live is a milestone, not an outcome. Not system deployment -- deployment is an event, not a result. Business outcomes: measurable improvements in operational efficiency, reduction in cycle times, improvement in order fulfillment accuracy, reduction in manual workarounds, achievement of the specific KPIs that were defined in the business case.

Outcome-based contracting is rare in the industry because it requires the consultant to share risk. Under an outcome-based model, if the implementation does not deliver the promised results, the consultant's compensation is reduced. This is precisely the incentive alignment that the industry needs, and it is precisely the model that the large SIs resist, because it requires them to put their revenue at risk rather than transferring all risk to the client.

Not every element of a consulting engagement can be outcome-based. Technical configuration, for example, is better compensated on a time-and-materials or fixed-deliverable basis. But the advisory and governance components -- the workstreams that influence whether the transformation delivers business value -- should have an outcome component. When the advisor's compensation is tied to the client's success, the advice gets better. The recommendations become more honest. The risk assessments become more rigorous. Because now the advisor has skin in the game.

What the Data Tells Us About Success

The research from our work across more than a thousand implementations is remarkably clear about what separates successful transformations from unsuccessful ones. And the findings consistently point away from the variables the industry emphasizes and toward the variables it neglects.

The specific system integrator appeared to have less of an impact on results than other variables. The type of software selected showed no statistical correlation with success or failure. The variables with the strongest impact on outcomes were: scope, magnitude of change, complexity of operations, level of organizational change management support, and level of software customization.

There is little to no impact from the specific SI partner on implementation outcomes.

Read those findings together. The SI does not determine your outcome. The vendor does not determine your outcome. What determines your outcome is how well you manage the organizational dimensions of the transformation: the leadership alignment, the change readiness, the process clarity, the governance rigor, and the cultural capacity to absorb disruption. These are the variables that the machine underinvests in, because they do not generate software revenue or consulting hours. And they are the variables that determine whether your tens of millions of dollars produce a transformation or an expensive disappointment.

The organizations that succeed invest heavily in these dimensions. They conduct organizational readiness assessments before the implementation begins. They fund change management at 15 to 20 percent of the total program budget, not the 3 to 5 percent that most organizations allocate. They define their business processes before they configure the software. They build internal capability throughout the implementation rather than outsourcing everything to the SI. They establish governance structures that give the client's leadership real-time visibility and decision-making authority.

None of these investments require a specific vendor or a specific SI. They require leadership, discipline, and a willingness to prioritize the hard, unglamorous, organizational work over the exciting, visible, technology work. The organizations that make this choice succeed at rates that far exceed the industry average. The organizations that do not make this choice join the majority.

The Canary in the Coal Mine: 13 Warning Signs

Even in well-structured engagements, things can go wrong. The key is detecting the problems early enough to course-correct before the damage compounds. Based on our experience recovering failed and troubled implementations, here are the thirteen warning signs that your consulting engagement is going off the rails.

1. You are too reliant on your SI. If your internal team cannot articulate what the SI is doing, why they are doing it, or how it connects to your business objectives, you have ceded control. The SI should be in a supporting role. If they are driving every decision, you are a passenger, not an owner.

2. There is no integrated program plan. If the only project plan is the SI's technical implementation plan, the program is under-planned. An integrated plan should cover all workstreams: technical, OCM, data migration, integration, business process, and governance. If you are six to eight weeks into the project without one, you are in trouble.

3. Expectations are unrealistic. If the timeline, budget, or benefit projections have not been independently validated, they are probably wrong. Take every SI proposal with a grain of salt and validate against independent benchmarks.

4. The implementation started before planning was complete. Jumping from software selection to configuration without a Phase Zero -- implementation planning, future-state process design, change strategy, resource mobilization -- is the most common precursor to failure.

5. There is no realistic business case. If you cannot articulate, in measurable terms, where the business value will come from, you have no North Star for decision-making. Every scope change, every customization request, every resource conflict will be resolved by gut feel instead of business logic.

6. Executive alignment is absent. If the CEO, CFO, and CIO are not aligned on the objectives, the program will be pulled in different directions. Governance without executive alignment is theater.

7. Change management is an afterthought. If OCM is funded at less than 10 percent of the program budget, or if the SI claims to handle change management through technical training alone, the organization is not being prepared for the transformation. It is being informed about it. Those are different things.

8. The wrong technology was selected. If the software cannot support your core business processes without extensive customization, the technology choice is wrong. No amount of consulting hours can fix a fundamental platform mismatch.

9. The SI is resisting independent oversight. If the SI objects to a third-party quality assurance advisor, offers "free" alternatives, or trains its team to deflect independent scrutiny, they are protecting their revenue, not your project.

10. Key resources keep rotating off. If the named resources from the proposal have been replaced by people whose resumes you never reviewed, the bait and switch is in progress. Demand an explanation and invoke the contractual protections you negotiated -- or should have negotiated.

11. Status reports do not match reality. If the steering committee presentations show green across the board but the project team is working nights and weekends, the reporting is filtered. Demand access to the raw project data, not the curated summary.

12. Testing is being compressed. If the testing timeline is being shortened to maintain the go-live date, defects are being discovered in production rather than in test. This is the single most dangerous compression in any implementation.

13. Nobody is talking about post-go-live. If the project plan ends at go-live with no stabilization period, no hypercare plan, and no benefits realization framework, the hardest phase of the transformation has not been planned for. The morning after go-live is when the real work begins.

If you see three or more of these warning signs simultaneously, your project is at significant risk. The earlier you address them, the lower the cost of correction. The longer you wait, the more the damage compounds, and the more expensive the recovery becomes.

Size Is Not the Problem. Culture Is.

I want to address a misconception that I encounter frequently: the belief that only large, prestigious consulting firms can deliver enterprise-scale implementations. This belief persists because the large firms have the marketing budgets to reinforce it and because the brand names carry a perceived safety that smaller firms do not.

The data does not support this belief. As the research cited earlier in this chapter shows, the specific SI has minimal statistical impact on outcomes. A prestigious brand on the proposal does not correlate with a successful implementation. What correlates with success is the quality of the people, the alignment of incentives, and the culture of the firm.

After leaving PricewaterhouseCoopers, I went to a smaller company. That company was eventually acquired by a larger firm, and I still enjoyed the work. The large-company environment worked because the culture was right. The dysfunction of the Big Four is not inherent to scale. It is inherent to a business model that rewards billing over outcomes, staffing over delivery, and vendor partnerships over client independence. A large firm with the right culture can deliver excellent work. A small firm with the wrong culture can be just as dysfunctional as any Big Four engagement.

The variable that matters is not size. It is whether the firm's incentives are aligned with your success. A firm that profits when you succeed and suffers when you fail will behave differently from a firm that profits regardless. A firm whose people are measured on client outcomes will staff differently from a firm whose people are measured on utilization. A firm that welcomes independent oversight will deliver differently from a firm that trains its managers to deflect it.

When you evaluate consulting firms, evaluate the culture, not the logo. Ask how they measure success. Ask how they handle failure. Ask what happens when a project is not going well -- do they add bodies, or do they change the approach? Ask their references the same questions. The answers will tell you more about the firm's ability to deliver than any proposal, any presentation, or any brand name ever will.

The Standard to Demand

Based on everything described in this chapter, here is the standard that every organization should demand from every consulting engagement:

Independence. The advisor must be structurally independent of the software vendor and the system integrator. No vendor partnerships. No referral fees. No commissions. One set of interests: yours.

Transparency. Real-time visibility into project status, risks, resource utilization, and decision rationale. No filtered status reports. No curated steering committee presentations. The raw data, available to the client's PMO at all times.

Accountability. Contractual commitments to named resources, knowledge transfer milestones, and defined exit strategies. Outcome-based compensation for advisory and governance workstreams. Financial consequences for under-delivery, not just for the client, but for the consultant.

Capability building. The engagement must leave the organization more capable than it was before. Training for the core team. Staffing support for the PMO. Documentation that transfers knowledge, not just records configuration. The goal of every consulting engagement should be to make the consultant unnecessary.

Client ownership. The client owns the program. The client owns the PMO. The client owns the governance. The SI delivers a workstream within a program the client controls. The advisor supports the client's decision-making. Nobody -- not the vendor, not the SI, not the analyst, not the advisor -- makes decisions on behalf of the client.

This is what good looks like. It is not what the machine delivers by default. But it is what the machine can be forced to deliver, when the client understands the dynamics, demands the standard, and refuses to accept anything less.

In the next chapter, we will zoom out to examine the ecosystem as a whole: the circular economy of vendors, consultants, analysts, and media that reinforces itself and marginalizes independent voices. Understanding the ecosystem is the final piece of the puzzle -- the context that explains why the machine persists and why breaking free from it requires not just better decisions but a fundamentally different relationship with the industry that surrounds you.

Chapter 23

The Ecosystem

In the previous six chapters of Part III, I described the individual actors in the machine: the system integrators with their perverse incentives, the bait-and-switch staffing practices, the unrealistic timelines, the knowledge hostage, the corrupted selection process, and the rare cases where the advisory relationship works as it should. Each chapter examined a component of the machine in isolation.

This chapter zooms out. Because the machine is not just its individual parts. It is the ecosystem that connects them -- the web of financial relationships, marketing partnerships, industry events, research publications, and social media ecosystems that reinforces the machine's narrative, marginalizes the voices that challenge it, and ensures that the client's information environment is dominated by the very parties who profit from their decisions.

Understanding the ecosystem is the final piece of anatomy. You cannot navigate the machine without understanding how the information that reaches you was produced, who paid for it, and whose interests it serves.

The Circular Economy of Digital Transformation

The enterprise technology industry has built one of the most efficient circular economies ever constructed. Every actor in the ecosystem feeds every other, the money flows in predictable circuits, and the client is the only party at the table who is not part of the circuit.

Here is how the circuit works.

The vendors make the software. They invest billions in marketing -- conferences, analyst sponsorships, partner programs, co-marketing funds -- to ensure that their products are perceived as essential, their migration timelines as urgent, and their cloud platforms as the inevitable future. The marketing budget is not a cost. It is an investment with a measurable return: every dollar of vendor marketing that drives a software sale or a cloud migration generates recurring subscription revenue that compounds over years.

With investors and vendors both investing heavily in cloud, the rest of the ERP ecosystem falls into line. Consultants and system integrators, paid by the vendors, reinforce the vendors' pro-cloud philosophy. Industry analysts, who are also paid by the vendors, have been touting the death of on-premise for years. The industry has built a fully integrated ecosystem that is crushing on-premise into oblivion.

The system integrators implement the vendor's products and receive commercial benefits from the vendor partnerships: preferential pricing on licenses, co-selling support, access to vendor expertise, and in some cases direct commissions on software deals. Their economic survival depends on the vendor's continued market dominance. A world in which SAP is replaced by a competitor or fragmented by composable alternatives is a world in which the SAP practice -- with its hundreds of trained consultants -- becomes valueless overnight. The SI has as much economic interest in the vendor's success as the vendor does.

You have a whole ecosystem of implementation partners, system integrators, resellers, and technical consultants that focus on SAP. The Big Four -- Deloitte, Accenture, KPMG, PwC -- all focus heavily on S/4HANA. Their goal is to get you to implement SAP and go to S/4HANA Cloud using their services.

The analysts validate the cycle. Gartner, Forrester, IDC, and their peers publish research that buyers rely on to evaluate technologies and partners. These analysts are paid by the vendors they evaluate -- through access programs, sponsorships, speaking fees, and co-branded research engagements. The financial relationship is substantial, ongoing, and structural. When an analyst publishes a Magic Quadrant or a Wave report, the report is produced within a commercial context in which the firms being evaluated are also paying customers of the analyst firm. The analyst's independence is genuine within the constraints of these relationships. It is not absolute.

The circuit closes when the analyst's favorable coverage drives buyer confidence, the buyer selects the vendor and the SI, the implementation begins, and the fees flow back into the ecosystem -- vendor revenue, SI billable hours, analyst access fees, conference sponsorships, and the whole cycle begins again.

The client pays for all of it. Not just through the license fees and the consulting fees. Through the information environment the circuit creates. Every analyst report that the client reads, every conference presentation they attend, every thought leadership article they encounter, every LinkedIn post that confirms their belief that they must migrate to the cloud now -- these are all produced within a commercial ecosystem that has a financial interest in specific outcomes. The client's information environment is not neutral. It is curated, funded, and distributed by parties whose interests diverge from the client's. And in most cases, the client does not know it.

The circular economy has one more dimension that deserves attention, because it represents the ecosystem's most powerful lock-in mechanism yet: the convergence of cloud and AI.

In Chapter 10, I described how the cloud subscription model gave vendors unprecedented recurring revenue and high switching costs. In Chapter 14, I described how AI is being embedded into every vendor's platform as the next investor-rewarded capability. What I want to emphasize here is what happens when you combine the two -- because the combination creates a form of vendor lock-in that the industry has never seen before.

In the cloud model, the vendor controls your infrastructure, your data, your SLAs, and your renewal terms. That alone creates substantial switching costs. But add AI to the equation and the lock-in deepens by an order of magnitude. The vendor's AI is trained on your data -- your transactions, your demand patterns, your operational history. Over time, the AI learns your business. It builds models that are specific to your operations, your customers, your supply chain. Those models become valuable. They become, in a sense, your institutional intelligence -- but they live on the vendor's platform, governed by the vendor's terms, and accessible only through the vendor's tools.

If you decide to leave, you do not just migrate your data. You abandon the AI models that were trained on that data. You lose the institutional intelligence that the system built over years of learning your operations. You start over, with a new vendor, a new AI, and a blank slate where your operational knowledge used to be. The switching cost is no longer just the cost of reimplementation. It is the cost of re-learning -- of rebuilding the intelligence that your business spent years teaching the old system.

This gives vendors unprecedented pricing power over their customers. At every renewal, the vendor knows that the cost of leaving includes not just the reimplementation but the loss of AI-driven intelligence that the customer has come to depend on. The customer's negotiating leverage -- already weak in the cloud model -- approaches zero. The vendor can raise prices, bundle additional services, change terms, and the customer's rational response is to pay, because the alternative is more expensive than the increase.

Cloud was the lock. AI is the deadbolt. And the ecosystem -- the SIs who implement it, the analysts who validate it, the conferences that celebrate it -- is building the walls around you while telling you it is building your future. The vendors are not just selling you software anymore. They are selling you a dependency that deepens with every transaction your AI processes, every model it trains, and every insight it generates. The longer you stay, the harder it is to leave. That is not a side effect of the technology. It is the business model.

Conference Culture

The annual vendor conference is the machine's most visible expression of ecosystem alignment, and it deserves specific attention because of how effectively it shapes the market's perception of reality.

SAP Sapphire. Oracle OpenWorld. Microsoft Ignite. Salesforce Dreamforce. Workday Rising. These events attract tens of thousands of attendees, generate hundreds of millions of dollars in sponsorship and registration revenue, and serve as the primary public stage on which the vendor announces its direction, celebrates its successes, and defines the narrative for the coming year. Every major SI is a gold or platinum sponsor. Every major analyst firm sends its research team. Every media outlet that covers enterprise technology has reporters on site.

The conference is a controlled environment. The keynotes are scripted and rehearsed to the last detail. The case studies presented on stage are curated selections from the vendor's happiest clients. The analyst sessions are briefed in advance by the vendor's analyst relations team. The media coverage is shaped by the access that the vendor grants -- exclusive interviews, product demonstrations, executive briefings -- which flows preferentially to journalists and outlets that have historically covered the vendor favorably.

What you experience at a vendor conference is not the industry. It is the vendor's version of the industry: a version in which the product is transformative, the migration is necessary, the partners are capable, and the future is cloudward. The organizations that failed on the platform are not presenting case studies. The consultants who delivered poor work are not on stage. The customers who are questioning whether the forced migration makes business sense are not in the keynote. The conference is a celebration, and like all celebrations, it presents a selective version of reality.

The power of the conference is not just in what is said. It is in who is there. When the CIO attends SAP Sapphire and sees thousands of their peers, every major consulting firm, and dozens of analyst firms all expressing enthusiasm for S/4HANA, the social proof is overwhelming. The herd is moving. The experts have validated the direction. The fear of being left behind -- which the vendor has cultivated deliberately through its forced migration timeline -- is intensified by the spectacle of an entire industry aligned behind a single direction. The client does not feel like they are being sold to. They feel like they are joining a movement.

This is the conference's deepest function: not information transfer, but social conformity. It is the annual renewal of the machine's energy, the moment at which the ecosystem reaffirms its alignment and sends its collective participants back to their organizations with the conviction that the vendor's path is the right path. For the organizations represented at the conference, the message lands. For the organizations that could not afford to attend -- the mid-market manufacturers, the regional distributors, the public sector agencies -- the echo of the message reaches them through the media coverage, the analyst reports, and the LinkedIn posts of the attendees who dutifully amplified what they heard.

How Thought Leadership Became Vendor Marketing

The enterprise technology industry produces an extraordinary volume of content: white papers, research reports, blog posts, webinars, podcasts, YouTube channels, LinkedIn articles. This content is presented as thought leadership -- independent analysis and insights offered to help buyers make better decisions. Most of it is vendor marketing with a byline.

The mechanisms are varied and often subtle. Some content is produced directly by vendors and labeled as such: product brochures, implementation guides, case studies. This is transparent and relatively harmless. The buyer understands they are reading vendor-produced content and discounts it accordingly.

More influential is the content produced by the ecosystem on the vendor's behalf. The SI publishes a white paper on digital transformation best practices -- which happens to recommend the vendor's platform and the SI's implementation methodology. The analyst publishes a report on cloud ERP market trends -- which is sponsored by three of the five vendors being discussed.

The media outlet publishes an article on AI in the enterprise -- which is based on a vendor-funded study that the vendor's communications team distributed to journalists with a ready-made narrative.

The content is not necessarily false. It may be accurate in its facts. But it is framed -- selected, organized, and interpreted -- within a commercial context that systematically favors certain conclusions. The studies that show positive outcomes from cloud migration are published and distributed. The studies that show mixed or negative outcomes are not. The case studies that demonstrate successful implementations are promoted. The case studies of failed implementations are anonymized, minimized, or not published at all.

Social media has amplified this dynamic to a scale that was impossible in the pre-digital era. LinkedIn, in particular, has become the primary distribution channel for enterprise technology thought leadership. The algorithms that govern what content surfaces reward engagement -- likes, comments, shares. The content that gets the most engagement tends to be the content that confirms what the audience already believes, that presents a compelling narrative, and that comes from recognized voices with large followings. The recognized voices with large followings in the enterprise technology space tend to be vendor executives, SI partners, and industry analysts -- the same parties whose interests are served by the ecosystem's preferred narrative.

The result is an information environment in which the client's LinkedIn feed, their conference agenda, their reading list, and their analyst briefings all reinforce the same message: the technology is essential, the migration is necessary, the partners are capable, and the future is determined. The dissenting voices -- the independent consultants who question the migration's business case, the clients who speak honestly about their failed implementations, the researchers who find that SI choice has minimal impact on outcomes -- are present but quiet. The algorithm does not amplify them. The conferences do not platform them. The analyst firms do not cite them. And in some cases, as I will describe shortly, they face active pressure to be quiet.

The Marginalization of Independence

The ecosystem does not merely ignore independent voices. It actively works to marginalize them. This is not conspiracy theory. It is business strategy, executed through the specific tactics described throughout this book.

The system integrators train their account management teams to deflect independent advisors. At least one of these firms has shared directly with me that they have specialized training as part of their management program on how to deflect advisory firms that attempt to offer additional services to their clients. The "free" OCM offering that appears whenever an independent change management firm is being considered. The account manager who schedules a meeting with the client's executives the same day the independent advisor is presenting. The subtle suggestion that adding another consulting firm creates confusion, introduces conflict, and slows the project. These tactics are not accidental. They are institutionalized.

The vendors use a different set of tools. Access programs that reward media outlets and analysts who cover the vendor favorably with early product announcements, executive interviews, and conference invitations. The opposite for those who are consistently critical: fewer invitations, less access, slower responses to press inquiries. The vendor's communications team does not need to threaten journalists. It simply redirects the flow of information, and the content environment adjusts accordingly.

The conferences enforce conformity through inclusion and exclusion. The speaking slots at the major vendor conferences go to customers who share success stories, consultants who recommend the platform, and analysts who have validated the vendor's strategy. The critics are not invited. The independent advisors who consistently challenge the vendor's narrative are not on the agenda. The conferences do not need to censor dissent. They simply do not fund it.

The result is an information environment that looks diverse -- many voices, many sources, many perspectives -- but is structurally homogeneous. Every voice that receives amplification from the ecosystem's resources has, in some form, been pre-qualified as aligned with the ecosystem's interests. The apparent diversity of opinion masks a deep uniformity of commercial interest.

The Price of Speaking Out

In organized crime, there is a principle called omertà -- the code of silence. Nobody talks about the family's business. Nobody cooperates with outsiders. Nobody validates the people who ask uncomfortable questions. Those who break the code face consequences. The enterprise technology ecosystem operates on its own version of omertà. Nobody in the ecosystem publicly criticizes the family's partners. Nobody validates the independent voices who challenge the vendor's narrative. Nobody breaks ranks at the conference. And when someone does speak out -- when someone names the conflicts, documents the failures, and refuses to participate in the code -- the family responds.

I want to be direct about something that I have not discussed publicly in as much depth as it deserves.

Being tech-agnostic, being a trusted client advisor, being someone who refuses to drink the Kool-Aid -- these positions make powerful people uncomfortable. And powerful people with uncomfortable positions do not always respond professionally.

Over the years, I have received anonymous threatening phone calls from people who did not appreciate what I had to say. I have received intimidating voicemails. One message, left by someone who never identified themselves, said simply: "Eric, I saw your article and I would be careful if I were you."

I want to be clear about how that feels. It does not feel like a business dispute. It does not feel like competitive friction between consulting firms. It feels like a scene from a movie about organized crime. It is a threat, delivered anonymously, with no accountability. And it has happened to me on multiple occasions.

The anonymous calls are not the only form of pressure. I have also received formal cease and desist orders from organizations that do not want their failures discussed publicly.

In one case, a large software vendor sent a legal letter demanding that I take down a YouTube video in which I discussed some of that vendor's well-documented implementation failures. The video contained publicly available information -- court records, media reports, industry analysis -- that anyone with an internet connection could find. The vendor's lawyers did not dispute the accuracy of what I had said. They objected to the fact that I had said it. The demand was clear: stop talking about our failures, or face legal consequences.

In another case, attorneys representing Queensland Health in Australia sent a similar demand. I had posted a video discussing their ERP payroll disaster -- the same case I described in Chapter 17 of this book, a case that is already extensively documented in public inquiry reports, government proceedings, and media coverage around the world. The attorneys viewed the video as a public relations problem and demanded that I remove all content discussing their implementation. Not because it was inaccurate. Because it was embarrassing.

In both cases, I refused to comply. But refusing required me to hire attorneys of my own, to spend money defending my right to discuss publicly documented failures in the enterprise technology industry. The cost was financial and personal. The message from the other side was unmistakable: we have more lawyers than you do, and we are willing to use them to make the truth expensive to tell.

This is what we are dealing with. Not just the anonymous threats from unknown callers. Not just the institutional training to deflect independent advisors. Not just the ecosystem's soft marginalization through conference exclusion and algorithm suppression. But formal legal action -- cease and desist letters, the threat of litigation -- deployed against individuals who have the audacity to discuss, publicly and accurately, the failures that this industry produces at a rate of 55 to 75 percent. The industry's response to its own failure rate is not to reduce the failures. It is to silence the people who talk about them.

The technology industry is a trillion-dollar ecosystem. The firms within it have significant resources, significant incentives, and in some cases, significant willingness to protect those resources through means that go beyond legitimate competition. I am not the only independent voice in this space who has experienced pressure, intimidation, or attempts to silence criticism. I am, perhaps, one of the few who is willing to say so publicly.

I am not sharing this to dramatize my own experience or to position myself as a martyr. I am sharing it because it illuminates something important about the ecosystem: the depth of its self-protective instincts. An industry that responds to honest criticism with anonymous threats is an industry that knows, at some level, that the criticism is accurate and that transparency would be damaging. The intensity of the resistance to independent voices is, itself, evidence of what those voices have found.

The machine does not appreciate being described from the outside. That is, in a strange way, the most honest endorsement this book could receive.

The Client's Information Gap

The consequence of all of this for the client is an information gap that is profound and largely invisible.

There are recent studies that show that 80 to 85 percent of people distrust big organizations, and they distrust big technology providers at an even higher rate. The distrust is real and widespread. But distrust alone is not sufficient protection. The client may distrust the vendor while still consuming the vendor-funded analyst report, attending the vendor-funded conference, and choosing from the vendor-recommended list of implementation partners. Distrust without alternative sources of information produces cynicism, not clarity.

The information gap has a specific shape. The client knows a great deal about the vendor's product, because the vendor has invested billions to ensure they do. They know the cloud is the future, because every analyst, every SI, every conference, and every piece of sponsored content has told them so. They know which implementation partners are available, because the vendor's partner ecosystem directory is comprehensive and prominently marketed. They know what success stories look like, because the vendor has curated and promoted them carefully.

What the client does not know: what the actual failure rates are for the vendor's platform. How their implementation experience compares to the market average. What the managed services dependency looks like three years after go-live. What the organizational and cultural prerequisites for success actually are. What the realistic cost and timeline look like for their specific situation, not the generic benchmark the SI uses to win bids. What options exist outside the vendor's recommended partner ecosystem. What the real business case looks like when someone other than the vendor constructs it.

This is the information that the ecosystem does not produce, because producing it would reduce the market for the ecosystem's services. The ecosystem's economic interest is in a client who believes the technology is essential, the timeline is urgent, the partner selection is straightforward, and the outcome is all but guaranteed. A client who knows the full picture -- who knows the failure rates, the cost overruns, the knowledge hostage dynamics, the bait and switch, the ecosystem's incentive structure -- is a client who asks harder questions, demands better terms, insists on independence, and reduces the machine's margin. The information gap is not accidental. It is structural.

The Wild West

There is a question that I have asked myself repeatedly over the past twenty-five years, and it is a question that I believe deserves a place in this book: why is any of this legal?

Consider how other industries that handle large sums of money and significant client risk are regulated. In financial services, advisors are required by law to disclose conflicts of interest. Fiduciary standards mandate that the advisor act in the client's best interest, not their own. Investment products must be sold with transparent fee structures. Audit firms, as I described in Chapter 17, are prohibited from consulting for the same clients they audit, because the Enron-era collapse demonstrated that the conflict of interest was too dangerous to tolerate. In healthcare, pharmaceutical companies must disclose payments to physicians. In real estate, agents must disclose dual representation. In nearly every consumer-facing industry where significant money changes hands and information asymmetry exists, regulation requires some degree of transparency, independence, or fiduciary duty.

The enterprise technology industry has none of this. No fiduciary standard. No mandatory conflict disclosure. No prohibition on the same firm advising and implementing. No requirement that the vendor disclose the financial relationships between its partner ecosystem and the analysts who evaluate it. No transparency mandate for pricing. No building codes for implementations. No inspection regime for go-live readiness. No regulatory body that reviews whether the vendor's sales claims match the product's actual capabilities.

If ERP vendors and system integrators were selling to consumers instead of businesses, they would have been regulated decades ago. A financial advisor who recommended investments based on the commissions they earned rather than the client's needs would face SEC enforcement. A home builder who started construction without blueprints or inspections would face code violations and lawsuits. A pharmaceutical company that sold a drug based on a scripted demo rather than clinical trials would face FDA action. But because enterprise technology is sold to businesses rather than consumers, the assumption is that the buyer is sophisticated enough to protect themselves. Nobody feels sorry for a billion-dollar corporation that gets taken advantage of by a consulting firm.

The problem with that assumption is that most organizations are not sophisticated technology buyers. They undertake major transformations once a decade. Their executives are experts in their own industries -- manufacturing, distribution, healthcare, financial services -- not in enterprise software procurement. The information asymmetry between the vendor ecosystem and the typical buyer is as severe as the asymmetry between a financial advisor and a retail investor. The difference is that the retail investor has regulatory protection. The enterprise technology buyer does not.

The result is the wild west. A market where the vendor can promise $200 million in benefits that never materialize. Where the SI can propose an eighteen-month timeline they know is unrealistic. Where the analyst can publish a ranking funded by the firms being ranked. Where the consulting firm can implement a system and then evaluate its own work. Where the vendor can force a migration that serves investors rather than customers. Where none of this is illegal, because no law says it has to be otherwise.

But here is the argument that will ultimately force the regulatory reckoning: end consumers are harmed by these dynamics. Not just the businesses that buy the software. The people those businesses serve.

When a healthcare company's ERP implementation fails, patient services are disrupted. When a defense contractor's system migration goes wrong, the supply chain that supports national security is compromised. When a medical device company's quality management system is botched, the products that people depend on for their lives are at risk. When a government institution's technology fails, taxpayers pay the price -- literally.

I was interviewed by CBS News about a case that illustrates this perfectly. Cook County, Illinois implemented a Tyler Technologies system for property tax administration. The implementation failed so badly that over 25,000 taxpayers were left waiting for property tax refunds totaling $56 million. These are not businesses absorbing cost overruns. These are individual homeowners -- people waiting years for money that is rightfully theirs, trapped in a bureaucratic nightmare created by a failed technology implementation that they had no part in selecting, no voice in managing, and no ability to escape. One taxpayer described it simply: "It is just so annoying and ridiculous and stupid." He is right. And he is one of 25,000.

This is the point that the "nobody feels sorry for big businesses" argument misses. The businesses are not the only ones harmed. The harm cascades. Bloated, expensive project costs are passed on to consumers in the form of higher prices. Disrupted operations are passed on to customers in the form of delayed orders, incorrect invoices, and degraded service. Failed government implementations are passed on to taxpayers in the form of delayed refunds, broken services, and institutions that cannot perform their basic functions. The Queensland Health payroll disaster that I described in Chapter 17 left doctors and nurses unpaid. The Target Canada collapse cost 17,600 people their jobs. The Cook County failure left 25,000 families waiting for money they were owed. These are not abstract corporate losses. These are real consequences for real people.

The regulatory reckoning is not just possible. It is inevitable. There are only so many government institutions that will tolerate these failures before stepping in. There are only so many healthcare disruptions, defense supply chain breakdowns, and taxpayer revolts before legislators conclude that an industry with a 55 to 75 percent failure rate and no accountability framework is an industry that needs oversight. The enterprise technology industry's era of self-regulation -- or more accurately, its era of no regulation -- will end. Not because the industry reforms itself. Because the harm to consumers and citizens becomes too visible and too costly for governments to ignore.

The question is not whether regulation will come. It is whether it will come soon enough to prevent the next wave of failures from producing the next wave of harm. The EU's antitrust investigation, the AI Act, and the Digital Markets Act are the first signals. Other jurisdictions will follow. But regulators move slowly, and the vendors have deep pockets, experienced lobbyists, and a long history of navigating regulatory scrutiny without fundamental change. In the meantime, the enterprise technology industry remains one of the least regulated trillion-dollar markets in the world. The organizations that navigate it successfully are the ones that build their own protections -- because the market will not provide those protections for them. Not yet.

Breaking Out of the Information Ecosystem

Understanding the information ecosystem is the first step to navigating outside it. Here is how the organizations that make better decisions do it.

Seek out the voices that the ecosystem marginalizes. The independent consultants, the disgruntled clients who posted honest reviews, the researchers who found that SI choice has minimal impact on outcomes -- these voices are harder to find than the ecosystem's promoted content, but they are more valuable. The information that requires effort to obtain is usually more honest than the information that is delivered to your inbox.

Treat sponsored content as a data point, not a conclusion. The analyst report sponsored by the vendor you are evaluating is not independent research. It is one perspective, produced within a commercial relationship. Read it. Consider it. But cross-reference it against sources that are not commercially affiliated with the parties being assessed.

Attend conferences with appropriate skepticism. The vendor conference tells you what the vendor wants you to believe. That information has value -- it tells you the vendor's strategy and roadmap. But it is not a balanced view of the market. Calibrate accordingly.

Find the clients who failed, not just the ones who succeeded. The vendor's reference list and the conference case study roster are curated for success. The organizations that struggled, overspent, or abandoned their implementations are not volunteering for speaking slots. Find them through peer networks, independent review platforms, and advisors who have seen enough implementations to know which failures exist behind the success stories.

Engage advisors who are structurally independent. Not independent-as-a-marketing-claim. Structurally independent: no vendor partnerships, no SI referral relationships, no commissions. The advisor who has no financial relationship with the vendors and partners being evaluated is the one whose information is not shaped by those relationships.

The ecosystem is powerful. It is well-funded, well-organized, and extraordinarily effective at shaping the information environment. But it is not the only environment. The independent voices exist. The honest data exists. The organizations that find them and use them make better decisions, get better outcomes, and resist being processed by the machine.

In the next and final section of this book, we will turn from diagnosis to prescription. We have spent twenty-three chapters understanding how the machine works -- its clients, its technology, its consultants, and its ecosystem. The final three chapters are about what to do about it: how to diagnose your organization's specific situation, how to build a transformation that operates outside the machine's defaults, and why the machine will persist despite all of this -- but why your organization does not have to be consumed by it.

Part IV: BREAKING FREE

Escaping the Machine

"You don't have to accept the machine. But you do have to understand it."

Chapter 24

The Honest Diagnosis

In the previous twenty-three chapters, I have described the machine in detail. The organizational dysfunction that feeds it. The technology engine that powers it. The consultants who operate it. The ecosystem that sustains and protects it. The cases where it can be navigated, and the cases where it cannot.

This is Part IV. The final section of the book. And in the spirit of everything I have argued throughout -- that honesty is the rarest and most valuable commodity in this industry -- I want to begin it with the most honest chapter I can write.

Most organizations do not fail at digital transformation because they chose the wrong software. They do not fail because they hired the wrong system integrator, or because the technology did not work, or because the cloud was the wrong direction, or because AI was too immature. These factors contribute to failure, but they are not its root cause.

Organizations fail because they did not diagnose themselves honestly before they started.

They did not look clearly at their leadership alignment, their cultural readiness, their process maturity, their data quality, or their organizational capacity to absorb disruption. They did not assess whether the people at the top agreed on why they were doing this. They did not evaluate whether the governance structures existed to make difficult decisions quickly.

They did not investigate whether the workforce had the change capacity to absorb another major disruption. They went straight from "the board approved the budget" to "we need to select software," and everything that came after -- the cost overruns, the go-live disasters, the knowledge hostage, the lawsuits -- was the predictable consequence of skipping the most important step.

The honest diagnosis is that step. This chapter is about how to do it.

The Three Interlocking Failures

Before an organization can diagnose itself honestly, it needs to understand the failure pattern it is trying to avoid. Throughout this book, I have described three interlocking failures that together constitute the machine's mechanism of destruction.

The first is **organizational dysfunction**. Leadership vacuums that leave the transformation without genuine sponsorship. Cultural accountability gaps that make commitments aspirational rather than binding. The "ASC" dynamic -- Always Something Changing -- that depletes the organization's capacity for sustained effort. The inherited cynicism of workforces that have watched previous initiatives launch and fail. The hub-and-spoke breakdown that turns a transformation into a political proxy war. The opt-out culture that allows departments to simply refuse to participate.

The second is **technology misalignment**. Software selected because the vendor's sales pitch was compelling, not because it fit the business. Forced migrations that serve the vendor's cloud revenue targets rather than the customer's operational needs. Cloud products that are less functionally mature than the on-premise systems they replace. Integration landscapes that are three times more complex than anyone estimated. Data quality problems that turn a technically successful implementation into an operational disaster. The customization paradox that traps organizations between rigid standardization and runaway technical debt. AI capabilities that are sold before they are real and deployed before the organization is ready.

The third is **consultant conflicts**. Business models that profit from duration rather than delivery. Bait-and-switch staffing that replaces the team that won the deal with the team that was on the bench. Eighteen-month timelines that compress critical workstreams to create the appearance of competitiveness. Knowledge transfer that never happens because the SI's managed services revenue depends on the client's dependency. Selection processes that are curated by the vendor's partner ecosystem. An information environment funded by the parties whose interests diverge from the client's.

These three failures do not operate independently. They are interlocking gears. Organizational dysfunction makes technology misalignment more likely, because an organization without strong governance makes poor technology decisions. Technology misalignment makes consultant conflicts more destructive, because a complex, mismatched system generates more scope, more change orders, and more post-go-live dependency. Consultant conflicts amplify organizational dysfunction, because the SI's incentive is to maintain the dysfunction that creates revenue, not to resolve it.

The honest diagnosis requires examining all three simultaneously. You cannot fix one and ignore the others. The organization that invests in excellent change management but selects the wrong technology and hires a conflicted SI will fail. The organization that selects the right technology but has no cultural readiness and no independent oversight will fail. The organization that hires an independent advisor but has no executive alignment and no process clarity will fail (though using independent advisors are more likely to ensure that these risks are mitigated). All three gears must be addressed, and addressing them requires understanding where each one is today -- honestly.

Why Organizations Skip the Diagnosis

If the diagnosis is so important, why do so few organizations conduct it?

The machine is designed to skip it. The vendor wants to sell software, not conduct organizational assessments. The system integrator wants to staff an army of consultants, not diagnose cultural dysfunction. The board wants to see a timeline to go-live, not a readiness report that might delay the start date. The executive sponsor wants momentum, not a systematic examination of the organization's capacity to absorb change.

The diagnostic phase produces no tangible deliverable that can be presented to a board. It does not result in a signed contract or a deployed module or a go-live date. It results in a document that says "here is what is broken, here is what needs to be fixed, and here is what will happen if you start before the fixes are in place." That is an uncomfortable document to receive. It is even more uncomfortable to share. So it gets skipped.

The urgency that the machine creates -- the vendor's migration deadline, the competitor who is already on the cloud, the board mandate to "go digital" -- is specifically designed to make organizations feel that they do not have time for a thorough diagnosis. The message is: the burning platform demands action, not analysis. The cost of waiting exceeds the cost of proceeding.

This is false in the majority of cases. The cost of proceeding without adequate diagnosis is almost always higher than the cost of the diagnosis itself. A readiness assessment that costs $200,000 and takes three months is not a delay. It is an investment that reduces the probability of the 189 percent cost overrun, the 55-75 percent failure rate, and the post-go-live operational disruption that affects more than half of all implementations. The diagnosis does not slow the transformation. It makes the transformation survivable.

Consider the analogy I introduced in Chapter 19: building a house. No one builds a house without a blueprint. No one pours a foundation without soil testing. No one frames the walls before the foundation is cured. No one lets the plumber serve as the general contractor. The sequence is so obvious that it does not require explanation, because we can see a house. We can touch it. We can stand inside it and know, intuitively, whether the foundation is solid or the walls are straight.

A digital transformation is an invisible house. You cannot see it. You cannot touch it. You cannot stand inside it and feel whether the foundation is solid. And because it is invisible, executives who would never skip the blueprint for a physical building routinely skip the blueprint for a transformation that costs ten times more and carries a hundred times more organizational risk. They would never build a factory without an architect. They build digital transformations without a readiness assessment. They would never approve a $50 million construction project with a 3 percent contingency reserve. They approve digital transformations with no contingency at all. The invisibility of the work creates a false sense that the discipline can be lighter. The failure rate -- 55 to 75 percent -- tells you the opposite is true.

The Organizational Readiness Assessment

The organizational readiness assessment is the diagnostic instrument that tells you where your organization actually stands, as opposed to where leadership believes it stands. In my experience, these two things are almost never the same.

The assessment I use examines ten dimensions, each of which has been shown through our research to correlate with transformation outcomes:

1. Strategic Clarity. Does the organization have a clear, specific, and shared understanding of why it is undertaking this transformation? Not "we are going digital" but: what specific business outcomes will be measured, over what timeline, with what accountability? Can executives at every level articulate the same answer to this question? When the answer varies significantly from person to person, the transformation does not have a foundation.

2. Executive Sponsorship. Does the executive sponsor have genuine authority over the decisions required to drive the transformation -- resource allocation, scope decisions, escalations, the authority to require business units to participate? Executive sponsorship in name only -- a title without authority -- is worse than no sponsorship, because it creates the appearance of alignment without the reality. I have worked with organizations where the executive sponsor could not override a business unit leader who was refusing to participate. That is not sponsorship. That is decoration.

3. Change Readiness. What is the organization's history with change? How did previous initiatives end? What is the current level of change fatigue? What is the workforce's trust in leadership's commitments -- based not on what leadership says but on what it has done in the past? The change readiness score is a function of organizational history, not aspiration. An organization that has launched and abandoned three initiatives in five years carries a readiness deficit that cannot be overcome by a compelling town hall presentation.

4. Process Maturity. Are the organization's current business processes documented, understood, and owned? Is there clarity on which processes drive competitive advantage and which are commodity? Organizations with undefined, undocumented, or contested processes cannot design future-state workflows. They cannot evaluate software fit. They cannot make configuration decisions. And they cannot hold anyone accountable when the system does not do what they expected, because nobody agreed on what it was supposed to do.

5. Data Quality. What is the actual quality of the organization's master data -- customers, products, vendors, locations, financial structures? Not the quality that IT believes exists, but the quality that emerges when you run extraction reports and audit the results. As I described in Chapter 12, every organization believes their data is "pretty good." It is not. The diagnosis must quantify the actual gap, because the gap determines the data migration effort, and the migration effort determines a significant portion of the program's timeline and budget.

6. Technology Landscape. What systems does the organization currently operate? How many? How old? How well are they integrated? What customizations have been built? What institutional knowledge is embedded in the current systems and would be lost in a migration? The technology landscape assessment prevents the discovery, twelve months into the implementation, that there are forty-seven integrations that nobody inventoried during the sales cycle.

7. Governance. Does the organization have the decision-making structures to run a multi-year, multi-million-dollar transformation program? Are there clear escalation paths? Is there a program management office with authority to make and enforce decisions? Can the organization resolve conflicts between business units and the program team without months of political negotiation? Governance is not a project plan. It is the organizational infrastructure that keeps the project plan operational when reality diverges from the plan -- which it always does.

8. Resource Capacity. Does the organization have the people, the time, and the internal capability to participate meaningfully in the transformation? Are the key business resources -- the subject matter experts who must define processes, validate configurations, and absorb training -- available for the program, or are they already at capacity with their day jobs? Resource capacity failures do not show up in the program plan. They show up six months in, when the business resources who were supposed to be the program's core team are missing from workshops because they cannot keep up with both the program and their operational responsibilities.

9. Culture. Is the organization's culture compatible with the degree of change the transformation requires? A culture that prizes autonomy and has historically allowed business units to opt out of enterprise mandates will not be able to execute a program that requires universal adoption of a common system. A culture that avoids conflict will not be able to make the difficult process standardization decisions that the implementation demands. A culture that celebrates individual heroics over documented processes will resist the knowledge transfer and governance structures that determine whether the transformation sustains after go-live.

10. Accountability. When the organization makes a commitment -- to a timeline, to a resource allocation, to a process decision -- does it follow through? Are there consequences for non-compliance? Is there a track record of decisions being made and honored? The accountability score is not about intention. It is about pattern. An organization that scores low on accountability will produce a transformation program where commitments are treated as aspirational, decisions are revisited endlessly, and the SI fills the governance vacuum with its own interests.

Each dimension is assessed through a combination of interviews, surveys, document reviews, and facilitated workshops that include executives, middle managers, and frontline employees. The results are rarely uniform across levels. An organizational readiness assessment can determine the lay of the land and the temperature of a company, which helps identify pockets of resistance. It can also help you understand the root causes and severity of resistance across different departments, business units, and locations -- each of which has its own political undercurrents, social dynamics, culture, and motivators.

The most valuable finding from a readiness assessment is almost never the average score. It is the gap between how leadership sees the organization and how the rest of the organization sees itself. Executives who believe accountability is strong discover that their employees view it as nonexistent. Leaders who believe the culture is ready for change find that their frontline workers describe a culture of survival. The gap between the executive view and the workforce view is not a measurement error. It is the most important data point in the entire assessment, because it is the gap that will determine whether the transformation's governance structures are realistic or fantasy.

What the Data Says About Readiness

The variables with the strongest statistical impact on digital transformation outcomes are: scope, magnitude of change, complexity of operations, level of organizational change management support, and level of software customization. Notice what is not on this list: the software vendor, the system integrator, the implementation methodology, the cloud platform, or the configuration approach. The variables that determine whether your transformation succeeds or fails are organizational, not technological.

The variables that reduce operational disruption at go-live are: clarity of defined business processes prior to or early in the transformation, investment in organizational change management and training, executive alignment, and time and effort invested in user acceptance testing and conference room pilots.

Read those two sets of variables together. The factors that drive success and reduce failure are almost entirely within the organization's control. They do not depend on which vendor was selected or which SI was hired. They depend on the choices the organization makes about how to prepare before the implementation begins. The diagnosis is the mechanism by which those choices are informed.

The top five challenges organizations encounter in digital transformation are: organizational change management and the people dimension; transformation misalignment with strategic objectives; difficulty managing SI deficiencies; clarity of business processes; and data migration difficulties. Four out of five of the top challenges are organizational. Only one -- data migration -- has a significant technical component, and even that one is driven primarily by organizational failures: no data owners, no data governance, no accountability for data quality.

The machine wants you to believe that transformation success is primarily a technology problem. The data says it is primarily an organizational problem. The diagnosis is what tells you which specific organizational problems you have, so that you can address them before you spend tens of millions of dollars discovering them the hard way.

I want to add a personal observation that reinforces this point, because it comes from the most adversarial and most thoroughly documented environment in which digital transformation failures are examined: the courtroom. In my work as an expert witness, I have analyzed over fifty implementations embroiled in litigation. These cases span different vendors -- SAP, Oracle, Microsoft, Epicor, and others. They span different system integrators -- Accenture, Deloitte, Avanade, and dozens of smaller firms. They span different industries, different geographies, and different organizational sizes. And in nearly every case, you could have swapped out the vendor's name and the SI's name and ended up with the same result. The failures were not caused by a deficiency unique to SAP or a practice unique to Deloitte. They were caused by the same systemic problems, appearing in the same sequence, driven by the same misaligned incentives, regardless of which logos were on the software and the business cards.

Unrealistic timelines proposed to win the deal. Organizational readiness that was never assessed. Change management that was underfunded or outsourced to the SI. Data migration that was underscoped. Testing that was compressed. Knowledge transfer that never happened. Leadership that delegated rather than governed. The machine produces the same failures because the machine operates the same way, regardless of which vendors and consultants are feeding it. The diagnosis that matters is not "did we pick the right vendor?" It is "have we addressed the organizational conditions that cause every vendor and every SI to fail?"

The Formula Revisited

In Chapter 1, I introduced the formula that captures the essence of most digital transformation failures:

NS + OP = EOP

New Software + Old Processes = Expensive Old Processes

The diagnosis is the instrument that tells you whether your organization is at risk of living this formula. If the process maturity dimension reveals that processes are undefined and undocumented, you are at risk. If the accountability dimension reveals that commitments are aspirational and consequences are absent, you are at risk. If the change readiness dimension reveals that the workforce is exhausted and cynical, you are at risk. If the strategic clarity dimension reveals that executives cannot agree on why the transformation is happening, you are at risk.

The inverse formula represents the outcome that rigorous diagnosis makes possible:

NP + NT + CM = DEO

New Processes + New Technology + Change Management = Digital Enterprise Operations

This is what success looks like. Not new software dropped onto old processes, but new processes designed thoughtfully and deliberately, enabled by technology that was selected to fit them, and sustained by change management that prepares the organization to adopt and own the new way of working. DEO is not a destination that the machine delivers. It is a destination that the organization builds, starting with an honest assessment of where it is today and a clear-eyed plan for the gap between today and where it needs to be.

The diagnosis determines whether you are on a path to EOP or DEO. It is the most important work of the entire transformation, and it is the work that the machine will do everything in its power to convince you that you do not need.

Diagnosing the Machine's Hold on You

Beyond the organizational readiness assessment, there is a second diagnostic question that every organization must answer before it can navigate the machine successfully: how deeply is the machine already embedded in your decision-making?

The machine's hold manifests in specific, identifiable ways. If your technology selection was driven primarily by the vendor's migration deadline, the machine has set your agenda. If your SI selection was limited to the vendor's recommended partner list, the machine has limited your choices. If your program plan was written by the SI and has never been reviewed by an independent party, the machine is running your program. If your executive team reads analyst reports but has not sought out clients who failed on the platform, the machine is shaping your information environment. If your change management is being handled by the same firm that is implementing the software, the machine has eliminated your oversight.

Each of these conditions is addressable. But addressing them requires recognizing them. The diagnosis is not just about the organization's internal readiness. It is about the organization's relationship with the machine -- how deeply the machine's incentives have penetrated the decision-making process, and what it would take to reclaim agency.

The 13 warning signs described in Chapter 22 are the operational version of this diagnostic: the signals that tell you, during an in-flight implementation, that the machine has taken over. But the strategic version of the diagnostic comes before the implementation begins: an honest assessment of whether the vendor selection was genuinely independent, whether the SI selection process was genuinely competitive, whether the program governance is genuinely client-owned, and whether the organization's information environment is diverse enough to include voices that are not funded by the parties whose services are being purchased.

Making the Diagnosis Real

The honest diagnosis is not a document. It is a conversation. It is the conversation that the executive team needs to have about whether they are actually aligned on why this transformation is happening. It is the conversation that the board needs to have about what success looks like and who is accountable for delivering it. It is the conversation that the frontline workforce needs to have -- and usually has, in break rooms and parking lots, but not in steering committee meetings -- about whether they believe this initiative is real, whether they trust leadership to follow through, and whether anyone has thought about what their jobs will look like on the other side.

Conducting this diagnosis requires a specific kind of courage: the courage to find out the truth even when the truth is uncomfortable. The executives who commission readiness assessments and then act on the findings, even when the findings say "you are not ready, and here is why," are the executives whose transformations succeed. The executives who commission assessments and then dismiss the findings, or who skip the assessment entirely because they already know what they want to do, are the executives who wake up two years later in a courtroom or a stabilization crisis wondering how it went so wrong.

Seventy percent of all change initiatives fall short of their intended goals. The organizations in that 70 percent are not there because they chose the wrong technology. They are there because they did not look at themselves clearly before they started. They saw the burning platform and jumped, without checking whether the landing zone was safe.

The honest diagnosis is the check. It is the moment before the jump where you look down and make sure you understand what you are about to land in. It does not guarantee a safe landing. But it is the only tool you have for making an informed decision about whether to jump, when to jump, and how to prepare for the impact.

The machine will not conduct this diagnosis for you. The vendor does not profit from it. The SI does not bill for it. The analyst does not publish reports about it. It is unglamorous, uncomfortable, and essential. And it is entirely the organization's responsibility to demand it.

In the next chapter, we will move from diagnosis to prescription: the principles and practices that define a different way -- one that navigates the machine without being consumed by it.

Chapter 25

A Different Way

In the previous chapter, I described the honest diagnosis -- the organizational readiness assessment that tells you where you actually stand before you spend tens of millions discovering your gaps the expensive way. The diagnosis is the first step out of the machine. It is the moment where you stop accepting the machine's framing and start building your own.

This chapter is about what comes after the diagnosis. It is about the principles and practices that define a different way of approaching digital transformation -- one that operates outside the machine's defaults, that rejects the vendor's urgency and the SI's conflicts, and that puts the organization's interests, not the ecosystem's, at the center of every decision.

These are not theoretical principles. They are distilled from twenty-five years of work with organizations that succeeded, informed by equal time with organizations that failed, and validated by the data across more than a thousand implementations. They represent the rare but real cases where transformation delivers what it promises -- not because the vendor was better or the SI was more capable, but because the organization did the work that the machine is designed to skip.

Principle 1: Strategy Before Technology

The first and most important principle is the one the machine violates most systematically: define your strategy before you select your technology.

This sounds obvious. It is almost never practiced. The standard sequence is: board mandates transformation, executives evaluate vendors, vendor is selected, implementation begins, and somewhere during the implementation -- usually when the configuration decisions become contentious -- the organization realizes it never defined what it was trying to achieve.

Why are we changing? This is a fundamental question that needs a more comprehensive answer than just upgrading technology or being forced to move to a new system. Organizations need to have a clear and comprehensive reason for going through a digital transformation.

Strategy before technology means answering the why before you answer the what. It means defining the business outcomes you are trying to achieve -- specific, measurable outcomes, not aspirations -- before you evaluate which technology can enable them.

It means understanding what processes drive competitive advantage and what processes are commodity before you decide whether to standardize or customize. It means articulating what success looks like in terms that your board, your executives, and your workforce can understand and measure.

Drown out the industry biases and noise. Focus on your business needs and use that to dictate your digital strategy -- not the other way around. The vendor wants you to start with their technology and adapt your strategy to fit it. The machine wants you selecting software in month two and defining strategy in month twelve, if ever. The different way is the opposite: strategy in month one, technology selection once the strategy is clear.

This requires resisting urgency that the machine creates. The vendor's migration deadline is not your deadline. The competitor's cloud announcement is not your burning platform. The analyst's report declaring on-premise dead is not your strategic plan. Your strategy is your strategy, and it should be built from your business requirements, your competitive position, your organizational capacity, and your stakeholder needs -- not from the vendor's roadmap.

Principle 2: Independence in Advisory

As I described in Chapter 22, the bright line is between independence and affiliation. An advisor who is affiliated with a vendor -- who earns commissions, receives referral fees, or operates an implementation practice that depends on a specific vendor's pipeline -- cannot provide objective guidance. An independent advisor can.

Independence in advisory means engaging someone whose only economic interest is your success. Not "success" as defined by go-live or deployment. Success as defined by the business outcomes you defined in Principle 1. The independent advisor's compensation should be tied, at least in part, to those outcomes. If the transformation does not deliver measurable value, the advisor should share the cost of that failure, not just the client.

This model is rare because it requires the advisor to assume risk. The machine's default is to transfer all risk to the client: the vendor disclaims liability for outcomes, the SI caps their exposure, and the analyst publishes research with no accountability for the organizations that follow their recommendations. A different way means demanding a different allocation of risk -- one in which the parties providing advice have skin in the game.

Principle 3: Organizational Readiness Is Not Optional

Sixty-one percent of respondents said organizational change and the people dimension is the most important part of digital strategy. And yet 59 percent of organizations had no change strategy at all.

Read those two statistics together. The majority believes people and change are the most important factors. The majority has no plan for addressing them. This is not a paradox. It is the machine at work. The machine does not sell change management. It sells technology. The budget goes where the machine directs it, and the machine directs it toward licensing fees and consultant hours, not toward the organizational work that determines whether the licenses and the hours produce value.

A different way means inverting the budget. Addressing the technical issues of your ERP system is not nearly as important to success as managing the people who will be using the software. ERP change management will be the #1 key to your project's success. Fund change management at 15 to 20 percent of the program budget, not 3 to 5 percent. Start the change work before the implementation begins, not after the technical configuration is complete. Hire an independent change management firm -- not the SI's "change team" -- whose sole focus is preparing the organization, not protecting the SI's timeline.

Organizational readiness is the foundation. Pour it before you frame the house. If the foundation is not solid, everything built on top of it will crack.

Principle 4: Right-Size the Technology

Not every organization needs a Tier 1 ERP. This is one of the most important lessons in this book, and it is the one the machine works hardest to obscure.

The vendor wants to sell you the largest, most comprehensive platform in their portfolio. The SI wants to implement the most complex system possible, because complexity generates scope, duration, and revenue. The analyst firm ranks vendors by capability, not by fit, which creates a perception that the vendors at the top of the Magic Quadrant are the best choice for everyone. The machine creates a gravitational pull toward the Tier 1 platforms -- SAP, Oracle, the most sophisticated, most expensive, most complex systems -- regardless of whether your organization needs that level of capability or has the internal resources to sustain it.

A different way means right-sizing. Match the technology to your actual complexity, your actual resources, and your actual needs. A

$200 million manufacturer does not need the same ERP that runs a $50 billion multinational. A regional distributor does not need the supply chain planning module designed for global logistics networks. A mid-market services company does not need a multi-tenant SaaS platform when a well-implemented on-premise or private cloud solution would serve them better.

Best-of-breed and point solutions can provide lower risk and faster value than monolithic ERP implementations. The default assumption that you must select one vendor for everything is a vendor-created narrative. The reality is that a composable architecture -- finance from one vendor, HCM from another, supply chain planning from a third -- can deliver better functional fit, lower switching costs, and a risk profile that is spread across multiple smaller implementations rather than concentrated in one massive program.

Right-sizing also means knowing when not to transform at all. If your current system works, if the business case for replacement is weak, if the organization is not ready -- the right decision may be to defer, to extend the current system's life through third-party support, and to invest in the organizational readiness work that will make you successful when you do eventually transform. Patience is not a virtue the machine rewards. But it is a virtue that produces better outcomes.

Principle 5: Honest Timelines and Budgets

As I described in Chapter 19, the eighteen-month lie is the entry point of the machine. Rejecting it is the first practical step in a different way.

Demand that the SI present a timeline based on your actual complexity, not a generic number designed to win the bid. Use independent benchmarks -- not the SI's proposal, not the vendor's estimate -- to validate whether the timeline is realistic. For mid-size companies, most implementations require 14 to 16 months. For companies larger than $1 billion, this increases to 31 to 34 months. These are averages for straightforward implementations. Add for scope, geography, data quality, integration complexity, and organizational readiness. Build in 20 to 30 percent contingency, not 5 percent.

The more time and effort you devote to the implementation planning phase, the more time and resources you will save in the long run. Phase Zero -- the period between vendor selection and technical configuration where you define processes, assess readiness, plan change management, and build the blueprint -- is not a delay. It is the most valuable time investment in the entire program. Organizations that compress or skip Phase Zero to "get started" pay for it later in the form of scope creep, change orders, and post-go-live stabilization that costs more than the planning would have.

Honest budgets include the full program cost, not just the technical workstream. OCM at 15-20 percent. Data migration and integration at realistic levels. Post-go-live stabilization and hypercare. Internal staffing for the PMO. Independent advisory and quality assurance. Training for the core team. When you budget for the full program rather than accepting the SI's technical project quote, the number is larger but the overrun is smaller. The average cost overrun is 189 percent. Organizations that plan honestly from the beginning reduce that overrun dramatically, not because they spend less, but because they budget for reality.

Principle 6: Own Your Transformation

The machine wants you to outsource your transformation to the SI. The different way is to own it.

Whether you succeed or fail in your digital transformation is entirely up to you -- not your consultants, not your system integrator, not your software vendor. That is a statement that may sound harsh, but it is the most liberating truth in this book. If success depended on the SI, you would be at the mercy of the SI's business model. If it depended on the vendor, you would be at the mercy of the vendor's roadmap. But it depends on you -- on your leadership, your readiness, your governance, your willingness to invest in the organizational work that determines outcomes. That means the power to succeed is in your hands. Not the machine's.

Owning your transformation means the program management office is yours. Staffed by your people. Managed by your leadership. Accountable for your outcomes. The SI delivers a technical workstream within a program you control. The advisor supports your decision-making. But the decisions are yours, the governance is yours, and the accountability is yours.

As I discussed in Chapters 18 and 20, this requires building internal capability from day one. Hire internal program managers, change management leads, business analysts, data migration specialists. Train your core team on the software platform and on implementation best practices before the SI arrives. Embed your people in every workstream so that when the consultants leave, the knowledge stays. Use tools like Mission Control to document decisions, risks, and governance in real time so that the institutional knowledge does not live exclusively in the consultants' heads.

One way to mitigate dependency risk is to bring more capabilities in-house and avoid becoming dependent on a consulting or implementation partner. This is not just post-implementation advice. It is a design principle for the entire engagement: minimize external dependency by maximizing internal capability. The SI should be training your team to replace them, not training your team to need them.

Principle 7: Contractual Protection

The machine's contracts are written by the machine's lawyers. They protect the vendor and the SI, not you. A different way means negotiating contracts that shift the risk back toward the parties creating it. Most clients do not realize that approximately 95 percent of a software contract is negotiable. The vendor presents the contract as though the terms are standard and immutable. They are not. Nearly every clause -- pricing, renewal escalation, exit terms, liability caps, resource commitments, knowledge transfer obligations -- can be negotiated if the buyer understands what to ask for and has the leverage to insist. The number-one thing to consider from the very start is not just the contract you are signing today but how it positions you for the next contract. Vendors present pricing differently -- one might show high initial costs while another low-balls the first term and escalates aggressively at renewal. Always evaluate the full lifecycle cost, not just the headline number.

Exit rights. Cloud subscription agreements should include defined terms under which you can terminate without prohibitive penalties. If the vendor will not agree to exit rights, they are telling you they expect you to want to leave.

Data portability. Require contractual guarantees that your data can be extracted in standard formats at any time. If the vendor resists data portability clauses, they are protecting lock-in, not your interests.

Performance guarantees. The SI's contract should include specific, measurable performance commitments tied to financial consequences. If the timeline slips beyond a defined threshold, the SI's fees are reduced. If the system does not achieve defined acceptance criteria, the SI does not get paid. This is the outcome-based contracting model described in Chapter 22, and it should be standard, not exceptional.

Named resources with tenure commitments. The team in the proposal should be the team in the contract, with minimum tenure guarantees and client approval required for any substitutions. If the

SI rotates off key resources without your consent, they pay a penalty.

Knowledge transfer milestones. The contract should define specific knowledge transfer deliverables -- documentation standards, training completion, capability assessments -- tied to the SI's final payment. If the knowledge transfer is incomplete, the final invoice is reduced.

The SI will resist every one of these provisions. Their lawyers will say the terms are non-standard. That is precisely the point. The standard terms protect the machine. Non-standard terms protect you. If the SI will not accept contractual accountability, they are telling you they do not expect to deliver.

Principle 8: Neutralize the Five Forces

In Chapter 10, I introduced Michael Porter's Five Forces Model as a framework for understanding why the enterprise software industry's structure so thoroughly favors vendors over customers. Every force -- the threat of new entrants, the threat of substitutes, the bargaining power of buyers, the bargaining power of suppliers, and the rivalry among competitors -- tilts in the vendor's direction. The cloud model created a vendor utopia: high barriers to entry, captive installed bases, minimal substitutes, and pricing power that approaches monopolistic at renewal.

A different way means deliberately engineering your transformation to neutralize these forces rather than accepting them as fixed constraints.

Neutralize vendor lock by preserving optionality. Do not go all-in on one vendor's cloud. Adopt a composable or dual-track architecture that keeps your core data, your AI models, and your most differentiating processes under your control. Build independent data layers on platforms you own. Deploy third-party AI tools outside the vendor's ecosystem. Every architectural decision that preserves your ability to leave -- or credibly threaten to leave -- restores negotiating leverage that the cloud model was designed to eliminate.

Increase the threat of substitutes. Pursue third-party support options for legacy systems rather than accepting the vendor's forced migration timeline. Companies like Rimini Street and Spinnaker extend the lifecycle of your existing investment and give you time to make the migration decision on your terms, not the vendor's. The vendor's entire forced-migration strategy depends on you believing you have no alternative. Third-party support proves that you do.

Reclaim buyer bargaining power. Negotiate as an informed buyer, not a captive one. Use independent benchmarks to validate pricing. Time negotiations to the vendor's fiscal year-end. Demand transparent renewal terms before you sign the initial contract. Build internal technical capability so that you are not wholly dependent on the vendor's support organization. Every capability you build internally is a capability you do not have to purchase from the vendor at the vendor's price.

Protect your intellectual property. As I discussed in Chapter 13, the commoditization of cloud ERP means your competitors can buy the same software, configured the same way, running on the same infrastructure. The last remaining differentiator is your data, your proprietary processes, and the competitive advantages embedded in how you operate. Do not surrender these to a multi-tenant public cloud model that standardizes them away. Do not opt in to shared AI models that train on your data and benefit your competitors. Question the cloud for your differentiating processes. Protect the secret sauce that makes your business yours.

Lower the barriers to entry in your own favor. If you go all-in on vanilla cloud, a competitor can replicate your capabilities by buying the same software. But if you invest in proprietary processes, independent AI, and composable architecture, you raise the barrier for anyone trying to replicate what you have built. The Five Forces model works in your industry too, not just the software industry. Every decision that commoditizes your operations weakens your competitive position. Every decision that preserves your operational uniqueness strengthens it.

Porter's model explains why the machine behaves the way it does. But the model also shows you where the leverage points are. The vendor's power is not a law of nature. It is a function of industry structure -- and industry structure can be influenced by the decisions you make about architecture, contracts, data sovereignty, and how much of your competitive advantage you are willing to cede to a platform you do not control.

Principle 9: Continuous Validation

The diagnosis is not a one-time event. It is a practice that must be sustained throughout the transformation. Continuous validation means independent oversight at every major decision point: vendor selection, SI selection, go/no-go decisions, scope changes, timeline adjustments, and the ultimate go-live decision.

As I described in Chapter 22, the 13 warning signs are the operational diagnostic that tells you when the program is going off the rails. Continuous validation means monitoring those signs in real time and acting when you see them, not waiting for the annual post-implementation review.

Tools like Mission Control make this feasible at a scale that manual governance cannot achieve. Real-time monitoring of risk registers, utilization reports, defect trends, change order patterns, and resource deployment. Alerts when the SI's staffing exceeds the plan without a corresponding scope increase. Visibility when testing timelines are being compressed. Early warning when the knowledge transfer milestones are not being met. The technology to achieve continuous validation exists. The question is whether the client demands it and whether the SI tolerates it.

The organizations that succeed are the ones that treat oversight as a continuous function, not a quarterly event. They do not wait for the steering committee presentation to discover problems. They have real-time visibility into the program's health, and they intervene the moment the data suggests intervention is needed.

The Role of the Informed Buyer

I want to close this chapter by addressing the question that may be forming in your mind as you read these principles: if the machine is so powerful, so entrenched, and so profitable, can individual organizations really make a difference by demanding a different way?

The answer is yes. Not at the industry level, not yet. But at the level of individual transformations, absolutely.

The informed buyer changes the engagement. When you demand independence in advisory, the vendors and SIs that cannot provide it self-select out. When you insist on honest timelines, the SIs that lowball to win deals lose to the ones that are realistic. When you negotiate contractual protections, you shift risk back toward the parties best positioned to manage it. When you build internal capability, you reduce dependency. When you fund change management properly, you increase your probability of success.

None of these actions changes the machine. But each one reduces the machine's hold on your specific transformation. And when enough buyers make these demands -- when independence becomes expected rather than exceptional, when honest timelines become the standard rather than the outlier, when contractual accountability becomes non-negotiable -- the market begins to shift. Not because the vendors and SIs changed their business models out of enlightenment. Because the informed buyers forced them to compete on dimensions other than price and promises.

The machine will persist. I will argue that in the next and final chapter. But the machine's persistence does not mean your organization must be consumed by it. The nine principles in this chapter -- strategy before technology, independence in advisory, organizational readiness, right-sizing, honest timelines, ownership, contractual protection, neutralizing the five forces, and continuous validation -- are not abstract ideals. They are practices that organizations implement every day with the guidance of independent advisors like my firm, Third Stage Consulting. We help clients apply these principles from the earliest stages of their transformation through go-live and beyond -- from the initial readiness assessment and strategy definition, through vendor and SI selection, through program governance and quality assurance, through change management and internal capability building, and through the post-go-live stabilization that determines whether the investment delivers lasting value. We do this because these principles work. And we do this because the machine will not do it for you. The organizations that understand these principles, that demand them from every vendor and consultant they engage, and that invest in the organizational work that the machine skips -- those organizations navigate the machine without being processed by it.

You cannot dismantle the machine. But you can refuse to feed yourself into it. That refusal starts with understanding how it works, continues with demanding a different set of terms, and succeeds when you build the organizational capability that makes the machine's services less essential and its conflicts less dangerous.

In the final chapter, we will examine why the machine will persist despite everything in this book, and what that means for the organizations attempting to transform in the years ahead. The machine is too profitable to dismantle. Your job is not to dismantle it. Your job is to not be consumed by it.

Chapter 26

The Machine Will Persist

This is the last chapter of this book, and I want to begin it with the truth that the book's title implies but that the preceding twenty-five chapters have been building toward:

The machine will persist.

It will not be dismantled by this book, or by any book. It will not be reformed by regulatory action, though regulation may soften some of its harder edges. It will not be disrupted by the buyer's revolt described in Chapter 16, though the revolt will change the terms for the organizations that lead it. It will not be transformed by AI, though AI will add new gears to the machine and deepen the lock-in that powers it. The machine will persist because it is too profitable, too deeply entrenched, and too perfectly aligned with the economic incentives of every party except the one that matters most: you.

This is not a counsel of despair. It is a counsel of realism. And realism, as I have argued throughout this book, is the most valuable thing I can offer you.

Why the Machine Cannot Be Dismantled

The machine persists because the economics are too powerful for any single force to overcome.

The vendors are generating unprecedented revenue. SAP's market capitalization rose from $164 billion to $355 billion in four years, driven almost entirely by cloud conversion. Oracle's remaining performance obligations jumped 359 percent to $455 billion. Every major vendor is posting record earnings, record free cash flow, and record cloud growth. The investors who fund these companies are being rewarded handsomely. The executives who lead them are being compensated lavishly. The sales teams who close the deals are earning the highest commissions in the industry's history. There is no economic pressure on the vendor to change. The market is telling them, in the only language it speaks, that what they are doing is working.

The system integrators are equally entrenched. Deloitte, Accenture, and their peers have hundreds of thousands of consultants whose billable hours depend on the vendor platforms around which their practices are built. Every forced migration that the vendor announces creates a wave of implementation demand that fills the SI's pipeline for years. Every eighteen-month lie that wins a deal generates the change orders that expand the revenue. Every knowledge hostage that the engagement creates becomes the managed services contract that sustains it.

The SI's business model does not merely tolerate the machine's dysfunction. It depends on it. A world in which implementations succeeded on time and on budget, in which knowledge transferred effectively, and in which clients achieved independence after go-live would be a world in which the SI's revenue model collapsed.

The analyst firms are funded by the vendors and the SIs they evaluate. The conferences are sponsored by the ecosystem they celebrate. The media covers the industry through access that the vendors control. The entire information environment in which buyers make decisions is produced, curated, and distributed by the parties who profit from those decisions. The circular economy described in Chapter 23 is not a conspiracy. It is a market. And markets do not dismantle themselves.

The failure rate has been 55 to 75 percent for thirty years. The average cost overrun has been 189 percent. Only 23 percent of implementations are considered successful by the organizations that paid for them. These numbers have not improved in a quarter century of technological advancement, methodological evolution, and industry maturation. They have not improved because the machine is not designed to improve them. The machine is designed to generate revenue. And by that measure, it is performing brilliantly.

AI Will Not Save You. AI Will Deepen the Lock.

If there is a force that many believe will disrupt the machine, it is artificial intelligence. AI will make implementations faster, they say. AI will reduce consulting hours. AI will automate the tedious work and free people for higher-value activities. AI will finally break the cycle of failure that has defined this industry.

I described in Chapter 14 why I believe this optimism is premature. But here, in the final chapter, I want to address the structural question: even if AI works as promised, will it change the machine?

It will not. It will add new gears to it.

As I described in Chapter 23, cloud was the lock and AI is the deadbolt. The vendor's AI is trained on your data -- your transactions, your demand patterns, your operational history. Over time, the AI builds models specific to your business. Those models become your institutional intelligence. But they live on the vendor's platform, governed by the vendor's terms. If you leave, you abandon them. The switching cost is no longer just reimplementation. It is the cost of re-learning -- of rebuilding the intelligence your business spent years teaching the system.

AI gives the vendor unprecedented pricing power. At every renewal, the vendor knows that the cost of leaving now includes losing AI-driven intelligence the customer depends on. The customer's negotiating leverage approaches zero. The vendor can raise prices, change terms, bundle services, and the customer's rational response is to pay, because the alternative is worse.

Meanwhile, the system integrators that should be using AI to reduce their own delivery costs are instead using it to increase their margins. The consultant who used to take forty hours to write a module now takes twenty, but the client is still billed for forty. The productivity gains are captured by the firm, not passed to the client. AI for thee, but not for me.

AI will make the machine more efficient. It will not make it more honest. It will not align the incentives that are misaligned. It will not transfer knowledge that the SI has no interest in transferring. It will not prepare organizations that have not prepared themselves. AI is a new gear in the machine, not a replacement for it. And like every previous gear -- cloud, mobile, blockchain, IoT -- it will be sold before the prerequisites are in place, deployed before organizations are ready, and blamed for failures that are organizational, not technological.

But I want to be fair to AI, because the picture is not entirely bleak. If vendor-embedded AI deepens the lock, client-owned AI can pick it.

The same technology that gives vendors unprecedented pricing power can also give clients unprecedented independence -- if they deploy it on their own terms. AI tools in the hands of the client's internal team can reduce dependence on the SI in ways that were impossible five years ago. AI-powered code generation can allow a smaller internal development team to do work that previously required a squad of expensive consultants. AI-assisted documentation can produce the decision records, configuration rationale, and operational procedures that SIs have chronically failed to deliver -- automatically, continuously, and at a quality level that no manual process can match. AI-driven training development can accelerate the creation of role-specific learning content, reducing the organization's dependence on the SI's trainers. AI-enabled testing tools can compress testing cycles without the quality sacrifice that manual compression produces.

This is the liberating potential of AI that the machine does not want you to see. The machine wants AI to deepen your dependency -- on the vendor's platform, on the SI's consultants, on the ecosystem's services. But AI is a tool, and tools serve whoever holds them. In the vendor's hands, AI is a lock. In the client's hands, AI is a key. The organizations that recognize this -- that invest in AI capabilities on the client side, that use AI to build internal competency rather than outsource it, that deploy tools like Mission Control to document, govern, and oversee their transformations with a fraction of the manual effort -- those organizations are using AI to reduce the machine's hold rather than deepen it.

The question is not whether AI will change the machine. It will. The question is who captures the value: the vendor and the SI, or the client. The default answer, if you accept the machine's framing, is the vendor and the SI. The different answer, if you invest in client-side AI capability, is you.

The Pessimistic Case

The pessimistic case for the next decade is straightforward: the machine will process another wave of organizations through the same cycle of failure, at larger scale and higher cost than ever before.

Every major vendor is simultaneously forcing migration to the cloud. SAP's 2030 deadline alone affects 30,000 organizations. Oracle, Microsoft, and their peers are on parallel tracks. The combined effect is the largest wave of forced digital transformations in history, arriving at a moment when the cloud products are still maturing, the AI capabilities are still unproven at scale, and the organizations being forced to migrate are no more ready than their predecessors were.

Beyond the current forced migration wave lies another horizon that few are discussing: the cloud-to-cloud switching wave. The organizations that migrated to cloud platforms over the past decade will, within another decade, begin to outgrow those platforms, discover that the vendor's roadmap has diverged from their needs, or face the same obsolescence pressure that drove them from on-premise. When that wave arrives, the switching costs will be higher than anything the industry has seen -- data migration from cloud to cloud, AI models abandoned, integrations rebuilt, contracts unwound -- and the organizations that went all-in on a single vendor's cloud will discover that the marriage they entered has no affordable exit.

The pessimistic case is not that the machine will fail. It is that the machine will succeed -- at what it is designed to do. It will generate revenue for vendors, billable hours for SIs, and subscription fees for analysts, while producing the same failure rates, the same cost overruns, and the same organizational damage that it has produced for thirty years. The only thing that will change is the scale.

The Optimistic Case

The optimistic case is not that the machine will be dismantled. It is that individual organizations can escape it.

The evidence is real. Forty percent of SAP customers have refused to start the S/4HANA migration because they cannot justify the business case. Kingfisher refused publicly, deployed third-party AI on existing systems, and presented their alternative strategy at industry conferences. Buyers are demanding data portability, exit rights, and transparent pricing in their contracts -- provisions that did not exist five years ago. Composable ERP architectures are moving from theory to production. Independent advisory firms are growing faster than the large SIs in the mid-market, because buyers are choosing independence over brand names. The EU is investigating vendor lock-in practices. Regulators are beginning to recognize what I described in Chapter 23: that the enterprise technology market has operated as the wild west for decades -- a trillion-dollar industry with no fiduciary standards, no mandatory conflict disclosure, no building codes for implementations, and no regulatory body that holds vendors and SIs accountable for the gap between what they sell and what they deliver. If this industry were selling to consumers rather than businesses, it would have been regulated long ago. The regulatory reckoning is coming, slowly and imperfectly, but it is coming. The market is shifting, slowly but perceptibly, in the buyer's direction.

The optimistic case is also supported by the data. The variables that determine transformation success are organizational, not technological. They are within the organization's control. Leadership alignment, change readiness, process clarity, data governance, and program governance -- these are not capabilities that require the vendor's permission or the SI's cooperation. They are capabilities that the organization can build, invest in, and own. The organizations that do this succeed at rates that dramatically exceed the industry average, regardless of which vendor or SI they selected.

The optimistic case is that the machine's power is not absolute. It is structural. It operates through default behaviors -- default selection processes, default contracting terms, default staffing models, default governance structures. Every one of these defaults can be overridden by an informed buyer who understands the machine and demands a different set of terms. The machine does not force you to accept the eighteen-month lie. You can demand honest timelines. The machine does not force you to let the SI run the PMO. You can own the program. The machine does not force you to skip the readiness assessment. You can insist on diagnosis before deployment.

The machine's power comes from the buyer's ignorance. When the ignorance ends, the power diminishes. Not to zero -- the economic incentives remain, and the ecosystem will adapt rather than reform. But enough that the informed buyer can navigate the machine without being consumed by it.

What You Can Do Starting Monday Morning

This book has covered a great deal of ground -- twenty-six chapters across four parts, spanning the organizational, technological, consultant, and ecosystem dimensions of a machine that processes trillions of dollars and fails the majority of the organizations it is supposed to serve. The scope can feel overwhelming. So I want to close with something concrete: the actions you can take starting Monday morning, regardless of where you are in your transformation journey.

If you have not yet started: Conduct an organizational readiness assessment before you do anything else. Evaluate your strategic clarity, executive alignment, change readiness, process maturity, data quality, and governance structures using the ten-dimension framework from Chapter 24. Do not select a vendor. Do not hire an SI. Do not approve a budget. First, understand where you actually stand. The diagnosis will save you more money than any vendor discount.

If you are evaluating vendors: Engage an independent advisor who has no vendor partnerships and no SI relationships. Do not limit your evaluation to the vendor's recommended partner list. Insist on scripted demos conducted by the delivery team, not the sales team. Find your own references, especially the ones the vendor did not provide. Evaluate the delivery team, not the sales team. And remember: the vendor and the SI have minimal statistical impact on your outcome. The organizational work matters more.

If you are about to sign contracts: Negotiate exit rights, data portability, named resources with tenure commitments, knowledge transfer milestones tied to payment, and performance guarantees with financial consequences for underdelivery. If the vendor or SI will not accept these terms, they are telling you something important about their expectations. The standard terms protect the machine. Demand non-standard terms that protect you.

If you are in the middle of an implementation: Review the thirteen warning signs from Chapter 22. If three or more are present, your project is at significant risk. Establish independent oversight immediately. Audit the SI's staffing against the proposal. Review change orders for scope that should have been in the original agreement. Assess whether your internal team has the capability and the authority to govern the program. It is not too late to course-correct, but the cost of correction increases with every week you wait.

If you are post-go-live and struggling: Assess your position on the capability maturity model from Chapter 20. If you are at Level 1 -- dependent on external support for non-routine activities -- build a plan to reach Level 3 within eighteen months. Establish a Center of Excellence. Demand decision documentation from the SI before their managed services contract expires. Source independent technical specialists who can build institutional knowledge on the client side. Break the knowledge hostage before it becomes permanent.

Regardless of where you are: Remember the formula. NS + OP = EOP. New Software + Old Processes = Expensive Old Processes. And the antidote: NP + NT + CM = DEO. New Processes + New Technology + Change Management = Digital Enterprise Operations. The formula was developed by my team at Third Stage Consulting, and it has been validated across more than a thousand engagements. It works. But only if you invest in all three elements, not just the technology.

The Fellow Disruptors

I do not want to leave the impression that I am the only person chipping away at the machine. I am not. There is a growing community of individuals and organizations that are working, in different ways and from different angles, to tilt the playing field back toward the customer. They deserve recognition, because the machine's narrative would have you believe that the ecosystem is monolithic -- that every voice in the industry is aligned with the vendor's interests. It is not. And the disruptors are worth knowing about.

Raven Intel is building something the industry has never had: a platform for independent, validated customer reviews of system integrators. In a market where SI reference checks are curated by the SI's sales team and the only feedback the buyer receives is the feedback the SI wants them to hear, Raven Intel provides unfiltered client voices. It is not perfect -- no review platform is -- but it represents a genuine attempt to close the information gap that the machine depends on. The more organizations that contribute their experiences, the more valuable the platform becomes, and the harder it is for underperforming SIs to hide behind their brand names.

Jan Baan deserves particular mention because his career arc embodies the evolution this industry needs. Baan founded, scaled, and sold Baan ERP -- one of the most prominent enterprise software companies of the 1990s. He was inside the machine. He built part of it. And now, decades later, he is building the alternative. His newer company, Rappit, is developing a composable alternative to traditional ERP -- a platform designed around the principle that organizations should assemble capabilities modularly rather than buying monolithic suites that lock them into a single vendor's architecture for decades. Whether Rappit succeeds or not, the fact that one of the original ERP pioneers has concluded that the monolithic model is broken and is building something different is a powerful signal about where the industry needs to go.

Independent consulting firms across the industry are providing the alternative to the Big Four and the global SIs. Firms of all sizes -- some focused on specific industries, some on specific platforms, some on advisory, some on delivery -- are offering organizations a choice between the conflicted, vendor-aligned model and an independent one. These firms do not have the marketing budgets of

Deloitte or the conference sponsorships of Accenture. But they have something the large firms structurally cannot provide: the ability to tell the client the truth without worrying about how it affects a vendor partnership. Every independent firm that wins an engagement over a Big Four competitor is a vote for a different model.

Marcus Harris and attorneys like him are giving clients something they desperately need: a legal pitbull in their corner. When implementations fail, when vendors misrepresent capabilities, when SIs deliver less than they promised, the client's recourse is the courtroom. But most organizations enter litigation against vendors and SIs that have armies of specialized lawyers and decades of experience drafting contracts designed to limit their own liability. Attorneys who specialize in ERP and digital transformation disputes level that playing field. They understand the technology, the contracts, the industry dynamics, and the specific ways in which the machine's standard terms disadvantage the client. Having someone like Marcus Harris reviewing your contracts before you sign them -- not after the project fails -- is one of the most cost-effective investments an organization can make.

Software vendors like Acumatica, IFS, QAD, Odoo, and others are offering customers something that the Tier 1 vendors have increasingly abandoned: choice. These are vendors that are not trying to be everything to everyone. They are focused on specific markets, specific industries, and specific use cases where they can deliver genuine value without the platform lock-in, the forced migration timelines, and the take-it-all bundling strategies of the major vendors. Acumatica's consumption-based pricing model challenges the per-user subscription model that the industry has standardized around. IFS's focus on asset-intensive industries provides depth that horizontal platforms cannot match. QAD's manufacturing focus delivers fit that a generalist ERP requires extensive customization to approximate. Odoo's open-source model offers a fundamentally different economic relationship between vendor and customer. None of these vendors is perfect.

But each one represents an alternative to the machine's default, and the existence of alternatives is what gives buyers leverage.

There are countless others -- too many to list here -- who are contributing to the shift in their own ways. Independent YouTube creators and bloggers who share honest implementation experiences. Procurement consultants who help organizations negotiate better contracts. Data governance specialists who build the foundation that the machine ignores. Internal IT leaders who insist on owning their programs despite pressure from SIs who want to run them. Every one of these individuals and organizations is a crack in the machine's facade. None of them alone will break it. Together, they are bending it.

A Personal Note

I want to close this book the way I began it: with honesty about what it has cost to write.

I started my career at PricewaterhouseCoopers, twenty-four years old, naïve, and genuinely excited about the potential of technology to transform businesses. I sat in rooms where software evaluations were rigged. I billed clients for time spent politicking on the firm's behalf. I watched the machine process organizations and produce wreckage, and I was a junior participant in the processing. I left. I built an independent practice. I spent two decades helping organizations navigate the machine from the other side of the table.

Writing this book, like running that practice, has come with consequences. I have received anonymous threatening phone calls. I have received voicemails from people who said I should be careful. I have received cease and desist orders from a large software vendor and from attorneys representing an organization whose failed implementation I discussed publicly. I have been trained for deflection by the firms whose practices I challenge. I have watched the ecosystem marginalize independent voices through conference exclusion, algorithm suppression, and the simple economics of who pays for the information that buyers consume.

I mention this not for sympathy but for context. The resistance to transparency in this industry is fierce because the stakes are enormous. The machine generates trillions of dollars in revenue. The people who profit from it are smart, well-resourced, and motivated. They do not welcome scrutiny. The intensity of the resistance is, itself, evidence that the scrutiny is warranted.

The stories in this book -- from the $1.5 million rigged selection at PricewaterhouseCoopers to the $7 billion collapse of Target Canada to the anonymous voicemail that said "Eric, I saw your article and I would be careful if I were you" -- are why this work matters. Not because I am uniquely brave for telling them. But because someone needs to tell them, and the machine has designed an ecosystem in which very few people are positioned to do so without economic consequence.

The Machine Will Persist. You Do Not Have to Be Consumed by It.

I began this book with a lyric from Pink Floyd: "What did you dream? It's alright, we told you what to dream."

The machine tells you what to dream. It tells you that the cloud is the future and the future is now. It tells you that eighteen months is realistic and $15 million is enough. It tells you that the SI has your best interests at heart and the analyst report is independent. It tells you that AI will change everything, that the vendor's roadmap is a commitment, and that standardization is the path to excellence. It tells you these things because the telling is profitable, and it will keep telling you until you stop listening.

This book is my attempt to describe the machine from the outside. To show you the gears, the levers, the incentives, and the economic logic that makes it run. To arm you with the diagnosis, the principles, and the practical actions that can help you navigate the machine without being processed by it.

The machine will persist. The failure rates will not improve. The cost overruns will not shrink. The vendor lock-in will deepen. The AI deadbolt will engage. The ecosystem will continue to produce an information environment that serves its own interests. The system integrators will continue to profit from the dysfunction they are hired to resolve. The analysts will continue to publish research funded by the firms being evaluated. The conferences will continue to celebrate success while the failures happen in silence.

But you do not have to accept the default. You can demand an honest diagnosis before you start. You can define your strategy before the vendor defines it for you. You can fund change management before the timeline compresses it to nothing. You can own your program instead of outsourcing it. You can negotiate contracts that protect you instead of the machine. You can build internal capability instead of permanent dependency. You can seek independent voices instead of accepting the ecosystem's curated consensus. You can question the cloud. You can challenge the timeline. You can refuse the Kool-Aid.

No single organization can dismantle the machine. I have said that throughout this book, and I believe it. But the machine's durability depends on the buyer's compliance. It depends on organizations accepting the defaults, signing the standard contracts, trusting the curated information, and outsourcing their governance to parties whose incentives are misaligned. Every organization that refuses to comply weakens the machine's hold -- not just on themselves, but on the market. Every buyer who demands honest timelines makes it harder for the next SI to lowball. Every contract that includes exit rights and performance guarantees raises the standard for the next negotiation. Every organization that builds internal capability and reduces SI dependency demonstrates that the dependency was never necessary. Every reader of this book who applies its principles and shares what they learned tilts the playing field back toward the customer.

I do not know whether the machine can be broken. But I know it can be bent. And the more people who read this book and apply its concepts, the more likely it is that the bending begins. At the very least, it will create a market in which the informed buyer is the norm rather than the exception -- a market in which the vendors and SIs must compete on value delivered rather than ignorance exploited. That market does not exist today. But it is buildable. And every organization that demands a different set of terms is laying the foundation.

The organizations that do these things -- that understand the machine, demand a different set of terms, and invest in the organizational work that the machine is designed to skip -- those organizations will navigate the transformation and emerge stronger. Not because the technology saved them. Because they saved themselves.

The machine will persist. Your job is to not be consumed by it.

In Chapter 1, I introduced an analogy that I said I would return to. The enterprise technology industry operates on the same structural principles as organized crime. The protection racket of forced migrations. The shakedown of change order cascades. The territorial enforcement of account control. The made-man system of vendor partner tiers. The omertà that silences independent voices. The difference between the machine and the mob is not ethics. It is legitimacy. The machine collects the same tribute, enforces the same silence, and protects the same territory. It just does it with a press release and a keynote. The mob had the decency to operate in the shadows. The machine does it in plain sight, with a booth at the trade show and a sponsorship on the analyst report. And that, perhaps, is the most unsettling thing about it.

Welcome to the machine. Now you know how it works. What you do with that knowledge is up to you.

About the Author

Eric Kimberling is the CEO and Founder of Third Stage Consulting Group, a leading independent advisory firm specializing in digital transformation and enterprise technology selection. With over 20 years of experience in organizational change and technology implementation, Kimberling has guided hundreds of organizations through complex ERP selections, system implementations, and digital transformation initiatives.

As a recognized thought leader in the enterprise software industry, Kimberling has helped organizations across diverse sectors—from Fortune 500 companies to mid-market businesses and government agencies—navigate the critical decisions that determine the success or failure of their technology investments. His expertise spans strategic planning, vendor selection, risk mitigation, and change management for large-scale digital initiatives.

Kimberling is the author of *The Final Countdown* and *Welcome to the Jungle*, two previous works that established his reputation as one of the most candid and independent voices in the enterprise technology space. He is a frequent keynote speaker at industry conferences and has authored numerous articles and research studies on digital transformation best practices. His insights have been featured in leading business publications, and he regularly provides commentary on emerging trends in enterprise technology and organizational change management.

Through Third Stage Consulting Group, Kimberling has witnessed firsthand both the spectacular successes and costly failures that define the digital transformation landscape. This unique vantage point—working as an independent advisor rather than a vendor or systems integrator—has provided him with unbiased insights into what drives transformation success and failure across different industries and organizational contexts.

His practical, results-oriented approach combines strategic thinking with real-world experience, making him a trusted advisor to executives seeking to maximize their return on digital transformation investments while minimizing the risks that have derailed so many well-intentioned initiatives.